An Adopted Lancastrian

To

Dennis

With Best Wishes

from

Joan

An Adopted Lancastrian

The Life & Works of James Hugh Reginald Dixon
1886–1975

Joan Johnson

First published in Great Britain in 2012
on behalf of the author
by Scotforth Books
www.scotforthbooks.com

Copyright © Joan Johnson 2012

The moral right of the author has been asserted

All photos courtesy of Joan Johnson unless stated otherwise

All attempts have been made to acknowledge the original copyright holders

All rights reserved. Without limiting the rights under copyright reserved above, no part of this publication may be reproduced, stored in or introduced into a retrieval system, or transmitted, in any form or by any means (electronic, mechanical, public performances, photocopying, recording or otherwise), without the written permission of the publisher, except for limited personal and educational extracts or brief quotations embodied in articles or reviews.

Printed in Great Britain by Berforts Information Press

ISBN: 978-1-904244-89-9

Contents

Foreword	ix
Preface	x
Introduction	xi
The York Years	1
Lancaster (1909–1914)	23
The First World War	43
Return to Lancaster	53
Concerts and Recitals	
Letters and Articles	
The Society of Saint Gregory	
Organ Adviser and Consultant	71
Music for All	79
Lancaster Music Festival	
Broadcasting	
Mistaken Identity	
City Status for Lancaster	
Dixon the Inventor	97
Sacred and Secular	107
The Dream of Gerontius	
Operettas	
Ashton Hall Organ, Lancaster	

The Incorporated Association of Organists 123
    Dixon and the Earring Theory

A Golden Decade 133

Panis Vitae 145

The Autumnal Years 165

Postscript 173

Appendix 177
    The Dream of Gerontius
    Press Extracts

List of Works 189

Bibliography 201

Index 207

Acknowledgements

It is an honour for me that Dr Francis Jackson, CBE very kindly agreed to write the foreword to this book. His words are much appreciated.

I am greatly indebted to Mr Philip Mackay for his computer skills in scanning and digitally enhancing numerous photographs, also to his wife Wiebke Mackay-Engel for translating all the German newspaper reports on the performance of *Panis Vitae* and producing the music examples. A word of thanks is due to Jonathan Clegg for editing the music examples.

The help received from Dr J Dibble in securing a copy of two compositions by Dixon and his interest in my work is much appreciated. I am very grateful to the late Mr Douglas Carrington and his wife Linda for supplying material from their archive and also to Mr Bryan Hughes for archive material and help with my research.

I appreciate the assistance given to me in my research by Gerrard Boylan, librarian of Oscott College, Birmingham, Dr Meg Whittle, archivist at the Metropolitan Cathedral, Liverpool and to the staff of the following libraries: Bishop Auckland Library, The Borthwick Institute of Historical Research, York, The British Library, Carlisle Reference Library, Darlington Reference Library, Lancaster Reference Library, Liverpool Central Library (Archive Department), London University Library, Manchester Central Library (especially the Henry Watson Music Library, the Local Studies and Patent divisions), RTÉ Libraries and Archive Services, Dublin, The Talbot Library, Preston and York Central Reference Library. My appreciation is also extended to staff at the Lancashire Record Office and North Yorkshire Record Office.

My thanks go to members of the Darlington, Preston and York Organists' Associations for their support and sharing conversations recalling memories of Dr Dixon.

I wish to express my thanks and appreciation to the Very Rev. Canon Stephen Shield, the Rev. Andrew Allman, Dr Caroline Hull, Vivien Burke and Damian Howard of St Peter's Cathedral, Lancaster for their help and encouragement, access to archive material and the music library.

A very generous legacy left to me by my dear friend the late Miss Joan Penney has been put towards publishing this book. It was through a link with Dr Dixon that we first met and our friendship began, therefore I am truly grateful for such a gift.

The author wishes to thank copyright owners who have given their permission to reproduce photographs and quote published examples of text and music.

Finally a word of thanks go to my friends and acquaintances who have contributed in any way to this book: John Ainslie, (Former Chairman of the Society of St Gregory), Joyce Bond, David Bourne (Former Churchwarden of St Lawrence, Flaxton), Keith Brown, Barbara Burt, Edward Burt (Former pupil of Archbishop Holgate's Grammar School), everyone at Carnegie Book Production, Brian Casey, Rowland Chapman, Nigel Clegg, Dr Peter Chatfield, Geoffrey Coffin (Principal Pipe Organs, York), Jane Cole (the present owner of Lunehurst), Adrian Crawford, the Rev. John Davies (Former vicar of All Saints, Huntington, York), Dr Jeremy Dibble (Professor of Music at Durham University), Brian Dickinson, the Rev. Michael Dolan, Rev. W A Elkin, Pamela Elliott (Manager and archivist of the York Family History Society), the late Joyce Farrow (Former Churchwarden of Holy Trinity Church, Stockton-on-the-Forest), the Rev. Ian Grieves, Paul Hale, Philip Hall, the Rev. Canon Alec Harding, Leighton Harding, the late Tom Hudson, Eileen Hunt, Marion Jefferies (Present owner of Stockton House, Stockton-on-the-Forest), Dennis Kidd, Francis Kitts, Robert Matthew-Walker, the Rev. Canon Robert McTeer, Charles Miller, the late Joan Penney, Beverley Pilcher, Mary Pollyne of Stockton-on-the-Forest, Olwen Riley (née Hudson), Edward de Rivera (Director of Music, Oxford Oratory), the late Dorothy Smith of Flaxton, Jacki Smith, Margaret Spencer, Dennis Spiby, the late Nora and Ethel Taylor (Pupils and lifelong friends of Dr Dixon), Anthony Wadeson and Simon Walker.

Foreword

by Dr Francis Jackson, CBE

To have come within the orbit of someone of the character of Doctor J. H. Reginald Dixon, with his wide experience of music – and life – his many attributes, not to say idiosyncrasies; with his formidable list of achievements in so many fields of music as well as in non-musical areas; all this has been a life-enriching circumstance. His tally of musical compositions, for one thing, is notable, indicating a fertile imagination and a ready facility in the writing of music. His magnum opus would have been to him of great importance – the Eucharistic Oratorio, PANIS VITAE, undertaken for the prestigious Catholic World Eucharistic Congress.

The fact that it was not wholly to the taste of Munich at its first performance, as well as its failure to become widely used elsewhere must have been a bitter disappointment to him and his sister. But such can be the fate of many works of art due to whatever reason, and those examples that are blessed with longevity have won the battle to remain in use – a fierce battle in a crowded arena and one which probably does not always claim the right victor. Tastes can change with the years, and composers and their products can be resuscitated.

One remembers the few, brief, encounters with Doctor Dixon (and playing his original Ainscough organ in Lancaster Cathedral). It is a recurring and pleasurable bonus to pass by his erstwhile home in Stockton-on-the-Forest each time we make our way to York from East Acklam – a sure way to keep him in the memory.

Joan Johnson has done a superb job, with all its researching and bringing together of a mass of material. She merits our grateful congratulation in so successfully representing the life and accomplishment of so interesting and unique a personality.

Francis Jackson

East Acklam, February 2011

Preface

This is the first book to be written on the life and works of Dr James Hugh Reginald Dixon, not to be confused with his namesake whose music emanated from a famous north-west seaside resort. It is a record of his fascinating life, outstanding achievements and valuable contribution to music for those who knew him and for future generations.

While still a pupil of Dr Dixon I began making notes and collecting material on his life with the intention of writing a biography at a later date. After his death, many years were to pass before I had the opportunity to undertake any serious research. I have endeavoured as far as possible to present an accurate account of Dixon's life and works from his own writings, conversing with those who knew him, personal knowledge, analysing his music manuscripts, recital programmes, letters, miscellaneous documents, articles and newspaper reports. Some newspaper reports are not always a reliable source as they have been found to contain inaccurate material. Other information such as that found in the introduction to the works published by Hinrichsen while correct at the time is no longer accurate. The reason being that Dixon continued to compose for several years after these works were published. It has not always been possible to accurately date the compositions even when certain manuscripts were signed, due to the fact that some works began as an improvisation and were written down at a later date, other extant manuscripts are copies made by Dixon, some are revised versions of an earlier work and occasionally a piece appears under a different title.

There are still avenues to explore, but 23 December 2011 marked the 125th Anniversary of Dixon's birth so I feel it is time to bring this book to a close.

Introduction

James Hugh Reginald Dixon was born in 1886 and spent his early years in and around York. He held various organ posts in the city and became a popular recitalist, composer and teacher.

In 1909 he was appointed Organist and Choirmaster of St Peter's Church, Lancaster (later Lancaster Cathedral), a position he held for over sixty years. The following year he became Organist to Lancaster Corporation and so began a life-long association with the instrument in the Ashton Hall.

During the First World War he served in the Royal Army Medical Corps and was appointed Director of Music at a military station near Lyon. After the war he resumed his duties at St Peter's and devoted his life to performing, composing, teaching and lecturing. With friends he established the Lancaster Music Festival and was a founder member of several other organisations, including the Incorporated Association of Organists and the Society of St Gregory.

His compositions comprise piano pieces, organ works, sacred and secular choral music, instrumental pieces, orchestral works, and incidental music. Two major works are his setting of *The Dream of Gerontius* dating from 1943 and the Oratorio *Panis Vitae* performed at the 1960 World Eucharistic Congress held in Munich.

Throughout a teaching career spanning a period of over 60 years, Dixon's pupils became the next generation of amateur and professional musicians, who in turn passed on the knowledge and skills learnt to their students. For many years organists who had studied with Dixon held appointments at nearly all the churches in Lancaster and the surrounding area. Some pupils continued their careers far beyond the boundaries of Yorkshire and Lancashire.

Dixon was a brilliant organist who excelled in the art of improvisation, an internationally known composer, an inspiring teacher, a notable accompanist, popular lecturer, organ adviser and consultant, an inventor, a talented artist and a prolific writer of letters and articles.

He was a distinguished personality and well-known character, who in later years could frequently be found in a local hostelry or hotel having his nightcap, easily recognisable with his white hair, beard, earrings and high-heeled shoes.

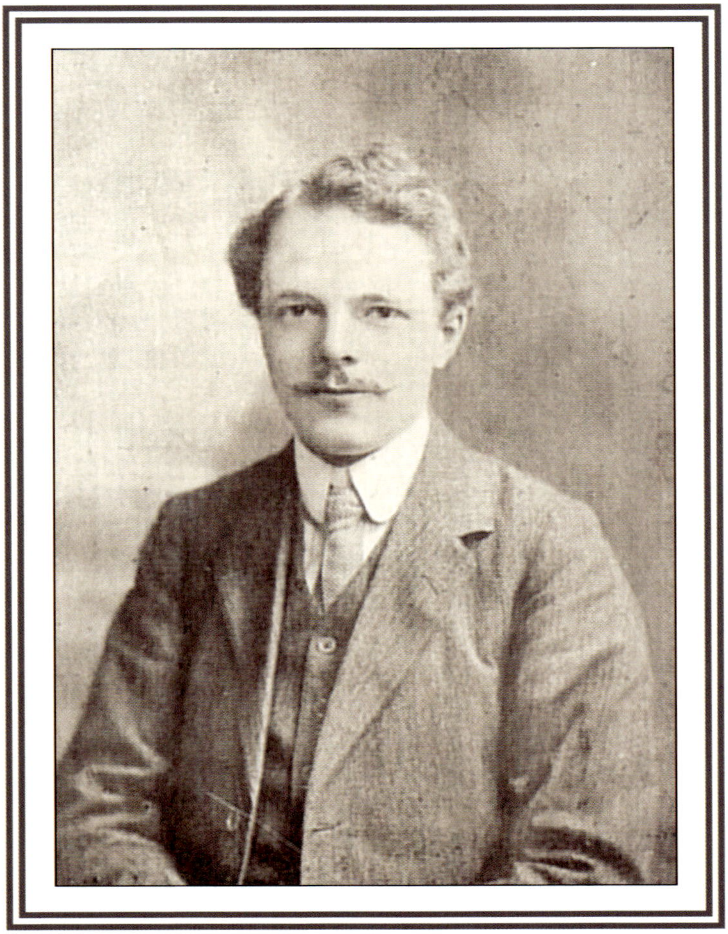

The York Years

Church registers, census returns and various nineteenth-century directories reveal that the ancestors of James Hugh Reginald Dixon were born, lived and worked in the York area.

For over a century the Dixon family were associated with the village of Huntington, which is situated on the banks of the river Foss approximately three miles north east of York. On 21 December 1795, William Dixon (Reginald Dixon's great-great-grandfather) aged thirty and Mary Lazenby aged nineteen, were married by licence in All Saints Parish Church, Huntington. Between 1796 and 1821 William and Mary had twelve children, six sons and six daughters, two of whom died in infancy. In the Parish Church Baptism Register of this period alongside the entry for each child, William's occupation was first listed as a carpenter, later a joiner and in the entry for the eighth child born in 1811 joiner and farmer. Mary came from a well-known farming family who owned and worked the land in several villages around York. It would appear that after the last child was born William changed his occupation, being listed in the Baines Directory of 1823 and the White Directory of 1840 as victualler of the local Hare and Hounds.

John, the first child of William and Mary, named after his maternal grandfather was born on 15 August 1796 and was baptised the following day. According to the 1841 census return, John was living in the village of Huntington with his wife Hannah and four of their seven children. The sixth child Jane had only lived for two days, the eldest son James aged eighteen and daughter Mary aged fourteen were not at home on the night of the census. Perhaps they were working and living at the residence of an employer or they may have been staying with relatives or friends. In the Parish Church Baptism Register alongside the entry for each of the seven children, John's occupation is listed as farmer, hay dealer or farm labourer.

James was born in 1822 and like his father went into farming and dealing in hay, but later he followed in the footsteps of his grandfather and became a publican. In 1850 he married Jane Creaser daughter of Matthew and Hannah Creaser (née

Opposite: James Hugh Reginald Dixon, c. 1907

Dawson) of York. The Creaser family were also in the brewing industry and at one time were known to have been proprietors of the Clock Inn, York. Like many of his neighbours James grew vegetables and flowers in his garden and exhibited a variety of these in the annual village show. Over a period of twelve years from 1851 to 1863 James and Jane had five sons and three daughters, the second son William died in infancy.

At the time of the 1881 census the youngest son George, now aged seventeen, was a pupil teacher in a board school and lodging with the Midgely family in the village of Huntington where he was born. Sometime between 1871 and 1881 his parents and two elder brothers James William and Matthew had moved to the Wind Mill Inn, St James Square, Boroughbridge, but by 1891 they had returned to live in York.

After completing his training George was appointed Master of Flaxton-on-the-Moor Church of England School succeeding Miss Annie Holgate who had resigned in February 1883.

The first entry in the school log book dated 5th–9th March written by Mr Dixon reads:

> I commenced my duties here. Rev. J Griffith opened the school and took upper standards at scripture on Monday morning. Worked according to the Time Table except on Wednesday when reading was substituted for the dictation. Good attendance in the earlier part of the week but decreased owing to the rough weather.[1]

During the next five years entries in the log book give an insight into the life of the school, describing the Reports from the Local Authority and Diocesan Inspectors, lessons, infectious diseases, participation in village events such as the Flaxton Feast, an annual day trip to Scarborough first introduced by Mr Dixon and the pupil attendance which fluctuated due to illness, inclement weather and the fact that the older children were required to work on the farms at busy times of the year.

As the August-September holiday of 1885 came to an end, the opening of the school on 21 September was postponed for two weeks owing to Mr Dixon having been involved in a railway accident which resulted in him having his left arm amputated.

On Christmas Eve 1885, George Dixon married Jane Abel in the Parish Church of St Mary and St Nicholas, Wigginton. The village of Wigginton is situated approximately four and a half miles north of York and at this time was relatively small.

Several generations of the Abel (Abell) family, whose surname can be traced back to the Norman Conquest worked in the agricultural industry, farming areas of land ranging from 30 to 198 acres. Unlike members of the Dixon family who

---

1 Flaxton School Log Book.

stayed in one village for many years, members of the Abel family through farming were associated with the villages of Cundall, Dunsforth, Farlington, Flaxton, Gateforth, Haxby, Huby, Sheriff Hutton, Stillington, Sutton-on-the-Forest and Wigginton.

The 1871 census shows that Hugh Abel (junior), his wife Elizabeth and their three daughters, Mary, (named as Annie in the 1881 census) Jane and Lilly were living at Toll Bar House, Wigginton. At this time Hugh Abel was a joiner and he employed an apprentice. By 1881 the family were living in Wigginton Road and the census reveals that Mr Abel was a carpenter and wheelwright employing two apprentice carpenters.

George and Jane Dixon, who had also trained as a teacher, settled down to married life in Flaxton. At this time it is quite likely that the Dixons were renting accommodation either from relatives, friends or a landlord. Research has revealed that the rent books for Flaxton during the 1880s were destroyed, their names did not appear on the Electoral Roll and the years the family spent in the village occurred between the census of 1881 and 1891, therefore attempts to locate the address have proved unsuccessful. The Tithe Award of 1843 and the census records between 1841 and 1871 show that members of the Abel family and the Creaser family owned land and property in Flaxton which may have been passed on to the next generation.

James Hugh Reginald Dixon, affectionately known as Reggie to his family, was born on 23 December 1886 in Flaxton. This new birth marked the first of three special days in the Dixon household, the next day being the first Wedding

Registration of Baptism

Anniversary for Jane and George, followed by Christmas Day when as a Christian family they would celebrate the Birthday of Christ. Reginald was baptised on 27 March 1887 at the village church of St Lawrence.

A sister Beatrice Lily was born in December of 1887. Shortly afterwards, Mr Dixon having received the highest Merit Grant resigned his post at Flaxton to become Headmaster of the school at Stockton-on-the-Forest. His duties were terminated on 15 April 1888 and the family moved to begin a new life at School House, Stockton-on-the-Forest. Two years later in 1890 a second son Ronald George was born.

As well as being a schoolmaster George Dixon was an insurance agent, his name appearing in Bulmer's Directory of North Yorkshire, 1890. In Kelly's Directory of the North Riding, 1893, the entry reads G. Dixon, schoolmaster, assistant overseer and agent to the British Equitable Fire Insurance and Life Assurance Company.

Both parents, who were musical, gave Reginald his first piano lessons from an instruction book, and it is quite likely that they initially taught the two younger children. Beatrice became an accomplished pianist and 'cellist and as a young boy Ronald, like his father, often sang in the village concerts. Reginald went on to have piano lessons from Mr Kinsley, a blind musician who later became Organist of Holy Trinity Church, Stockton-on-the-Forest.

In one of his lectures entitled 'Fashions in Retrospect', Reginald describes his earliest recollections of church-going when he was taken by his mother to the village church:

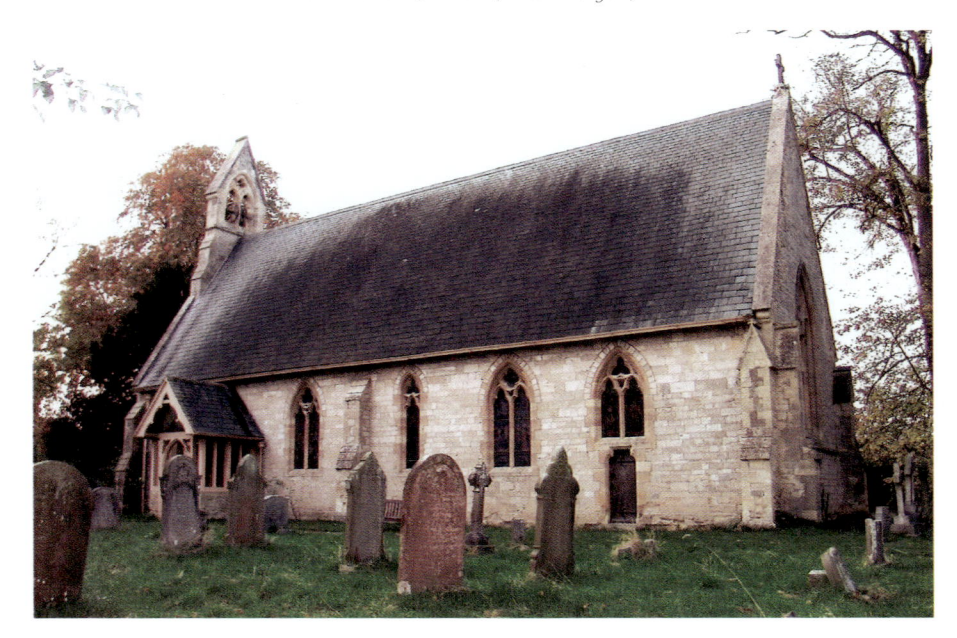

St Lawrence, Flaxton (Adrian Crawford)

The service was of the 'low Church' variety. A body of singers – lads and lasses – occupied the west end gallery in which there was a harmonium of one and a half rows of reeds. The parson occupied a solitary seat in the small chancel. Verses of the psalms were recited alternately by the parson and the congregation with the choir coming in at the Gloria. The Responses and Amens were said and Anthems were unknown. The Rector's wife or the assistant school teacher played the harmonium and as far as I can remember no voluntaries were ever played.

In 1895 the 'Restoration of the Church' brought great changes. The West end gallery was removed and a new larger chancel was built as well as a tower with four bells and a spire. The choir were now robed in cassock and surplice and to my great delight a new organ by Foster and Andrews of Hull was installed. A competent organist was appointed and things musically took on a new fashion. The psalms were sung by the choir who now had seats in the Chancel. Regular choir practices were held and the Responses, Amens and Litany were sung. On special occasions even an Anthem was performed.[2]

Holy Trinity Church, Stockton-on-the-Forest (Adrian Crawford)

About this time Reginald became a choirboy though he admitted that his interest in watching the organist change the stops on the organ was far greater than that of pointing the psalms. The first time he ever touched an organ was when he was chosen to assist the organ tuner by holding down the keys while the organ was tuned. This experience was the spark that kindled his determination to become an organist. During the school holidays Reginald often went to visit his grandparents who attended the local Methodist Church and he was fascinated by the different sounds of the organ, in particular the mixture and reed stops.

In addition to learning the piano Reginald now began organ lessons with Kinsley. His first tutor book was 'First Six Months at the Organ' by Stones, followed by

---

2 Dixon Lecture, 'Fashions in Retrospect'.

Stainer's 'Organ Primer'. Later, 'The Art of Organ Playing' by Best was carefully worked through, alongside the *Short Eight Preludes and Fugues* by J. S. Bach. At the age of ten Reginald became assistant organist at Holy Trinity Church.

Holy Trinity Church, Stockton-on-the-Forest
Foster and Andrews 1895
Original Specification

Great Organ		**Swell Organ**		**Pedal Organ**	
Open Diapason	8	Violin Diapason	8	Bourdon	16
Hohlflöte	8	Salicional	8	**Couplers**	
Dulciana	8	Voix Celeste	8	Swell to Great	
Principal	4	Oboe	8	Great to Pedal	
Waldflöte	4			Swell to Pedal	

An interest was shown in composition from the time he could write. Early pieces were inspired by daily adventures and village life. He wrote an Instruction Book for Piano, songs for schoolchildren and arranged miscellaneous pieces of music.

As well as having music lessons and composing Reginald took an active part in school concerts and musical life of the village. One such concert which was reported in the local press was given by the scholars of Stockton-on-the-Forest School:

> On Wednesday a most enjoyable and successful concert was given by the scholars of the above school. The part songs, recitations, musical drills, flag drills, and readings were so well rendered that the large number present frequently demanded encores. Miss Brooksbank must have been delighted to think that her careful training gave such entire satisfaction. The following was the programme (with additions): – Recitation, Annie Woodall; songs, Emily Marshall and Ronald Dixon, recitation, Florence Jane Sterriker; piano solo, Reggie Dixon; recitation, Sarah Dyson; song, Gertrude Dacre; recitation, Clarence Marshall; song, Ethel Cowper. Mr. Dixon sang two character comic songs during the interval, and Mr. Kinsley (organist) met with a well-deserved encore. The chairman (Rev. William Gell, M.A.,) congratulated Mr. Dixon and Miss Brooksbank on the excellent condition of the school. 'Excellent' reports had been received from both the Government and the diocesan inspector. J. H. Reggie Dixon ably presided at the piano.[3]

---

3 *Yorkshire Herald*, Friday 11 March 1898.

Organ console, Holy Trinity Church, Stockton-on-the-Forest

Later that year another report refers to the Harvest Festival and the tea followed by a concert held in the schoolroom on Monday evening, 3 October:

> The Harvest Services were continued on Sunday last. There were two celebrations of the Holy Communion, and the sermon in the morning was preached by the rector. The church in the evening was filled to overflowing, when an appropriate sermon was preached by the Rev. W. Johnson, Headmaster of Archbishop Holgate's School, York. On Monday evening the annual tea and concert was held in the school. A large number sat down to tea, the following ladies presiding at the tea tables:- Miss Agar, Mrs C Marshall, Mrs Sterriker, Mrs Berry, Miss Palmes, Mrs Lund, Mrs Gell, Miss A. Smith, and the Misses Cleveland. For the concert which followed and over which the Rev. W. Gell, rector, presided, the school was packed with an enthusiastic audience, whose encores were frequent and kindly responded to. During the interval the rector gave a short address, and at the close proposed a very hearty vote of thanks to all who had contributed to the decorations of the church and to those who kindly carried out the work; to the ladies who had presided at the tea tables; to all the ladies and gentlemen who had so kindly assisted at the concert; to Mr. F. Wharldall for the kind loan of the piano; and to Mr. H. E. Inman, the organist, for getting up of so good and enjoyable an

entertainment. The singing of the National Anthem brought the proceedings to a close. Last evening the children had tea. The following contributed to an excellent programme: Mr. H. E. Inman, Miss Spetch, Master Precious, Mr. Bert Hall, Ivy and Olive Hope, Mr. Arthur Hitchcock, Mr. Monaghan, Master Leonard Ankers, Master Reginald Dixon, Mrs Wharldall and Mr. Hindley Biggs.[4]

In September 1898 Mr George Dixon received a letter from Pocklington School, York, informing him that his son had been awarded an Elementary School Scholarship to the value of £7 10s. per annum.[5] There is no evidence as to why this offer was not taken up. Maybe his parents could not afford to send him there even taking into consideration the value of the scholarship.

Shortly after the Harvest services and concert reported above, Reginald became a pupil of Mr Henry Euston-Inman of De Grey Street, York. A member of the Incorporated Society of Musicians and the Guild of Organists Inman had studied with Tertius Noble, Organist of York Minster (1898–1912), R T White Mus. Doc. Oxon. and R W Oberhoffer who was Music Master at Ampleforth College and Organist of St Wilfrid's Church, York. As a teacher of pianoforte, organ, singing, theory, harmony and counterpoint, he successfully prepared his pupils for the Royal Academy, Royal College and Incorporated Society of Musicians Examinations. Inman was also Organist and Choirmaster at St Saviour's, Saviourgate (now an archaeological centre) and St Thomas', Lowther Street, York as well as being conductor of the St Thomas' Philharmonic Society.

It would appear that George Dixon resigned his position as Headmaster of the school in 1899. His successor at Flaxton, Mr R Wolsenholme, had been appointed to follow him at Stockton-on-the-Forest, but was taken ill and died before he could take up the post. It is not known where or to which new post Mr Dixon had been appointed. Wherever it was he did not go, but remained headmaster of the village school until he retired.

Initially having resigned his position meant that the family, who until now had lived in the School House were required to find accommodation elsewhere and presumably arrangements to move were already being made. If there had been an option of staying in the School House which was quite small, perhaps Mr Dixon felt it was no longer suitable with the family growing up, or maybe other decisions regarding the house were taken by the Local Authority.

At this time Mr Dixon decided to rent part of Stockton House which has a fascinating history. The original part of the house is thought to date from the

---

4 *Yorkshire Herald*, Saturday 8 October 1898.
5 Most references to monetary values in this book are cited in pre-decimal sterling (pounds, shillings and pence), in which: 12 old pence (styled as 12*d*.) = 1 shilling (1*s*.) = 5 new pence (5p); and 20 shillings (20*s*.) = £1.

Dixon family at School House, Stockton-on-the-Forest, c. 1898 (J W Cook, York)

early eighteenth century and in the first half of the nineteenth century it was used as a 'holiday home' by the Wilkinson family who lived in London. Mr Wilkinson senior, who died in 1850, introduced Methodism to the village and a room at the back of the house became a Chapel which remained in use until the 1950s. An extension to the house was built when the owner decided to provide a school to educate ten poor boys from the village and accommodation for a schoolmaster. It is thought that the Dixon family rented the former schoolroom and rooms above. In 1915 Mr Dixon bought part of the house and some adjoining land for £550, and Stockton House remained the family home until he died in March 1941. A pamphlet published by the *Yorkshire Herald* (date unknown) and an article published in *Modern Farming* October 1919, reveals that George Dixon was a leading authority in Britain on growing chicory.[6] He grew the crop on an extensive scale, organised other farmers to do the same and was a pioneer of the industry in re-establishing the cultivation of the crop in England.

---

6 'Why not grow your own chicory' *Modern Farming*, October 1919, p 16.

Stockton House

In July 1899 Reginald, now aged twelve, was awarded a Local Exhibition by the North Riding Technical Instruction Committee (NRTIC) tenable for two years at Archbishop Holgate's Grammar School, York. The school founded in 1546, was reorganised in 1895 when it became an 'Organised Science School', under the headmastership of the Rev. William Johnson who was appointed in January 1896. The present school having undergone many changes is now re-sited on the Hull Road and the old school became part of St John's College.

So Reginald began a new chapter in his academic education. By August 1900 all was not well as correspondence passed between the secretary of the NRTIC and the exhibitioner regarding his poor school performance and the amount of time he was devoting to music.[7] The Committee did not regard the study of music as part of the Award even though the subject had been added to the curriculum in 1895, previously having been a so called 'extra'.

Between July 1899 and December 1901 Reginald passed several examinations held by the Incorporated Society of Musicians, Preliminary, Elementary, Grade III (Intermediate) and Grade IV (Advanced) in pianoforte playing, followed by Grade I, II and III examinations in organ playing all with Honours, so it is not surprising that his school work did not satisfy the NRTIC. Also in 1901 he was successful in the Associated Board of the Royal Academy and Royal College of Music Examinations in Elements of Music and Pianoforte Junior Grade, and in 1902 the Senior Pianoforte Grade.

---

7 Letter, Dixon archive.

During this period Reginald was assistant organist to Henry Euston-Inman. The following two references refer to an application for an appointment:

De Grey Street, York.

J H Reginald Dixon, has been a pupil of mine for some years, and my deputy for three years and in spite of his youth, I consider him <u>quite capable</u> of fulfilling the post of Organist.

Signed
H Euston-Inman,
Organist and Choirmaster of St Thomas' Church York

Dec. 9th 1901[8]

***

I certify that during the absence of my organist, this year Mr Dixon supplied the place to our complete satisfaction.
J. L. M. Young M.A., Rector of S. Saviour York.

Decr. 9. 1901[9]

It is almost certain that these references refer to the position of Organist at St Denys (Dennis, Dionysius), Walmgate to which Reginald was appointed just before his fifteenth birthday. The organ he would have played was a small two manual Postill dating from about 1850. This instrument was replaced by a new organ in 1925, built by Thomas Hughes of Bradford who incorporated a small amount of pipe work from the old instrument into the new one.

In conversation with Dixon many years later when talking about St Denys, he recalled the occasion when he bought an E flat clarinet for £2, took it along to the church and played it during the service. The congregation thought the organ had a new stop! Another anecdote from his time at St Denys when the organ was still handblown, concerned a young lad who came to blow

---

8 Reference, Dixon archive.
9 Reference, Dixon archive.

for him. When the time came to play nothing happened. After calling 'blow up, Johnny, blow up' and still nothing happened Dixon went to investigate. He found the lad with the tell tale lead weight in his mouth puffing madly!

Sometime between 1899 and 1901 Reginald went to live with his maternal grandparents in Millfield Road, York. There could have been several reasons for the move. He was a strong character with an independent mind and was known to smoke from a young age, so perhaps his parents thought that the grandparents would instil a strict code of discipline in him. A more likely reason is that with attending school in York, having music lessons in the city, deputizing as an organist and performing in concerts, it was much more convenient to live in the city rather than travel several miles from home and back each day.

From an early age Reginald was quite mischievous and loved playing practical jokes on family and friends. He told me of the occasion when he and some friends entered a church and decided to put red ink in the holy water, then hid outside and waited for the people to come out with a red cross on their forehead!

It was said that Reginald used to sit in the organ loft at the Minster. He could have been introduced to Tertius Noble through Euston-Inman who may have recommended that his pupil gain experience in this way. The Minster choir boys were educated at Archbishop Holgate's Grammar School and Reginald would know some of these boys, therefore it is quite likely that he went along to the Minster after school to sit in the organ loft.

School Reports from 1901 to 1903 show that his attendance and diligence ranged from satisfactory to good, although the latter for the most part was only satisfactory.[10] It would appear that Reginald was still preoccupied with musical activities. Academically he was good at English, Mathematics, History, Geography, Chemistry and Physics, only fair at Latin and French, but excelled at Drawing and was awarded a silver medal for Drawing and Design.

Accounts reveal that although he was on a scholarship, books still had to be paid for each term, the cost of these ranging from 13*s*. 9*d*. to £1 5*s*. 8*d*. In 1901 there were external exam fees to pay and a tailor's bill of 7*s*. 3*d*., plus a charge of 1*s*. 5*d*. for chemistry laboratory breakages! From 1902 as well as paying for books, fees for education, paper, pens, extras and dilapidations had to be paid for as the scholarship came to an end. Fees now ranged from £2 17*s*. 11*d*. to £4 3*s*. 10*d*. with the cost of books being paid at the end of each term and tuition fees payable in advance for the following term.[11]

In the Cambridge Local Examinations for Senior Students held in December 1902 Reginald, now almost sixteen, passed the following subjects, English (Composition, Grammar and Shakespeare), Pure Mathematics and Applied

---

10 School Reports, Dixon archive.
11 School Accounts, Dixon archive.

Mathematics, Theoretical Chemistry, Electricity and Magnetism and Music with distinction. Also in 1902 he achieved a Second Class pass in Physiography, Mathematics, Magnetism and Electricity awarded by the Board of Education South Kensington Advanced Stage Examinations. A card dated 24 February, 1903 sent from Euston-Inman to George Dixon reads:

> Mr Johnson has just called to tell me that your son is placed first in the United Kingdom for Harmony Cambridge Senior and is the only candidate to obtain a distinction in music.[12]

At the Annual Speech Day in July 1903 the results for 1902–03 printed on the Programme show that James Hugh Reginald Dixon was one of four successful candidates entered by the School for the Joint Matriculation Exam of London University, gaining a 2nd Division pass in English, Mathematics, French, Chemistry, Electricity and Magnetism.[13]

His early interest in electricity and magnetism was to become widely known at a later date through one of his inventions and his theory on the wearing of earrings to improve one's eyesight.

There are various receipts in existence for exam fees and tuition.[14] One dated 27 June 1903 is from the Royal Academy for admission to the Metropolitan Examination in September of that year. Two others dated January and March 1904 relate to tuition given through the Cambridge University Correspondence College. It is not clear if this course was for academic or music tuition.

Accounts for music lessons, plus piano and organ music show that Reginald was still a pupil of Euston-Inman in March 1904. At this time he had also been studying via a correspondence course with Eaglefield-Hull. Tuition with different teachers during the same period would suggest that each was for a different aspect of music and to suit specific examination requirements. As well as lessons in piano, organ and theory Reginald studied violin with Arthur A Radcliffe of York. Learning the violin would enable him to have a greater understanding of string writing which was a requirement of some examinations. After Eaglefield-Hull became organist of Huddersfield Parish Church, Reginald was now able to make frequent trips to Huddersfield for further study of both theoretical and practical work.

While studying with Eaglefield-Hull, Reginald obtained his Associate Diploma of the Royal College of Organists in July 1904 and the Fellowship Diploma in July 1906, aged seventeen and nineteen respectively. He was one of 7 candidates out of approximately 150 to pass the latter exam and the only other organist in

---

12 Card, Dixon archive.
13 Annual Speech Day Programme, Dixon archive.
14 Receipts for exam fees and tuition, Dixon archive.

York at this time to have the Fellowship Diploma was Tertius Noble, the Minster Organist who was made an Honorary Fellow of the College.

In conversation Dixon recalled that he took the Associate examination at the College then situated in Bloomsbury Hall, Hart Street and that the instrument was a poor one to play. By contrast he took the Fellowship examination in the new Royal College of Organists (situated in Kensington Gore across the road from the Royal Albert Hall) which had a new three manual organ built in 1904 by Messrs. Norman & Beard.

Between taking the two diplomas, Dixon was one of 110 candidates out of a total of 328 applicants, who having taken a local exam were selected to attend the Royal College of Music in February 1905 to take a final examination for a free open scholarship. There were 10 organ candidates of whom two were accepted. The examiners were Sir Frederick Bridge MVO, Mus. Doc. and Sir Walter Parratt MVO, Mus. Doc. It would appear that Dixon was not awarded a scholarship and therefore continued to study privately.

In July 1906 as an external student of London University Dixon passed the Inter Mus. Bac., only one other student in the country at this time was successful in the same exam. The examiners on this occasion were Dr Bennett and Dr Bridge.

St Denys Church, York

A report in the *Yorkshire Herald* relating to Dixon's success in passing the Fellowship Diploma of the Royal College of Organists also mentions that:

> Quite recently this successful musician stood second for the position of Musical Director of Jesus College Oxford. He has had offers of several splendid appointments…Musical critics predict for him a great future.[15]

No information is available regarding offers of these splendid appointments, but in April 1906 he had succeeded J A Meale as Organist and Choirmaster at Selby Wesleyan Chapel, a post he held until 1908. At this time Dixon was teaching piano to an advanced level and it was recorded in the *Yorkshire Herald* that Miss Edith Coulton, a pupil of Dixon, had been successful in the Incorporated Society of Musicians pianoforte examination held that year.[16] During his appointment at Selby Dixon continued to live in York, travelling when necessary to fulfil his duties, as well as teaching there twice weekly.

After leaving Selby he took up an appointment for a short period of time in Dringhouses. When asked about this appointment Dixon referred to the dedication of the church as St Helen's. Although there were two previous churches on the present site by this name and the road opposite the church is St Helen's Road, the church is in fact dedicated to St Edward the Confessor. A foundation stone for this church was laid in 1847 and money to build the church was given by Mrs Lee, widow of the late Rev. Edward Trafford Lee Vicar of the church. On completion the church was dedicated to St Edward the Confessor in memory of the late vicar.

The exact dates of these early appointments are unknown as they were either not recorded or records have not survived.

Between 1900 and 1909 Reginald Dixon participated in many concerts and recitals both as a pianist and organist, as well as specialising in oratorio accompaniment. Some of the programmes from the early years of the twentieth century are lost, but enough have survived to give an idea of what audiences in those days heard and enjoyed.

In 1904 and 1905 Dixon took part in the Lord Mayor's (The Right Honourable R H Vernon Wragge) Lenten Sacred Concerts, which were held in the Guildhall, York each Sunday in Lent beginning at 8.15 p.m. and lasting approximately one hour. The doors of the main entrance were opened at 8.00 p.m., but early entry at 7.45 p.m. via another door was available for those who wished to make a contribution of one shilling or more. While programmes were free, a silver collection was taken at the door for the Hospital, Dispensary and the Minster Restoration Fund. These concerts organised by a number of local musicians proved to be very successful. They attracted a good audience, were noted for fine performances by

---

15 *Yorkshire Herald,* July/August 1906.
16 Ibid.

talented musicians and raised a substantial amount of money for the Lord Mayor's Fund. In a report on the third concert held in March 1904 Dixon was described as:

> A young pianist of great ability and his performance of the Beethoven's *Fantasia, op.* 77 was a very clever one.[17]

Also taking part in this concert were Miss May Gibbs (Soprano), Mr Edmund Bean who organised the concert, Albert Monaghan (Tenor) from the Minster Choir, Violinist Arthur A Radcliffe and Messrs. H Bartley and Sons' Band.

The second Lenten concert, held on 19 March 1905 was arranged by Mr M Rymer, Choirmaster of the Centenary Wesleyan Chapel York. As well as being the accompanist for the evening Dixon was also the solo pianist and played the *Etude de Concert*, No 2 by Chaminade. Other soloists taking part in the concert were members of the Chapel Choir and the grand piano on this occasion was kindly lent by John Grey & Sons of Coney Street.

For a time Dixon was a member of the Southlands Young Peoples' Association, where he was involved in organising several concerts, the connection arising through living with grandparents who were members of Southlands Methodist Church. During this period concerts given back in the village of Stockton-on-the-Forest were similar to those which took place prior to 1900.

The organ recitals Dixon gave were of three main types and were designed to suit the instrument, the occasion and the audience. There were classical recitals which included the major works of J S Bach, the Handel Organ Concertos, Mendelssohn Sonatas and compositions by Guilmant. Some recitals were described as Grand Popular Recitals and included arrangements, often by Dixon himself of well-known piano pieces by Mendelssohn, Chopin, Brahms and Grieg, orchestral works such as the second movement from the Bruch *Violin Concerto*, the *Peer Gynt Suite* by Grieg, Tchaikovsky's *Casse Noisette* and the *Eine Kleine Nachtmusik* by Mozart, and excerpts from Opera, for example the Overture from *Tannhäuser* by Wagner and selections from *Faust* by Gounod. The 'Hallelujah Chorus' from the *Messiah* was also a popular piece. Other recitals were those of a descriptive and dramatic nature in which pieces such as *The Storm* by Clegg (arranged Dixon), Rubenstein's *Russian Patrol* and the *Sicilian Mariners* by Meale were performed. Dixon frequently designed his programmes with a mixture of pieces from the above categories and usually included one of his own compositions the most popular being *Grand Chœur* and *Grand Offertoire in B flat*.

In January 1908 Dixon gave a Grand Organ Recital at Melbourne Terrace Wesleyan Church selecting a programme to suit all tastes. According to the writer in the *Yorkshire Herald* his popularity as a young talented organist was evident from the large audience and the applause he received.

---

17 *Yorkshire Herald,* 7 March 1904.

> Mr Dixon's descriptive work on the organ is particularly fine, and the audience readily voted the young musician's arrangement of *A Storm at Sea* the *pièce de resistance* of the recital.[18]

Some of these recitals were for organ alone while others featured vocal and instrumental soloists. Albert Monaghan and Daisie Sample, described as the York Prima Donna, both appeared on several occasions with Dixon. Other soloists around this time were Gertrude Dacre, Annie Wetherall, Miss Shipman and violinist George Oldroyd one time leader of the Leeds City Orchestra.

The recitals took place on various days of the week to celebrate the opening of a new organ, the anniversary of such an instrument or as part of the celebrations to mark a special occasion. Some recitals were given to raise funds (usually a silver collection) for new organs, restoration of instruments, the Boer War and occasions when disaster struck, for example the fire at Selby Abbey in October 1906. These programmes usually included a hymn sung at the beginning or in the middle and ended with the Doxology. Ticket prices ranged from 6*d*. to 2*s*., with the average cost of 1*d*. for a programme which usually contained mini programme notes. On some occasions there would be an afternoon and evening recital when it was common to have a public tea at a cost of 5*d*. or 6*d*.

In addition to performing in concerts and giving solo recitals Dixon specialised in accompanying oratorios, cantatas and similar works for Choirs such as St Thomas' Philharmonic Society, the Huddersfied Parish and Oratorio Society Chorus and Church Choirs throughout Yorkshire.

Compositions from the York years comprise church music, pieces for organ and piano, secular solo songs and choral music as well as arrangements of works by other composers. Several of these early compositions were modelled on works which Dixon was studying and performing. He assimilated a variety of styles and compositional techniques, some in preparation for specific examination requirements, but all his works display originality and show characteristic elements of his personality.

The anthems of this period range from those in a simple homophonic style to a more complex example such as the Easter Anthem *Praise for Redemption*, composed in 1905 and dedicated to the Choir of St Denys, York. This work scored for four-part choir, a quartette, tenor soloist and organ accompaniment is reminiscent of a verse anthem.

A setting of the Lord's Prayer and three hymn tunes were composed while Dixon was organist at Selby Wesleyan Chapel and therefore reflect the style of music associated with the Methodist Church at this time. Two of the hymn tunes to the words 'We Love to Sing' and 'The World looks very Beautiful' were specifically written for the Sunday School Anniversary Services of 1907.

---

18 *Yorkshire Herald,* 28 January 1908.

One of the most popular organ compositions of this period was the *Grand Chœur in D major* influenced by Guilmant who had written a piece with the same title and in the same key. The work, composed at the age of sixteen, is dedicated to J A Meale who performed the piece at the Nineteenth Annual Festival of the Nonconformist Choir Union, held at Crystal Palace on Saturday 22 June 1907.

Example 1, Grand Chœur, bars 1–8

Another early organ work is a so-called *Toccata in C,* which is not a toccata in the usual sense, but resembles the Menuet from the *Suite Gothique* by Böellmann.

Example 2, Toccata in C, bars 1–10

Three other works which frequently appeared on programmes about this time were *Pastorale, Intermezzo* and *Bell Rondo*.

The piano works include a *Gavotte,* a *Sonata Classique* and three pieces named after flowers: *London Pride, Wallflowers* and *Red Tulips*.

Dixon selected a variety of texts for his vocal compositions taken from the works of Oxenford, Shelley, Dryden, Burns and Foster. These include love songs, descriptive songs and others which are serious or humorous all scored for different voices. A letter was sent out by Dixon asking people to subscribe to a volume of songs price 2/- (2s) post free, and the letter contains a note to the effect that Sir Frederick Bridge to whom the Burns songs are inscribed speaks of the compositions as being melodious. There is no evidence that the collection was ever published. Songs such as 'The Simple Sailorman' and 'The Clang of the Hammer' often appear in programmes of the period and were usually sung by the composer himself. Another popular song entitled 'Love is ever at the Spring', composed in 1906 and dedicated to Miss Nellie Bolton, was published by Weekes and Co. Ltd in a collection of songs by various composers. Dame Nellie Melba apparently wrote to the composer saying how much she liked this song.

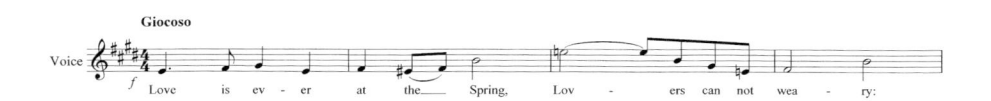

Example 3, Love is ever at the Spring, bars 5–8 (reproduced by kind permission of Stainer & Bell Ltd)

An important composition from this period is a cantata *Love and Music* which is scored for chorus, solo soprano or tenor, and string orchestra. In the preface to the work Dixon writes:

> An examination of many University exercises revealed to me that they are very often, academic, learned and sometimes ultra artistic, but possess no essential vitality. Their artistic effort being almost wholly confined to a high cultivation of certain ideas, hardly in themselves to be named ideals; and conforming in a very remarkable manner, to the standard canons of musical science; yet their musical qualities are not such as to make them live, or in any way affect – except in a small degree, the progress of this divine art. In 'Love and Music', I have tried to look up to a new ideal, in this form, and have endeavoured to set forward a new work, vital in character, learned in style, interesting in detail, artistic in spirit and above all, musically and pleasing to the senses.
>
> To ensure the above, and in the absence of any prescribed form, as at some other Universities, I have innovated some ideas; amongst which may be mentioned –
> 1. The substitution of a Quintette for a Quartette. The words suggesting 'weaving' of harmonies, and five parts were adopted instead of four to give this effect.
> 2. The introduction of an 'a la valse' movement to make a fitting background to the words 'When their light weight the tender feet shall bear'.

3. A new principle in the orchestral Prelude, whereby the subject matter for the latter part of the work, is taken from the prelude; and not, as is often done, the prelude built up of matter taken from the work.
4. The work is one continuous whole, not being divided up into separate sections, quite apart one from another. The contrasts are those of massive sections, rather than of fine detail, whereby the whole gains uniformity.
5. The dramatic feeling, especially of the Recit and Solo is shown in 'Play I could once' and 'Charm me asleep'.

> The objects named above may not be fully realised ... but my intention was to embody in a suitable form some of my art views; keeping the principle of essential vitality ever before me.

Although the work is a continuous whole, nine sections can be defined; Prelude, Choruses (with Solo), 'Come forth, O ye Children of Gladness, Come', 'O Music of My Heart', 'Away from the dwellings of care worn men', Quintette, 'Adorn thyself', Recitative, 'Play I could once', Aria, 'Charm me asleep', Chorus (with Solo), 'Away with melancholy', Fugue and Finale, 'Hail music!'

The dramatic feeling referred to above in the Recitative, 'Play I could once, but now you see my harp hung up there on the willow tree', is created by use of word painting, chromaticism, rhythm features, changes of tempo and dynamics ranging from *pianissimo* to *fortissimo*, while in the accompaniment use is made of double and triple stopping on the strings played *pizzicato*, interspersed with phrases played *arco*. Similarly in the Aria 'Charm me asleep', marked andante cantabile, embellishment of the melodic line, the lilting rhythm, use of chromaticism, and an accompaniment based on broken chords later changing to rapidly repeated semiquavers as the tempo and dynamics change to suit the text all contribute to the drama.

Technical devices used in the work include canon, canon by inversion (with added thirds), canon by diminution, canonic and free imitation, double, triple and quadruple counterpoint and fugue.

As mentioned earlier Dixon resigned his post in Selby and became Organist at St Edward the Confessor, Dringhouses, such a move being a temporary one as he was preparing to be received into the Catholic Faith. His conversion took place on 8 December 1908 at St Wilfrid's, York and attending Midnight Mass that Christmas must have been a spiritually moving experience. According to the Rev. B Lockwood in his article 'Profile',[19] Dixon was attracted to the faith when he met a friend one day on York railway station with a rosary. One can only speculate that the reasons for his conversion were much deeper than this. He probably had links

---

19 *Church Music*, August 1971, Vol. 3 No. 10, pp 15–16.

with the Catholic Church through friends and music. It may have been that he was influenced by reading about the faith or attending a Mass. Having been baptised and brought up in the Church of England, then experiencing Methodism, was he at the impressionable age of just twenty-two searching for some spiritual direction and therefore did the Doctrines of the Catholic Faith, the Latin Mass and its music surrounded by mysticism appeal to his emotions at this time? The true reason will never be known.

Very few appointments in Catholic cathedrals or churches were available at this time and Dixon was not sure where his career would take him. He continued to play at Dringhouses for a little while longer and it could have been either before or during this time that he studied the art of plainsong with Oberhoffer.

Early in 1909 Dixon answered an advertisement with a box number for an organist and choirmaster. Contact with Oberhoffer, with whom he had been acquainted for some time, was to prove an important link in his application. Oberhoffer introduced Dixon to the Prior at Ampleforth, who in turn discovered that Prior Burge of Liverpool and formerly of Ampleforth had been asked by Canon Billington of St Peter's Church, Lancaster to help in the appointment. Dixon was duly appointed Organist and Choirmaster of St Peter's on the recommendation of Prior Burge.

In May 1909 just before leaving for Lancaster Dixon gave one more recital in York at the Presbyterian Church, Priory Street, now St Columba's United Reformed Church with New Lendal. With the morning and evening services celebrating the Sunday School Anniversary, the organ recital took place in the afternoon. The following extract is taken from a report on the Anniversary celebrations:

> Mr Dixon had prepared an attractive programme, the selection varying in theme and mood, and not only were the congregation impressed by the wonderful power and beauty of the fine new organ, but with the striking capability of the organist. Probably the uppermost feeling in the minds of the audience was one of regret that York was losing the services of so versatile and brilliant a musician. It is to be hoped that at some future date a York Church will secure his services and bring him back to the Minster City.[20]

This was not to be.

---

20 *Yorkshire Herald*, 10 May 1909.

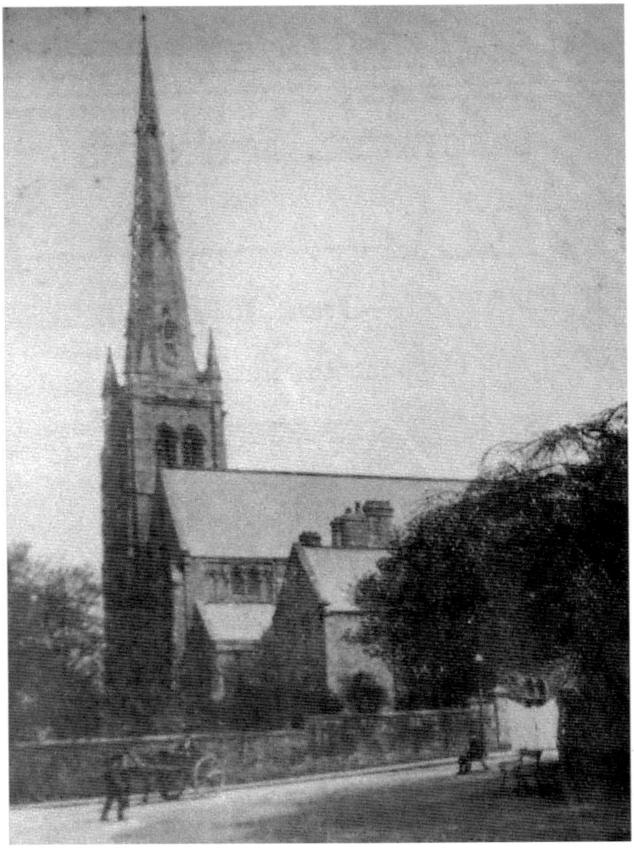

Lancaster 1909–1914

So the young Dixon left his native York in May 1909 and began a new chapter in his career, working with the clergy and choir at St Peter's, forming new friendships with local musicians and participating in the musical life of the historic town of Lancaster.

The foundation stone for St Peter's was laid on 29 April 1857. Edward G Paley a native Yorkshire man resident in Lancaster at the time, was the architect and his design for the church was in the early fourteenth-century Gothic style. Built by subscription, the church was consecrated on 4 October 1859 by Dr Alexander Goss, Bishop of Liverpool, and on the following day, the chapels and chantries were consecrated by Bishop Turner of Salford. These initial ceremonies took place in private, the church being officially opened to the public on 6 October. Pontifical High Mass was celebrated by Bishop Goss and the sermon was preached by Bishop Roskell of Nottingham who took as his text 'Go make disciples of all the nations, baptise them in the name of the Father, and of the Son and of the Holy Ghost' (cf. Matthew 28:19).

Music for the occasion was Haydn's Imperial Mass, which was sung by a choir and soloists accompanied by an orchestra from Manchester, with Laurenz Schmitz as organist and Gustav Arnold as conductor. A former organist at the Catholic Chapel, Dalton Square from 1850 to 1854 Arnold left Lancaster for Manchester. He taught the children of Charles Hallé who in 1857 founded the Hallé Orchestra. Was the Hallé Orchestra in Lancaster for this special occasion?

Laurenz Schmitz, born at Buederich Neuss, Rhineland in 1823 was appointed the first Organist of St Peter's. As well as being a teacher of music and languages he had been Organist at the Catholic Chapel since 1855.

The first organ in St Peter's was the one which had been built for the Catholic Chapel in August 1841 by J C Bishop. It was removed from the Chapel in 1859 and placed in the south transept of the new church. This instrument remained there until 1888 when it was replaced with a new organ built by Henry Ainscough of Preston.

Opposite: St Peter's Church later Lancaster Cathedral (Parish Magazine)

Ainscough was born in Lancaster in 1851 and spent his early years in the town where he attended the Catholic Chapel in Dalton Square. After leaving school Ainscough served his apprenticeship with the firm of Thomas Harrison in Union Street, Rochdale and sometime later was appointed foreman. In 1872 when Harrison closed the Rochdale works and moved north to establish a factory in Durham, Ainscough decided to set up his own firm in Derby Street, Preston. At the time of the 1881 census, records show that Henry was married and employed three men. It is interesting to note that Ainscough was a pioneer among riders of the so-called safety bicycle, which was invented in 1876 and went into production in 1885 superseding the pennyfarthing. At a later date he was one of the first motor-cyclists to ride through the streets of Preston and he also owned a yacht which he often sailed out of Lytham where he lived. Ainscough could afford these luxuries having secured many contracts to build new instruments which were required for the increasing number of Catholic Churches being built in Lancashire. Having seen photographs of Henry Ainscough dressed in breeches and thick woollen stockings, Francis Kitts described him as an Elgar look-alike.

A west end gallery was erected to accommodate the organ which was a gift from Mr Richard Leeming of Greaves House. Both the gallery and the organ case were designed by Paley and Austin. The eight granite pillars on which the gallery is supported were constructed by Mr Heap and the organ case of Dantzic oak was made by Mr Charles Blades. On a panel in the gallery there is a shield bearing the Leeming family coat of arms beneath which is the inscription 'Garde bien la foi' (Guard well the faith).

The instrument is divided on either side of the great west window, the great and choir organ being on the north side and the swell organ on the south side with the pedal organ divided on either side. This window made by Hardman of Birmingham and generously donated by Mr Joseph Smith illustrates the 'Te Deum'. Scolls of the text are woven around scenes of our Lord in glory, surrounded by angels and archangels, the emblem of the Holy Ghost surrounded by angels, the apostles, prophets, martyrs, saints, our blessed Lady, St Joseph, St John the Baptist, St Elizabeth, St Anne, SS Ambrose and Augustine authors of the great hymn, Kings, the company of women saints and patrons of the donor. The setting of the sun in the west lighting up this magnificent window is one that will be etched on my memory for life.

A detached console with horizontal tiers of stops and a straight pedal board was situated in a central position, near the edge of the gallery with the organist facing the west window and terraced seating which was provided for the choir. Some writers have referred to the console as being reminiscent of the Cavaillé-Coll instrument in Sainte-Clotilde, Paris which César Franck played, but the Ainscough console was not terraced. It is quite likely that Ainscough attended the opening of the Cavaillé-Coll instrument built for Blackburn Cathedral in 1875

*Interior of Lancaster Cathedral
(G Wynspeare Herbert,
Lancaster)*

and may well have seen other instruments by this builder, which could account for the similarities in console design. The design of the instrument Ainscough built for St Peter's was not the first of its type. In 1880 he had built an organ for St Joseph's, Preston, which was the same size, divided and had a detached console of similar design. The organ at Lancaster was built upon the most advanced principle of pneumatic action (tubular pneumatic), which was noted for its promptness of attack and repetition and light touch. Originally the 1,886 speaking pipes were supplied with various wind pressures from six reservoirs, which in turn received their supply from a very large main bellows worked by a three-throw crank, and blown by one of Duncan's Patent Hydraulic Engines.[1] In 1905 the instrument was the first in Lancaster to be electrified. The following specification is taken from an Ainscough booklet containing details of instruments, specifications and testimonials.

---

1 Ainscough Booklet of Organ Specifications and Testimonials c. 1896.

Specification of the Grand Organ In St Peter's, Lancaster

SPECIFICATION OF THE Grand Organ in St. Peter's, Lancaster,

BUILT BY

HENRY AINSCOUGH, of Preston.

The following is a Specification of the Organ which contains three complete Manuals and Pedals, viz:—

GREAT ORGAN, CC to A,—58 NOTES.

On a wind pressure of $3\frac{1}{2}$ inches.

No.				
1.	Double Open Diapason		Metal	16 Feet.
2.	Open Diapason		Metal	8 "
3.	Small Open Diapason		Metal	8 "
4.	Hohl Flöte		Wood	8 "
5.	Principal		Metal	4 "
6.	Flute Harmonic		Metal	4 "
7.	Twelfth		Metal	$2\frac{2}{3}$ "
8.	Fifteenth		Metal	2 "
9.	Mixture, 3 and 4 Ranks		Metal	various

On a wind pressure of $4\frac{1}{2}$ inches.

| 10. | Trumpet | | Metal | 8 " |

SWELL ORGAN, CC TO A,—58 NOTES.

On a wind pressure of $3\frac{1}{2}$ inches.

No.				
1.	Lieblich Bourdon		Wood	16 Feet.
2.	Open Diapason		Metal	8 "
3.	Salcional		Metal	8 "
4.	Voix Celestis		Metal	8 "
5.	Principal		Metal	4 "
6.	Mixture 2 and 3 Ranks		Metal	various
7.	Oboe		Metal	8 "
8.	Vox Humana		Metal	8 "

On a wind pressure of $4\frac{1}{4}$ inches.

| 9. | Horn | | Metal | 8 " |
| 10. | Clarion | | Metal | 4 " |

Tremulant acting on Nos. 1 to 8.

CHOIR ORGAN, CC TO A,—58 NOTES.

On a wind pressure of $2\frac{3}{4}$ inches.

No.				
1.	Gamba		Metal	8 Feet.
2.	Dulciana		Metal	8 "
3.	Lieblich Gedacht		Metal	8 "
4.	Flauto Traverso	Wood and Metal	8 "
5.	Salicet		Metal	4 "
6.	Clarionet		Metal	8 "
7.	Orchestral Oboe		Metal	8 "

PEDAL ORGAN CCC TO TENOR F,—30 NOTES.

On a wind pressure of $3\frac{3}{4}$ inches.

No.				
1.	Open Diapason		Wood	16 Feet.
2.	Contra Bass		Metal	16 "
3.	Bourdon		Wood	16 "
4.	Violoncello		Metal	8 "

On a wind pressure of $4\frac{1}{2}$ inches.

| 5. | Trombone | | Wood | 16 " |

Couplers—No. 1. Swell to Great.
No. 2. Swell to Octave.
No. 3. Swell to Choir.
No. 4. Swell to Pedals.
No. 5. Great to Pedals.
No. 6. Choir to Pedals.

Four self-reversing pistons acting upon the couplers, 1, 2, 4, and 5.
Two double-acting compositions to Swell Organ.
Three double-acting compositions to Great and Pedal Organs.
One Pedal reducing Pedal Organ to Bourdon, and also taking in great to Pedal Coupler.
One Pedal bringing on the FULL ORGAN and Swell to Great and Great to Pedal Couplers.
Handsome Oak Case, designed by Paley & Austin, Lancaster.

The organ was dedicated on the Feast of the Epiphany, Sunday 6 January 1889. Pontifical High Mass was celebrated by the Right Rev. Dr O'Reilly, Bishop of Liverpool, and the sermon entitled 'The use of music as an aid to religion' was preached by the Rev. R N Billington, then of St Augustine's, Preston. He took as his text 'Now bring me here a minstrel. And when the minstrel played the hand of the Lord came upon him,' (cf. Kings II, 3: 15). According to the local press his sermon traced the origin and development of music from its creation to the present time and showed its intimate connection with the people of God and Religion both in the Old and New Testaments.[2] Other clergy taking part were the Very Rev. Canon Walker, Rev. R Walsh, Rev. T Murphy, Rev. J Corbishley, Rev. J Preston, Rev. Dr Preston and Rev. R Etherington. Mr R Preston along with the Rev. R Etherington was master of ceremonies.

The choir sang Haydn's Imperial Mass and the soloists were, Miss Smithers (Soprano), Mrs Troughton (Contralto) and Mr Howson all of Lancaster, and Mr MacMahon (Tenor) and Mr Myerscough (Bass), both from St Wilfrid's, Preston. During the Offertory the choir sang *Ave Maria* by Lambillotte. Organ music included *Marche Romaine* by Gounod for the entry of the Bishop's procession, 'Larghetto' from Beethoven's Second Symphony during the Elevation and the *Grand Triumphal March* by Smart at the end of Mass. The organist on this occasion was James Tomlinson, a native of Lancaster, born in 1850. He was initially taught music by his father and became organist of the Wesleyan Chapel, Morecambe at the age of 11. Further study was undertaken with Edmund Sharpe and in 1868 Tomlinson was appointed Organist of St Thomas' Church, Lancaster. At the time of the dedication Tomlinson was organist of St Wilfrid's, Preston, appointed there in 1876 and he was also organist to Preston Corporation, a position he had held since 1882. In addition to these appointments he was a composer and joint lessee of the Theatre Royal Preston.

Celebrations continued in the afternoon with a service at which the Bishop was again present. In his address the Bishop spoke about the generous benefactors who had contributed to the magnificent building and Richard Leeming, donor of the organ. Following the example of the benefactors the Bishop encouraged the congregation to attend Mass and offer their gifts and prayers. The service ended with Benediction sung by the Bishop. Music heard during the afternoon included a *Barcarolle* by Sterndale Bennett and Gounod's *Marche Cortège* for organ, as well as the *Splendente* and *Deus Tibi Laus* by Mozart, Gounod's *O Salutaris* and *Tantum Ergo* for choir and soloists by Rossini.

As one would expect on such a special occasion as this the Church was full to capacity for High Mass and a large congregation was present in the afternoon. The dedication of the organ on such an important day as the Feast of the Epiphany was one to remember, and some may well have considered it to be one of the

---

2   *Lancaster Guardian*, 12 January 1889.

outstanding days in the life of the church since its Dedication in October 1859. This great occasion was tinged with sadness as Mr Richard Leeming had passed away on 22 September 1888. Both the Bishop and the Rev. Billington remembered him with affection, and hoped that his charity and love of sacred music had gained him a place with the blessed in Heaven.

A recital on the new instrument was given by James Tomlinson on Tuesday 8 January. According to the local press it was attended by an enthusiastic audience of approximately 1,000 which included the elite of the town and many music critics.[3]

Tomlinson began his programme with a piece in memory of the donor, Richard Leeming.

March Funèbre et Chant Séraphique	Guilmant
Storm Fantasie	Lemmens
Prelude and Fugue in A minor	Bach
Communion	Grison
First Concerto	Handel
Andante con variazioni	Beethoven
Elevation	Saint-Saëns
Marche Cortège	Gounod

Another press report describes the tonal qualities of the organ:

> It is of rich and mellow tone and leaves a grand impression as its full tones peal out in majestic roll. Of the solo stops the vox humana is remarkable for its effectiveness, and the clarinet, orchestral oboe, horn and the swell oboe are each excellent examples of very fine voicing. Stops of almost equal merit are the gamba, hohl flöte, gedact and vox celestes. The diapasons are as they should be a real foundation bass for the whole organ, which is superbly balanced in every department. The materials, workmanship and finish are undoubtedly of the very highest quality.[4]

Henry Ainscough received the followings testimonials concerning this instrument:[5]

> 8, Starkie Street, Winckley Square, Preston.
>
> *It gives me great pleasure to express my opinion on Mr AINSCOUGH'S powers as an Organ Builder. I am well acquainted with a number of excellent instruments built by him, the most recent example being the large one at St. Peter's, Lancaster, which I opened a few weeks ago.*

---

3 Ibid.
4 *Lancaster and Morecambe Chronicle,* 11 January 1889.
5 Ainscough booklet of Specifications and Testimonials.

This instrument is a noble specimen of a modern organ, and it is sufficient for me to say, that as regards mechanism, tone, soundness of material, and construction, it is unsurpassed by any instrument I have ever tried.

JAMES TOMLINSON
Organist to Preston Corporation.

* * *

MONS. WIEGAND'S opinion on the Organ built by Mr. Ainscough of Preston, for St. Peter's, Lancaster:

I have had great pleasure in touching your beautiful Organ. Really you have an instrument perfect in its mechanism and materials, its polished and admirably finished wood-work and pipes. The metal pipes are of excellent composition. The touch of the keys is very prompt, and excessively easy, as are also the pedals, which I myself would like heavier. Concerning the tone (soronite) it is truly beautiful. I should like the Choir Organ in a Swell box; with that you would certainly have a real gem of an organ. I consider you have a superb instrument.

The above is a translation of Mons. Wiegand's letter in French. You will understand it better than I can. He gave his opinion in answer to my express wish, and I am sure you will be gratified to have it.

W. WALKER (Canon), St. Peter's, Lancaster

***

St. Thomas', Waterloo, Liverpool, 19th February, 1890

Dear Sir,
I was exceedingly pleased with the Lancaster Organ. The touch of your Organs is always good, but the pneumatic action on the instrument at Lancaster makes the touch nearly perfect, and I noticed this especially in the pedal action, which is quite unique.

The tone quality of the Organ was also excellent, though owing to some defect in the hydraulic blowing apparatus, I was unable properly to test the great Organ. The whole instrument is however, of very high class in tone and workmanship, and does you great credit.

Believe me, Dear Sir,
Very truly yours,
ALBERT A. BENNETT

***

Mr. AINSCOUGH. Preston.

St. Peter's, Lancaster
November 26th 1894.

Dear Sir,

I have the pleasure to preside at one of your Organs built in the above Church, and it gives me intense satisfaction to testify to its wonderful capabilities, and to the beautiful work it contains; work, I believe, executed at not too great a cost; reflecting greater credit on its conscientious builder.

I am afraid to give too great a vent to my own private opinions, as many remarks made, and justly so, have been classed as 'big', only to be verified and more than verified by an attendance and a tune; however, compared with other instruments of a like construction, which I have not only played but been used to, I feel bound to vote on every point in favour of Mr. Ainscough's.

The points in which this Organ excels any others I know of are first, the large amount of variety he obtains out of the few number of stops, in this case I have thirty-eight, but I have as much, and better at that, than I've had out of fifty or even more. There is not a duplicate stop in the Organ, i.e., no two stops are alike, save in one or two cases in name only. There is no sign of competition between even the reeds, each having its own respective tone, colour, and intensity, and the same could be said of all the work throughout.

Secondly, the excellent way in which these stops, individually so good, combine; and yet it is difficult to state in which this or that set of pipes excel, singly or combined.

Thirdly, the grandeurs of the action— the point in which Organs built by those spoken of as the 'only and best Englishmen' have failed miserably. I myself have played on such, and set my mind against the action,—poor action; it was reserved for Lancaster and Preston to show what could be done in the way of perfection in tubular pneumatics.

Faithfully yours,
JOHN HUGHES HOLLOWAY,

Organist and Ch. M., St. Peter's, Lancaster,
Associate of the Royal College of Organists
Late of Portsmouth Cathedral.

Henry Ainscough, Esq.

John Hughes Holloway (brother of F W Holloway, Organist at the Crystal Palace and Conductor of the Palace Orchestral and Choral Society) had succeeded Laurenz Schmitz who retired from his post in 1894. When Holloway moved to

Ushaw College in 1904, Mr T Morrison became organist and he was succeeded by James Hugh Reginald Dixon who took up his appointment on 20 May 1909.

Enclosed in a letter from Ainscough to Dixon dated 23rd June 1909 is an estimate for improvements to the instrument, which Dixon must have suggested and thought necessary.[6]

> Choir Organ:
> Complete the Clarinet to CC with all stays and fittings   £10 – 0 – 0
> Complete Orchestral Oboe to CC with all stays and fittings,
> alteration to upper boards and providing a supply of wind   £10 – 0 – 0
> To enclose the Choir Organ using same materials as the Swell Box
> Alter the position of the off basses and put them at the back of the
> Choir Organ
> Shutters vertical. Opening to the nave of the Church
> To have two Balanced Pedals close together so that they can be
> used alone or together
> Price for box, fitting up, grooving off basses and the two
> balanced pedals   £22 – 0 – 0
> Add a tremulant of a different beat to the present swell one
> Price with all draw stop movement and fittings   £6 – 10 – 0
>
> Swell Organ:
> Add Open 8ft Flute of either wood or metal, or wood throughout
> Open pipes from tenor G sharp to top 38 pipes 20 pipes being closed
> This stop to be placed in the space occupied by the oboe which it is proposed to be move to the space occupied by the present 4ft clarion and revoice the oboe to the same tone it has now upon the heavier wind pressure
> Make provision of another slide and block with upper board and all fittings for the clarion and the requisite draw stop movements   £31 – 0 – 0
> Swell Bass of Bourdon suggested to be borrowed for the pedal organ and with all requisite pneumatic movement, wind chest and draw stop movement
>   £18 – 10 – 0

From information written by Dixon on the back of the letter it would appear that if only some of the suggested alterations could be done then his preference was for the Choir to be enclosed and the Swell Bass of Bourdon to be borrowed for the Pedal. Some of the above suggestions were never to materialise in his lifetime, but the Choir Organ was eventually enclosed in the restoration of 1956.

With regard to wind pressures those given by W A Roberts of Liverpool in his article entitled 'Henry Ainscough: Organ Builder of Preston' for the swell

---

6   Letter, Dixon archive.

Ainscough console
(Bernard Stephenson)

flues, pedal flues and choir vary slightly from those given by Ainscough and Dixon.

Roberts also gives a few more details on the stops than is indicated in the Ainscough Organ Builders Booklet, having examined the instrument in detail on a visit to Lancaster in 1928. Great: Double Open (Zinc), Hohl Flute stopped bass tenor C, Mixture 4rks in upper 1½ octaves and 3rks below. Swell: Celestes tenor C, Mixture 3rks upper 1½ octaves and 2 below. Choir: Gamba (straight slotted pipes), Flauto Traverso harmonic, Salicet (octave gamba), Clarinet to B flat. Pedal: Contra Bass (Zinc), Trombone lower octave wood and upper octave metal. Couplers: Swell octave on own keyboard and to Great. Roberts refers to the flutes as delicious in their ripple, especially the triangular hohl flute, the choir flauto traverso and the gedackt of quintadena timbre.[7]

During the early months of his appointment Dixon would find considerable

---

7   *The Organ*, April 1929, Vol. VIII, No. 32, p 213.

alterations taking place in the church, which affected the services. The work included a new high altar designed by Gilbert Scott, made of black marble with a frontal of white marble, which replaced the original altar given by the widow of Gabriel Coulston, a marble reredos and a triptych designed after the school of Dürer; new flooring – the black and white tiles in the chancel being replaced with black and white marble blocks; new flooring in the nave, aisles, chantries and transepts; new seating, the old dark-stained pitch pine being replaced with new oak; new oak doors and a screen was erected around the west door; the walls were re-coloured and the stone work cleaned. All these alterations were completed by the end of September in time to celebrate the fiftieth anniversary of the consecration of the church.

Prior to the official celebrations on Sunday 3 October, several events took place, including the veneration of the relics of SS. Urban and Valerian which were to be sealed in the new altar after its consecration. Pontifical High Mass was sung by Dr Singleton, Bishop of Shrewsbury, in the presence of Dr Whiteside, Bishop of Liverpool. The Bishop of Newport, Dr Hedley, preached the sermon taking for his text a sentence from the Epistle for the day 'I give thanks to my God that in all things you are made rich in Jesus Christ.'

As the Bishop entered the church the choir sang the anthem 'Ecce Sacerdos Magnus', the music being specially composed for the occasion by Prior Burge OSB, who dedicated the work to Canon Billington and the choir of St Peter's. An arrangement by Dixon of Gounod's Mass *Angeli Custodes* was used for the main parts of the Mass, while the introit, gradual, offertory and communion were sung to Solesmes plainchant. Prior Burge conducted the choir and the organ accompaniment was provided by Dixon. The concluding voluntary was the *Song of Triumph* by John E West. In the evening Benediction was given by Bishop Whiteside. The music at this service included the hymn 'Faith of our Fathers', 'Salve Regina' and the solemn 'Te Deum' sung to plainsong, *O Salutaris* by Gounod and Palestrina's *Tantum Ergo*.

The Rector at St Peter's in 1909 was Canon Richard Newman Billington whose writings included 'A History of St Peter's', published in 1909 and the first part of the 1913 Lancaster Pageant. He was assisted by the Rev. Dr James Kenny and Rev. Richard Bilsborrow, who according to Dixon were both keen golfers, and Rev. Edward Stephens.

At this time the choir of men and boys numbered approximately 30 members. Their repertoire included a variety of Masses and Motets by Palestrina, Vittoria, Viadana, Tallis and Byrd. The Proper of the Mass was regularly sung to plainsong melodies found in the Graduale. As a choirmaster, Dixon was a strict disciplinarian who demanded high musical standards and commitment from his choir.

Dixon gave his first organ recital in St Peter's on Wednesday 3 November 1909 (the proceeds being for the Jubilee Fund). The programme read as follows:

Ancient Organ Music
a) 'Voluntary for ye single Organ' Dr John Blow
(From a Seventeenth Century MSS in the British Museum)
b) Toccata in F J S Bach

Modern Music
a) Prelude 'Dream of Gerontius' Elgar
b) Finale 'Symphony Pathetic' Tschaikowski

Antiphon
'Salve Regina' Roder
St. Peter's Choir Men

Descriptive Pieces
a) Legend 'St. Francis preaching to the Birds' Liszt
b) March Rubenstein
c) A Storm at Sea R.D.

Pieces in Various Styles
a) 'O Sanctissima' Meale
b) 'Pastorale' Dixon
c) 'Grand Chœur' Dixon

Well-known musicians in the town at the time included Wesley Martin, Organist of the Priory Church, E A Taylor Mus.Bac., A K Hawthenthwaite Mus. Bac., Robert Stavely, Organist of St Michael's and All Angels, The County Asylum, Alfred Moreland, a blind organist who played at St Luke's, Skerton, Mr C Chadderton, Mr A Douthwaite from the Wesley Methodist Church, Mr J W Aldous, Music Master at the Royal Grammar School as well as Conductor of the Aldous Choir and Orchestra, and Mr R T Grosse, Conductor of the Male Voice Choir and the Centenary Quartette. Mr Grosse was also an organist and in the late 1890's held an appointment at Over Kellet Parish Church. Later he became organist at the Centenary Congregational Church before taking up an appointment at Christ Church, Lancaster. In addition to these organists many of whom taught music, there were several highly qualified instrumental and singing teachers in the town.

On first coming to Lancaster Dixon became Conductor of the Yealand Choral Society. In December 1909 they gave a performance of Dvořák's *Te Deum* and the *Christmas Oratorio* by J S Bach, at a venue in Kendal, under the direction of Henry J Wood Conductor of the Queen's Hall Orchestra. The Choral Society entered competitive music festivals and it was at the Morecambe Music Festival one year that Dixon met Elgar, who was a regular visitor to the Festival and an enthusiastic supporter of amateur music making. Dixon also conducted the Lancaster Amateur Dramatic and Operatic Society (LADOS) until joining up in the First World War. In a lighter vein he played the piano in Beeley's Dance Band and formed a concert party known as 'The Merry Ones'. In addition to these activities Dixon had a private teaching practice and soon became a popular recitalist in the area.

When Dixon arrived in Lancaster the Town Hall was in the process of being built. This building, which was a gift from Lord Ashton at a cost of approximately £350,000, was finally officially opened on 27 December 1909 after being postponed twice before Christmas. The Public Hall, known as the Ashton Hall, within the Town Hall building was to become a valuable asset as a Concert Hall to the musical life of the city for future generations. A new organ built for this Hall by Messrs. Norman & Beard of Norwich was also given by Lord Ashton and is situated in a special gallery above the platform with the console in the centre. The richly carved oak case with pipes gilded in gold leaf was the work of craftsmen employed by the world renowned firm of Messrs. Gillow & Co., Lancaster.

Wesley Martin gave the first recital on the new organ as people gathered for the opening ceremony of the new Town Hall, then after dinner invited guests went to Lord Ashton's home where Dixon entertained them.

In a report on the opening proceedings the following comments were made about the organ:

> The volume of sound from full organ is truly awe-inspiring, but more pleasing still is the full rich exquisite beauty of the stops, especially the vox humana which is certainly as near the reproduction of a perfect tuned human voice as one can expect a mechanical contrivance to come.[8]

On the evening of the opening day there was a subscription Ball at which music was provided by Mr Beeley's Dance Band. The following day there was a children's dance and entertainment in the form of a Punch and Judy show and a ventriloquial performance.

Due to the delay in opening the building the Lancaster Choral Society had to rearrange their performance of Handel's *Messiah* which took place on Wednesday 29 December with soloists, Madame C Siviter (Soprano), Miss Ada Phillips (Contralto), Mr Charles Saunders (Tenor) and Mr Frederick Austin (Bass). The orchestra was augmented by some professional musicians with Miss Hothersall LISM at the organ and Mr John Paley (Trumpet) was the soloist in the air 'The trumpet shall sound'.

Early in the New Year (4–14 January 1910), several receptions were held by the Mayor and Mayoress. Each evening from 6.00 p.m. to 10.00 p.m. invited guests were given a tour of the new buildings, provided with refreshments and

---

8   *Lancaster Guardian*, 1 January 1910.

Ashton Hall Lancaster, Norman & Beard 1909.
(Original specification)

Great Organ
Double Open Diapason	16
Large Open Diapason	8
Medium Open Diapason	8
Geigen Principal	8
Clarabella	8
Octave	4
Hohl Flute	4
Twelfth	2 2/3
Fifteenth	2
Mixture	3 rks
Trumpet	8
Clarion	4
Sub Octave Coupler to Great Reeds	
Ped. Compos to Great Pistons	

Swell Organ
Contra Gamba	16
Open Diapason	8
Rohr Flöte	8
Viol d'Orchestre	8
Voix Céleste	8
Principal	4
Flageolet	2
Contra Fagotta	16
Horn	8
Oboe	8
Vox Humana	8
Clarion	4
Tremulant	
Swell Octave	
Swell Sub Octave	

Solo Organ
Harmonic Flute	8
Concert Flute	4
Clarinet	8
Orchestral Oboe	8
Tuba	8
Tremulant	
Solo Sub Octave	
Solo Octave	

Choir Organ
Gamba	8
Lieblich Gedact	8
Dulciana	8
Flauto Traverso	4

Pedal Organ
Sub Bourdon (from Bourdon)	32
Open Diapason (Wood)	16
Violone (from Great Bourdon)	16
Bourdon	16
Bass Flute (from Bourdon)	8
Octave (from Open Diapason)	8
Trombone	16
Tromba (from Trombone)	8

Couplers
Solo Unison off
Solo to Great
Solo to Choir
Swell Unison off
Swell to Great
Swell to Choir
Choir to Great
Solo to Pedal
Swell to Pedal
Great to Pedal
Choir to Pedal

Accessories
5 pistons to Great
5 pistons to Swell
3 pistons to Choir
4 pistons to Solo
Reversible piston, Swell to Great
Reversible piston, Solo to Great
Reversible pedal, Great to Pedal
5 composition pedals to Pedal
5 composition pedals to Swell (duplicate)
Balanced pedals for Swell and Solo
Compass of manuals: CC to C, 61 notes
Compass of pedal: CCC to G, 32 notes

entertained in the Ashton Hall with instrumental and choral music performed by local musicians.

Six organists took turns to perform and compete for the appointment of Corporation Organist. Dixon was selected for the position (although there was no official written confirmation as such) and so began a lifelong association for him with this instrument, the building, local musicians and others from afar, both amateur and professional singers and instrumentalists.

On Wednesday 23 February 1910, the Lancaster Male Voice Choir conducted by Mr R T Grosse held their sixth annual concert in the Ashton Hall. The principal soloists on this occasion were Miss Gertrude Lonsdale (Contralto), who had been engaged to appear in the forthcoming Beecham Grand Opera season at Covent Garden, Mr John Harrison regarded as a fine English tenor and Mr J H Ditchburn (Bass) noted for his extensive range and pure tone. Several pieces sung by the Centenary Prize Quartette formed a contrast between the soloists and the choir. As well as acting as accompanist Dixon played some organ solos including works by Handel, Elgar, Wagner, Widor and by special request *Storm at Sea* arranged Dixon. Having been in Lancaster less than a year Dixon had already made his mark on the musical scene.

Dixon at the Ashton Hall Organ (G Wynspeare Herbert, Lancaster)

The following quote is taken from a report on the concert:

> Reference must not be omitted to the fine work at the organ and 'Grandette' piano of Mr J H R Dixon, a gentleman who in addition to being an accomplished musician, is also a collector of letters. At present he is entitled to write about half the alphabet after his signature, but he is young and we have hopes of his annexing the remaining letters in due course.[9]

The 'Grandette' piano mentioned in the report was a new instrument designed by Arthur Allison of London and supplied by Bearman Brothers of Lancaster. It was a small grand piano (four feet eight inches in length) of symmetrical construction, noted for its quality of tone and touch.

A Grand Organ Recital and Concert was held in the Ashton Hall on Wednesday 12 October 1910. On this occasion Dixon was joined by Madame Sadler-Fogg (Soprano), John Sheridan (Violinist), and The Centenary Quartette, Messrs. R T Grosse, T Whittaker, E Ellis, and F Cockerill. The ticket prices ranged from 6*d.* to 3*s.* and the programmes cost 2*d.*

The programme began with Dixon introducing each stop on the organ in turn and in combination displaying the range and quality of the instrument through improvisation. Organ solos in the first half of the programme included, Overture *Zampa* by Herold, Bach's Chorale Prelude *Herr Jesu Christ, dich zu uns wend*, excerpts from *Casse Noisette* by Tschaikowski [sic], 'In Hammersbach' from *Three Bavarian Dances* by Elgar and ending with Lemare's *Toccata di Concerto*.

Madame Sadler-Fogg, wife of the celebrated organist C H Fogg and known before her marriage as the Scottish Soprano, sang the aria 'With Verdure Clad' from Haydn's *Creation* and several songs including the well-known *Solveig's Song* by Grieg. It was reported in the local press that 'She sang admirably and trilled out the higher passages with wonderful clarity of tone.'[10]

The same reporter commenting on the performance given by the Quartette wrote:

> The Centenary Quartette sang charmingly. They presented delicately-harmonised old English Melodies and again proved what consummate artists they are. As usual they sang unaccompanied except when the Town Hall chimes yielded to the impulse of the moment and burst into song on their own account. The Singers breathed gently: 'If e'er a sigh had learned to leave my breast' and the chimes cut in boldly 'ding-dong, ding-dong', and intimated with a loud voice that no matter what the Quartette said this was the year of grace, 1910 and it was nine of the clock and a stormy night. The effect was very weird.[11]

---

9 *Lancaster Mail*, 25 February 1910.
10 *Lancaster Mail*, 14 October 1910.
11 Ibid.

Mr John Sheridan of Liverpool, making his first appearance in Lancaster as a solo violinist, chose a selection of pieces to demonstrate his technique and artistic interpretation. These included two compositions by Schubert one being an arrangement of *Ave Maria* (Wilhelmj), the other a piece entitled *L'Abeille*, Wieniawski's *Legende*, and a *Canzonetta* by Victor Herbert.

Again the soloists were accompanied by Dixon on the Allison Grandette piano. Organ solos in the second half of the programme included a Grand Selection from *H M S Pinafore* by Sullivan, Rossini's *William Tell Overture* and the first performance in Lancaster of a *Prelude and Fugue* by the Bohemian composer Josef Segart. Another piece performed for the first time was Dixon's own composition *A Shepherd's Idylle*, which depicts the myriad-voice song of nature, rustling leaves, the babbling brook, gentle zephyrs, the hum of insects and bird song interspersed with the shepherd boy imitating their notes on his pipe. In these early days of popular recitals no programme seemed complete without Dixon playing his arrangement of the famous *Storm at Sea* piece! From the report quoted above the writer gives a description of Dixon's performance:

> The outstanding feature of a most enjoyable concert was the artful jugglery of Mr Dixon. Other gifted persons can produce rabbits and white mice out of a top hat, but Mr Dixon's sleight of hand was much more stupendous. He seized the organ gently but firmly with both hands and produced choirs of angels, shipwrecks, earthquakes, and piping arcadian shepherds. He caressed the instrument dreamily and cast his audience into woods where rippling brooks harmonized with the rustling of the leaves and the voices of birds. He assaulted the organ with demoniacal fury and straightway the thunder roared through the hall, the waters surged, the winds were unloosed and the lightnings unchained. One felt like reaching out for a life-belt. It was a time of exquisite peril. Again he pressed a button and unveiled a musical cinematograph. We saw a grey old monastery, tinged with the red autumn sun, and heard voices of the choir rising on the rose-scented air. If we burnt magicians in these days, Mr Dixon would be a cinder now.[12]

Throughout 1910 the concerts described above and similar musical events had taken place, but members of the Town Council were encouraged to make fullest use of the new hall and its fine organ, by promoting Municipal Concerts and Recitals for the people at popular prices. This was a period when recitals were given on magnificent organs in Town and City Halls throughout the country. It was an era when notable organists played arrangements of orchestral pieces and when the appointment of a city organist was fashionable. The idea of having

---

12 Ibid.

Saturday evening concerts and recitals was suggested and as an experiment one such recital was given by Dixon (thought to be in December 1910 but the exact date is unknown) under the auspices of the Corporation.

Dixon chose the following programme of popular pieces which was designed to appeal to a wide public taste and to show off the instrument to the full.

Toccata in F (brilliant pedal passages)	J S Bach
Siegfried Idyll (exquisite)	R Wagner
Fantasia on Popular Melodies of a patriotic nature	J H R Dixon
Christmas Music: Adeste Fidelis	J A Meale
Nazareth	C Gounod
William Tell Overture	G A Rossini
National Anthems of the Allies	

Miss Alice Webb vocalist for the evening sang two solos: *Caro Mio Ben* by Giordani and *Morning Bright* by Goring Thomas. The recital was attended by a large enthusiastic audience and proved to be a success.

Saturday 4 February 1911 saw the first of a series of recitals for the people promoted by the Corporation. An improvised Prelude introducing all the stops on the organ was repeated by request. Other pieces in this recital included the Andante from the Unfinished Symphony by Schubert, A Grand Selection from *Carmen* by Bizet, works by Meale, West, Guilmant, Handel and the first performance of Dixon's own composition *Melodie in D flat* which is based on the opening eight note phrase.

Example 4, Melodie in D flat, bars 1–4

The success of this first concert encouraged the Town Hall Committee and the Corporation as a whole to continue providing the Saturday Evening Concerts. Apart from the desire to make full use of the Ashton Hall and the organ provided by Lord Ashton, it was also considered that the provision of good music whether instrumental or vocal, would exercise an elevating and refining power upon those who attended the concerts.

These recitals attracted huge audiences of over 1,000 people at any one time and proved that those who advocated introducing such recitals and concerts were indeed wise. Dixon put a great deal of effort into making these recitals successful by playing popular pieces and believing that at the bottom of '99 per cent' of people there was a real love of music, though it was sometimes undeveloped.

A visit to Lancaster by King George V on 24 August 1912 was the first of many Royal visits when Dixon as Corporation Organist would give a special recital. The programme on this occasion was as follows:

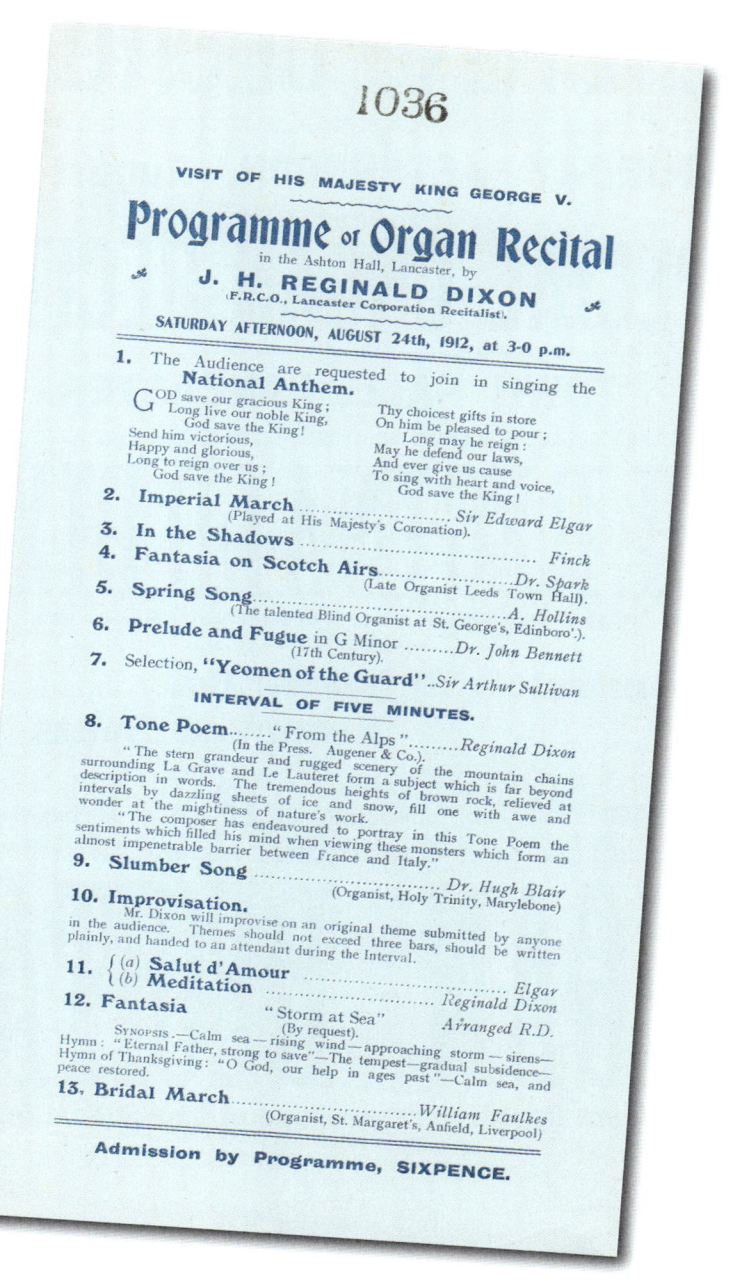

> **1036**
>
> VISIT OF HIS MAJESTY KING GEORGE V.
>
> ## Programme of Organ Recital
>
> in the Ashton Hall, Lancaster, by
>
> **J. H. REGINALD DIXON**
> (F.R.C.O., Lancaster Corporation Recitalist).
>
> SATURDAY AFTERNOON, AUGUST 24th, 1912, at 3-0 p.m.
>
> 1. The Audience are requested to join in singing the **National Anthem.**
>
> GOD save our gracious King;
> Long live our noble King,
> God save the King!
> Send him victorious,
> Happy and glorious,
> Long to reign over us;
> God save the King!
>
> Thy choicest gifts in store
> On him be pleased to pour;
> Long may he reign;
> May he defend our laws,
> And ever give us cause
> To sing with heart and voice,
> God save the King!
>
> 2. **Imperial March** .... Sir Edward Elgar
> (Played at His Majesty's Coronation).
> 3. **In the Shadows** .... Finck
> 4. **Fantasia on Scotch Airs** .... Dr. Spark
> (Late Organist Leeds Town Hall).
> 5. **Spring Song** .... A. Hollins
> (The talented Blind Organist at St. George's, Edinboro').
> 6. **Prelude and Fugue** in G Minor .... Dr. John Bennett
> (17th Century).
> 7. Selection, **"Yeomen of the Guard"** ...... Sir Arthur Sullivan
>
> **INTERVAL OF FIVE MINUTES.**
>
> 8. **Tone Poem** .... "From the Alps" .... Reginald Dixon
> (In the Press. Augener & Co.).
> "The stern grandeur and rugged scenery of the mountain chains surrounding La Grave and Le Lauteret form a subject which is far beyond description in words. The tremendous heights of brown rock, relieved at intervals by dazzling sheets of ice and snow, fill one with awe and wonder at the mightiness of nature's work.
> "The composer has endeavoured to portray in this Tone Poem the sentiments which filled his mind when viewing these monsters which form an almost impenetrable barrier between France and Italy."
> 9. **Slumber Song** .... Dr. Hugh Blair
> (Organist, Holy Trinity, Marylebone)
> 10. **Improvisation.**
> Mr. Dixon will improvise on an original theme submitted by anyone in the audience. Themes should not exceed three bars, should be written plainly, and handed to an attendant during the Interval.
> 11. { (a) **Salut d'Amour** .... Elgar
> { (b) **Meditation** .... Reginald Dixon
> 12. **Fantasia** "Storm at Sea" Arranged R.D.
> (By request).
> SYNOPSIS.—Calm sea—rising wind—approaching storm—sirens—Hymn: "Eternal Father, strong to save"—The tempest—gradual subsidence—Hymn of Thanksgiving: "O God, our help in ages past"—Calm sea, and peace restored.
> 13. **Bridal March** .... William Faulkes
> (Organist, St. Margaret's, Anfield, Liverpool)
>
> **Admission by Programme, SIXPENCE.**

VISIT OF
H.M. KING GEORGE V.

SATURDAY AFTERNOON, August 24th.

SPECIAL ORGAN RECITAL.

TOWN HALL, LANCASTER.

J. H. REGINALD DIXON
(F.R.C.O., Lancaster Corporation Recitalist).

Admission (by Programme) 6d.
Reserved Seats, 1s.

Doors open 2-30 p.m.   Commence at 3-0 p.m.   Carriages 4-30.

ORGAN RECITAL.

Magnificent Organ.   Programme of Exceptional Interest.

The First World War

The outbreak of war in July 1914 interrupted Dixon's career as it did for countless musicians and for many it was to be the end of their career. Dixon joined the City of London Sanitary Company, RAMC, but in between training and being assigned to various tasks he continued to study via a correspondence course, compose and give recitals whenever the opportunity arose.

In 1914 Dixon set to music John Dryden's 'Song for St Cecilia's Day' written in 1687. The work scored for contralto solo, vocal quartette and chorus with an accompaniment for strings is dated 14 October 1914 and was submitted for his Bachelor of Music Exercise. Originally Dixon intended to set the whole poem, but for this exercise omitted verses 3, 4 and 5 hence the abrupt change of key from F major to E flat major between verse 2 and 6. The choice of keys, tempi and dynamics all reflect the mood of the text. This composition displays unison, homophonic and contrapuntal vocal writing with some use of chromaticism and word painting. There are antiphonal phrases between the instrumental and vocal parts as well as contrast between the lower and upper strings and voices.

One Saturday afternoon in 1915 while on training in Yorkshire, Dixon appeared in army uniform at Hull City Hall to give an organ recital. It was a popular programme with works by J S Bach, Wagner, Mascagni, Ravel and Dixon, including the first performance of his *Stanzas on a Martial Theme*. It was reported that the large and appreciative audience requested several encores.

In May 1915 Dixon wrote a letter to the editor of the *Musical Standard* endorsing the idea of a monthly column on Roman Catholic Church Music suggested by John Donald in a previous letter.[1] As a Catholic musician Dixon felt that such musicians had little opportunity of comparing notes and experiences and were to a certain extent isolated. In his letter he went on to suggest various topics for such a column and this resulted in Dixon being invited by the editor to write a monthly series of articles entitled 'Roman Catholic Church Music Notes'. With the exception of cathedrals and a few other notable places of worship, it was observed that the state

---

1 *Musical Standard,* 1 May 1915, Vol. V, No. 122.

of music in Roman Catholic churches at this time was poor, so the principal aim of these notes was to improve the standard of music through practical help and advice along the lines laid down in the 'Moto Proprio' of 1903 by Pope Pius X. In addition it was hoped to foster a spirit of mutual self-help among Catholic choirmasters, stimulate readers into action and be of interest to the general reader. A letter from Wallace L Crowdy, editor of the *Musical Standard,* was sent to Dixon thanking him for his first contribution and saying 'its originality and practicability are admirable.'[2] Topics for discussion included composition of the choir, a review of music in current use, music publishing and the art of plainsong. Dixon was of the opinion that there was a place in Catholic services for the best music from each century and referred to the word 'Catholic' meaning universal as to time, as well as place. It was not possible for Dixon to maintain a regular contribution to the magazine in 1916. In the first three articles of that year, one published in January and two in April Dixon writes about his experience of attending services in London. On the fourth Sunday of Advent 1915 he was in Westminster Cathedral and describes the architecture, the atmosphere and the music sung at High Mass.[3] Later that day he visited St Etheldreda's, Ely Place and writes a short paragraph on the history of the church, followed by some notes on the Lewis organ and the small choir of men and boys. He was impressed by the enthusiastic congregational singing at Vespers and Benediction and derived great pleasure from this and other visits there.[4] In April 1916 Dixon was again in Westminster Cathedral attending services throughout Holy Week and gives an account and appreciation of the music sung by the choir directed by Dr Richard Terry.[5] After further unavoidable disruption Dixon resumed writing for the *Musical Standard* in November 1916.

Between December 1915 and January 1916 Dixon was in Lancaster during which time he appeared at the Ashton Hall on three occasions. He gave an organ recital on 4 December, and later that month on 29 December accompanied the Aldous Choir in a performance of Handel's *Messiah* in aid of the Red Cross Society, followed by another organ recital on 8 January assisted by Mr T Howarth (Bass) and Sergeant Menzies (Violin), the proceeds being for the Mayoress' Comfort Fund.

Organ recitals at the Ashton Hall continued throughout the war. Moving the Minutes of the Town Hall Committee, March 1916, the Mayor said that the last organ recital was a success owing to the efforts of Mr Gooch, but if the war got over and they got their organist back the recitals would be an even greater success.[6]

---

2   Letter, Dixon archive.
3   *Musical Standard*, 22 January 1916, Vol. VII, No. 160.
4   *Musical Standard,* 3 April 1916, Vol. VII, No. 170.
5   *Musical Standard,* 29 April 1916, Vol. VII, No. 174.
6   *Lancaster Guardian,* 4 March 1916.

Meanwhile Dixon had returned to London and continued to perform whenever possible. His name appears on a programme as assistant accompanist with J A Meale solo organ and accompanist at the 106th Popular Concert held in the Wesleyan Central Methodist Hall, 12 February 1916.

On Easter Sunday evening 1916 Dixon made a return visit to Stockton-on-the-Forest (the village where he grew up and where his parents still lived), to give an organ recital at Holy Trinity Church with Sergeant C Dawson (Asc) in aid of the Red Cross Fund.

In May 1916 Dixon appeared in army uniform at the Royal Albert Hall to receive his Bachelor of Music Degree which he had obtained as an external student of London University in 1915, gaining a distinction in playing at sight from vocal and instrumental score. At this time he was on training in Chelsea and as Director of Music of his corps his musical abilities were much in demand both as a performer and in arranging a variety of concerts. While the organ at St Peter's remained silent Dixon could be found playing the organ for services at several notable places including Westminster Cathedral and Brompton Oratory.

A postcard dated 27/7/1916 showing a group of soldiers entitled Crowboro Camp was sent home to his mother. On the reverse side the message reads;

> How do you like this? It is our detachment here. We all live together and have a jolly good time. I am developing into a Water colour painter and a champion 'Ping Pong' player. I'm lighting the cigarette.
>
> Reg

Crowboro Camp (Dixon archive)

Dixon always had a sense of humour. During the war on the front of a folded piece of scrap paper he wrote the following inscription for his tombstone:[7]

**HERE LIETH
THE BODY OF**

PRIVATE DIXON

WHO
Fell ASLEEP
At 6 – 5 A.M.
ONCE

'When the Roll is called up
Yonder, I'll be there'
(His favourite Text)

NO COAL BY REQUEST IT'S QUITE HOT ENOUGH
REST IN PEACE

Inside there is a pencil sketch and several rough water colour brush strokes, with the following message on the opposite page:

NOTICE

THE CONTENTS OF THE FAMOUS
<u>DIXON GALLERIES</u>
HAVE BEEN LOST

ANY INFORMATION LEADING TO THE RECOVERY OF THE SAME WILL BE
GRATEFULLY RECEIVED BY THE SAID DIXON

On the back is a drawing of the points of a 'crowbro' compass with a funny face in the middle.

---

7 Dixon archive.

Male Voice Choir (Dixon archive)
(Eug. Oulmann Lyon)

For some time Dixon was Music Director at a military station near Lyon. It was here that he had a band and a male voice choir. This not only gave him the opportunity to arrange well-known pieces for the resources he had, but also to compose music for the group.

A manuscript book of composition sketches and arrangements of works by other composers is dated 23rd June 1917 and labelled Pte. J H Reginald Dixon 528210 No. 2 Mediterranean Rest Camp, St. Germain Mont d'Or France. Many years later on a return visit to this area some people in the village recognised him and remembered him playing the organ.

Dixon spent Christmas Day 1917 with his family in Stockton-on-the-Forest and in the afternoon gave a recital at Holy Trinity Church in aid of the Belgium Relief Fund.

A Concert under the direction of Pte J H Reginald Dixon was given on 17 April 1918, venue unknown. The musicians taking part were those in the orchestra, the Pierrot Troupe and the following soloists, Spr. Wellstead, Pte. Goodall, Q. S. Stewart, 2/Lt. Knowles, Sgt. Weedon, Pte. Wigglesworth, Mlle. de Vincent, L/Cpl. Shrive, Spr. Parker.

In June 1918 Dixon for reasons unknown transferred from one section of the RAMC to another and below is a copy of a testimonial written by A G Trollope:[8]

---

8 Ibid.

Pierrot Troupe (Eug. Oulmann Lyon)

> Rest Camp, St Germain Au Mont.
> D'Or, France
> 17th June, 1918

Pte J. H. R. Dixon 109th Sanitary Section has been in this camp over a year. He is a F.R.C.O. and Bachelor of Music, trained our Male Voice Choir and Conducted our Orchestra. He is an immense loss to this camp. Through being able to give High Class Concerts we have amused troops passing through this camp in thousands, and it has thereby stopped men breaking out of camp and many other crimes.

At the same time we have been able to send away to Prisoners of War Funds and other Charities substantial sums of money.

I can highly recommend Pte Dixon: he is a first class musician and fine character.

> A. G. Trollope,
> Lt. Col.- Commandant.

Army Camp Orchestra (Dixon archive)

While at this camp Dixon composed a piece for orchestra entitled *Les Fleurs de Mont d'Or* which he dedicated to Lt. Col. Trollope.

Dixon not only performed and composed music, but was also a creative writer of stories and poems. Here are two poems written in October 1918 when he had moved to Driencourt in northern France, a town reduced to rubble in the war.[9]

> The Raiders
>
> 'Swallow flying – tell me, who
> can wing the sky as fleet as you?'
> 'Birds of prey – by hunger sped
> swiftly pounce on live or dead:'
> 'Dread eyed eagle from the air
> who with you such trophies share?'
> 'Hellish Fledglings – born of hate
> have wrenched from us our dreaded state.'
> 'Quinted drone on murder bent
> In whose service you are sent?'
> 'Lucifer – first fiend of the war
> Him we own – and his we are!'
>
> *Driencourt: Oct. 1918 J H Reginald Dixon Mus. Bac. FRCO*
> *(Pte. R A M C 48th Sanitary Section)*

---

9   Ibid.

> ### Happy Valley
>
> 'Yes – there they lie; where vengeful sickle reaped
> midst shattering roar – its harvest grim of death.
> A week has scarce elapsed, and now, no breath
> of wind can pass the place – but it is steeped
> In rotting stench; Disgusting, nauseous – vile,
> Their goulish faces, gorged with blackened blood –
> Their gaping mouths, and hideous sightless eyes, the
> food which countless crawling maggots do defile.
> They are but Huns, – yet, British Soldiers lie
> In earthly hells – who long since passed away.
> And you and I, and yours and mine – shall die,
> And dust to dust – corruptions toll shall pay.
> O! Soul of man – immortal – free – sublime
> Thou, thou alone dost reign for endless time.'
>
> *Driencourt 2.10.18. J H Reginald Dixon Mus.Bac.FRCO*
> *(Pte. R A M C 48th Sanitary Section)*

Towards the end of the war Dixon was in Charleroi, Belgium, a town situated on the river Sambre, and after the Armistice he stayed on there until 1919.

Dixon told an amusing story (though not funny at the time) of the occasion when he was asked to play for Mass which was attended by the Mayor and some notable dignitaries. At the end of Mass he should have played the Belgium National Anthem which he knew well, but unfortunately when the time came he inadvertently played a French Army marching song with a very similar melody, thus creating an embarrassing situation for everyone.

While in Charleroi Dixon composed an orchestral piece *Suite Carolorégienne* dated June 1919 which has three movements entitled, 'L'Entrée' (The Entry of British troops into Charleroi November 1918), 'Merci' and 'Le Départ' (British troops leave Charleroi). Two small manuscript books from this period containing compositional exercises reveal that Dixon was undertaking some kind of study, possibly in Charleroi, though this work may relate to a correspondence course which at some time he had taken with A G Iggulden Mus. Doc. Dunelm FRCO.

It was in Charleroi that he met Alice Marie Victorine Jamart, a young concert pianist and Professor at the Academie de Musique there.

A card home says:

> We have fixed July 23rd (Wednesday) for the Happy Day,' and on the front of the card showing a picture of L'Hotel de Ville the words 'Our names are duly affirmed up here.'[10]

This was followed by another card:

> Just a hurried note to say that the Wedding is postponed for a few days on account of one of the necessary papers not having arrived from England. With a stroke of luck it might be Sat: next or even next week.'[11]

After the Wedding in July 1919, Dixon and his wife spent their honeymoon in Namur and returned there for a holiday in the summer of 1921, visiting Bruges and Brussels en route.[12]

---

10 Dixon archive.
11 Dixon archive.
12 Cards, Dixon archive.

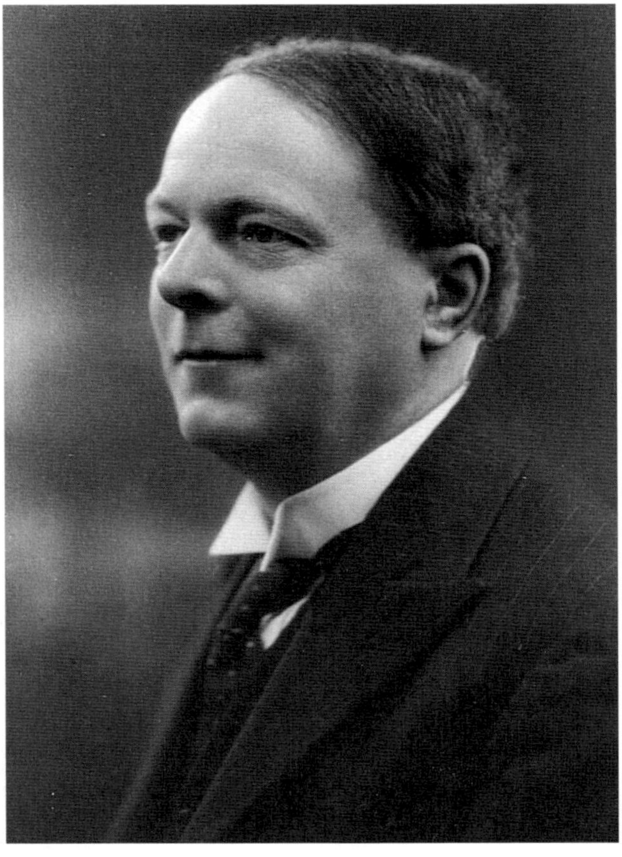

Return to Lancaster

ON RETURNING TO LANCASTER the newly married couple took up residence at 2 South Road, and Dixon resumed his position as Organist at St. Peter's and the Ashton Hall.

His first recital after the war took place in the Ashton Hall, on 15 November 1919 and was given in aid of the War Memorial Village, Lancaster.

In January 1920 the first in a series of subscription concerts, known as the Dixon-Jamart Concerts was launched. These were monthly concerts, held on Wednesday evenings in the Ashton Hall, featuring James Hugh Reginald Dixon at the organ, Madame Alice Dixon-Jamart at the piano and guest artists. All the concerts began at 7.30 p.m. and judging from the programmes and taking into account several encores probably ended quite late, the final item always being the National Anthem.

The organ solos were similar to those given in earlier recitals, adaptations of piano pieces, transcriptions of orchestral pieces, one of his own compositions and an improvisation. The first concert ended with a performance of the ever popular Dixon arrangement of *The Storm*. An unusual piece in this programme was *The Magic Harp* by J Arthur Meale in which the theme is played on the pedals accompanied by arpeggios representing the harp played on the manuals.

The first appearance in Lancaster of Mr Dixon and Madame Dixon-Jamart on the concert platform together was on 11 February 1920, when they played Liszt's tone poem *Les Preludes* as a duet for piano and organ. According to the local press report the technique was superb, and the 'echo' on the piano was quite captivating.[1] Madame Dixon-Jamart played two piano solos in this programme, *Soir d' Automne*: *Causerie sous bois* by Raoul Pugno and the 'Spinning Chorus', from *The Flying Dutchman* by Wagner-Liszt, which were reported to be enrapturing.[2] A special feature of this second concert was that the second half of the programme was devoted to the music of Sullivan.

---

1 *Lancaster Guardian*, 13 February 1920.
2 Ibid.

Opposite: Portrait (G Wynspeare Herbert, Lancaster)

Interestingly the third concert in the series featured the music of Wagner. Probably the first time a Wagner concert had been held in Lancaster, the programme included the March from *Tannhäuser,* 'The Prize Song' (*Die Meistersinger*), sung by Mr Bridge Peters, 'The Ride of The Valkyries' (*Die Walküre*) and in complete contrast the Good Friday Music (*Parsifal*). This concert was given under the patronage of Sir Norval and Lady Helme and Members of the Committee of the Royal Lancaster Infirmary. As it was held on St. Patrick's Day, Dixon ended the first part of the programme with *An Irish Fancie*, in which he blended popular Irish melodies with the squealing of a pig and the sound of Irish instruments. There is no other evidence of this composition, so it may have been an improvised piece for the occasion.

Guest artists in the first series of concerts included the local Centenary Quartette led by Mr R T Grosse, Muriel Brunskill (Contralto) who studied opera scores with Dixon, Mr C Harold Dawson (Tenor), Mr Bridge Peters (Baritone) and Miss M Atkinson (Mezzo-soprano). Vocal solos included well-known songs and excerpts from opera and oratorio.

Admission charges for the concerts were as follows; seats at the back of the hall, 9*d.*, area and side gallery, 1*s.* 3*d.* and reserved seats in the centre gallery, 2*s.* 4*d.* Admission charges for the next season were to be increased to 1*s.* 3*d.*, 2*s.* 4*d.* and 3*s.* 6*d.* respectively. A season ticket was introduced at a cost of 12*s.* 6*d.* for seats in the back stalls, second seats and side gallery and 18*s.* 6*d.* for seats in the centre gallery. Later on in the season due to the increased cost in the production of the programme, the promoters were compelled to raise the cost of the programme to 4*d.* All the prices included tax.

The second series of concerts began in October 1920 and ended in March 1921. Guest artists in this series included Doris Clegg (Soprano), Tom Child (The well-known Yorkshire Tenor), Nancy Ainsworth (Soprano, pupil of Marchesi), Walter Barrett (Baritone), John Sheridan (Violinist), Muriel Brunskill (Contralto), Mr Bell-Walker (Tenor), Mr F Crewe (Violinist), Bridge Peters (Baritone), Miss Stephanie Baker (Contralto), Robert W Sporne (Tenor), Mrs Arthur Benson (Soprano), Thomas Haworth (Tenor), Rev. J Harold Hastings (Elocutionist) and Monsieur Armand Lenain (Violoncellist).

In the first concert Muriel Brunskill sang 'Memories' (Souvenir), one of only two songs composed by Dixon-Jamart in 1919, the other one being 'Westward Bound' (Chant de Départ), which was performed in the March 1921 concert and sung by Mr Thomas Haworth. Herbert J Brandon wrote the words to both songs and the compositions were published in 1922 by Escott & Co Ltd as royalty songs sung by Walter Saull. The songs could also be sung in French to a text by Georges Fay. Both songs have a piano accompaniment with an optional violin obligato part for 'Memories'.

A performance of the Schumann Piano Concerto in A minor with organ accompaniment was given by Madame Dixon-Jamart and Mr Dixon in the November concert of this series. Also in this programme Tom Child was welcomed back to the town after an absence of over twenty-five years when he had sung at the Old Palatine Hall.

The December concert was held under the distinguished auspices of the British Music Society. According to an advert for the concert an address was to be given by Dr Eaglefield-Hull (Hon. Director of the British Music Society), inaugurating a Branch of the Society in Lancaster. However, from the programme it appears that Dr Hull never made it to Lancaster, and the address was given instead by Mr Cecil H Bateson, Hon. Organiser for Lancaster on behalf of the British Music Society.

In honour of his former teacher Dixon had included in the programme an organ piece by Dr Eaglefield-Hull, entitled *Variations Poetiques*. Also on this occasion Dixon played the Elgar Organ Sonata, each movement being interspersed with operatic arias from Meyerbeer, Puccini, Leoncavallo and Verdi, sung by Nancy Ainsworth and Walter Barrett. The special guest artist for the evening was the famous violinist John Sheridan, who studied with Ševčík, the teacher of Kubelík.

The fifth concert in the series was advertised as Mr Dixon's Grand Benefit Night. An extract from the cash book of the Dixon-Jamart Concerts for the current season dated December 1920 was printed on the back of the programme:

| Receipts | £155 5s. 9d. |
| Expenditure | £159 4s. 0d. |

There was also an extract from Shakespeare's 'Romeo and Juliet', Act IV., Sc. 5:

Peter: 'Then music, with her silver sound -'
Why 'silver sound?' Why 'Music with her silver sound?'
1ˢᵗ Musician: Marry, sir, because silver hath a sweet sound.
2ⁿᵈ Musician: I say 'silver sound' because musicians sound for silver.
Peter:- It is 'Music with her silver sound', because musicians have seldom gold for sounding.

It is clear from this information that all was not well regarding the financial situation of presenting these concerts.

Proceeds from the last concert in the series which took place on Wednesday 30 March were given to the Royal Lancaster Infirmary by arrangement with the work people's Committee. A special guest in this concert was Monsieur Armand Lenain who played the Lalo Violoncello Concerto and a Sonata by Grieg.

For the third season which began in October 1921, the following soloists were engaged; Madame Gwladys Bateson (Contralto), Henry Brearley (Tenor), Miss Muriel Robinson (Soprano), Mr T H Smethurst (Baritone), Baroness Olga de Korff (Soprano), Mr R Sporne (Tenor), Miss E Rogerson (Contralto), Mr I Young

(Baritone), Mr Stephen Pye (Baritone), Master Stanley Govan (Violinist) and Miss Dora Neville (Manchester's Popular Entertainer at the Piano).

In the October concert Dixon and Madame Dixon-Jamart played the Debussy *Petite Suite* on two pianos. According to the local press report they 'played in perfect accord, bringing out the ethereal charm and studied vagueness of effect that marks many of the composer's works.'[3]

There were only five concerts in this season. In December instead of the usual concert in the Ashton Hall, pupils of Dixon and Madame Dixon-Jamart gave a Students Invitation Concert in the Storey Institute. The following pupils took part: Miss W Hargreaves; Mr Arthur Preston; Miss Verity; Miss Elsie Rogerson; Miss A Gabbert; Miss Blanche Jones; Miss F Ellam; Miss Linda Robins; Miss Amos; Mr Aubrey Curwen; Miss Mary Chamberlain; Miss Elsie Bell (sometime later organist of St Thomas' Church) and Mr John Samson (sometime later organist of Moor Lane Methodist Church).

Throughout the three seasons in addition to solo performances Madame Dixon-Jamart performed three piano concertos, Schumann A minor, Grieg A minor and Beethoven No. 3 in C minor.

Dixon usually included one major organ work in these concerts, such as a Widor Symphony, the Sonatas of Mendelssohn, Rheinberger, Guilmant and Elgar, as well as Preludes and Fugues by J S Bach.

For the final concert of the series on 25 March 1922 there were two performances as a twice nightly experiment. It is sad to think that this was not only the last concert in the 1921–22 series, but the last one in which Dixon and his wife would appear together.

Later that year Reginald and Alice were to go their separate ways and sadly the marriage came to an end, but they did keep in touch by correspondence. This was a sad and difficult time for both parties personally, and as professional musicians who had become so well-known locally. Madame Dixon-Jamart, perhaps feeling that she could not return to her native land, decided to stay in her adopted country and went on to teach French in several different schools, ending her career at Barnstaple High School in Devon. After her retirement she continued to live in the town in Higher Church Street, next to the old St Mary's Catholic Church. In later years whenever the Incorporated Association of Organists held their annual Congress in the South West Reginald would visit her.

Between 1922 and 1924 Dixon must also have considered leaving Lancaster as he applied for several teaching and organ posts. He looked into the possibility of exchanging his post with that of a fellow musician and even considered emigrating, applying to teach in a Montreal High School, Canada. Other applications included a teaching post at Downside and two contrasting high profile

---

3 *Lancaster Guardian,* 28 October 1921.

organ posts, that of Organist and Choirmaster at Westminster Cathedral and the position of Birmingham City Organist. Despite glowing testimonials from Dr Eaglefield-Hull, Sir Richard Terry and the Mayor of Lancaster regarding the various applications none were successful. Dixon received a letter from Cardinal Bourne's Private Secretary informing him that the post at Westminster Cathedral had been filled and from another letter it appeared that he was not even included in the shortlist for Birmingham.[4]

Now facing life alone and perhaps feeling disappointed at not securing any of the posts he had applied for, Dixon continued giving recitals and teaching as well as immersing himself in further study via a correspondence course with Norman Sprankling Mus. Doc. (London) of Bristol. About this time he began lecturing first for the Women's Institute (WI), the Rural Adult Educational Movement and the Workers' Educational Association (WEA), then in 1924 he was appointed to the staff of Liverpool University as a Lecturer in extra mural studies. From this time until the late 1950s he gave a series of weekly lectures throughout the academic year, as well as lecturing at Summer Schools. In addition to the WI and the WEA there were other groups of students including Civil Servants. Courses were of one to five years duration and some were one-off lectures to such groups as Organists' Associations, the Rotary Club, and the Lancaster Catenian Association. The topics, which numbered well over two-hundred, included History of Music, Appreciation of Music, Elements of Music and Instruments. He would often run three courses in a week, each one held in a different place, delivering a variety of lectures. The area covered included many towns and villages throughout Lancashire from Barrow-in-Furness to Birkenhead. His lecturing took up a great deal of time not only in preparation, but in travelling and delivering the lecture. There is no evidence that he ever had a car or drove one, but he was known to ride a motorbike, buying his first one in 1914. Maybe he used this form of transport for local trips and the train or bus for longer journeys, the latter two perhaps more reliable and efficient in those days than they are at the present time.

During the 1920s Dixon became Honorary Conductor of the Liverpool Metropolitan Cathedral Choir which comprised 250 voices, members coming from 26 choirs in the Diocese including the Cathedral Choir. The Choir made frequent appearances at St. George's Hall and the Pro-Cathedral.

Dixon's pilgrimage to Lourdes in 1924 was the first of many and it was here that he would become well-known and often play the organ.

In 1924 Dixon became interested in local politics and made an unsuccessful attempt at Municipal Honours. He was, however, rewarded with a seat on the Education Committee and later became a governor of the Catholic schools, a position which he held until 1963. A letter from his mother sympathises with him over his defeat at the polls but adds that,

---

4   Testimonials and letters, Dixon archive.

> Dad thinks professional men should not take a prominent part in political or civic affairs, as they will be seen to offend some of their clients or pupils etc. Have your own opinions but keep them to yourself and probably that's wise.[5]

A series of illustrated lecture-recitals were given by Dixon between 1924 and 1925 in the Ashton Hall, Lancaster, each attracting a large audience. In the introduction to one of these lecture-recitals entitled 'What the organ said' there is a description of a sunset:

> The setting sun was tinging the majestic Town Hall and graceful Clock Tower with a soft warm radiance that moved my whole soul to deep admiration, and I was thankful for my years of training in drawing and painting, which enabled me to fully appreciate the beauty of the structural lines, and the exquisite harmony of colour then visible.
>
> Behind the stately building, the serenity of the grey-blue-black sky was not ruffled even by a single cloud, and unshaded windows nearby were luminous with reflected brightness of the glorious orb of day, which would very soon disappear behind the blue hills of Morecambe Bay.[6]

This is a scene Dixon was very fond of and one which was significant in two of his later compositions.

1925 was a momentous year not only for Dixon, but for those of the Catholic Faith and many inhabitants of Lancaster and the surrounding area.

On 22 November 1924 Pope Pius XI signed a decree creating the new Diocese of Lancaster and raising St Peter's Church to Cathedral status. The new Diocese within the Archdiocese of Liverpool covered an area which stretched from north of the River Ribble at Preston to the Scottish Borders and comprised 108 Parishes.

The first important ceremony to be performed in the new Diocese was that of installing a new chapter which took place in the Cathedral on Monday 16 February 1925; Archbishop Keating of Liverpool presided. This was followed by the consecration of the Right Rev. Thomas Wulstan Pearson OSB as Bishop on Tuesday 24 February.

Music for this occasion included 'Ecce Sacerdos' (composed by Abbot Burge OSB, first performed at the Jubilee celebrations and dedicated to the late Canon Billington and the Choir of St Peter's); 'Sacerdotes Domini' by Byrd and Palestrina's Mass *Ite Confessor*. Plainchant was used for the Proper of the Mass. Dr Dixon presided at the organ, but it was reported in the local press that he had been

---

5   Letter, Dixon archive.
6   Dixon archive.

confined to his house and risked his health to be present for the occasion.[7]

The sermon was preached by Abbot Ramsey of Downside Abbey on the text from St Matthew's Gospel (XXVIII: 18–22).

After the Consecration a reception was held in the Ashton Hall for the new Bishop. Dixon played the organ and the standard of music was highly praised by Canon Blundell. When the Diocese of Lancaster was established Dixon was appointed as a member of the Diocesan Music Commission, such a body being required in each diocese since 1903 when Pope Pius X issued his 'Motu Proprio' on sacred church music.

Between 1838 and 1922 only sixteen students had the Doctorate of Music Degree conferred upon them by the University of London. Dixon was the first to be awarded a double distinction in this exam (a rare honour) for playing at sight from a full score and extempore composition. His written composition submitted for the Mus. Doc. Exercise completed in November 1924 was a setting of a tenth-century miracle play entitled *Mysterium Resurrectionis, Domini Nostri Jesu Christi.* Dixon selected words from a thirteenth-century manuscript in the Library of the City of Orléans, as printed by Thomas Wright (Ex: 'English Miracle Plays'- Pollard). The work, which takes approximately one hour to perform, consists of twelve sections and is scored for full orchestra, double choir and six soloists. It is interesting to note that in the recit 'Noli flere, Maria' a duet for the two angels, the harp has a prominent role and a similar treatment is applied to the 'Angel's Song' in *The Dream of Gerontius* and the solo section of 'Ecce panis' in *Panis Vitae*. The work begins with an overture and there is an orchestral interlude in the middle. Four movements are written in eight parts, two for double chorus, 'Eamus ergo propere' and 'Noli flere, Maria', the motet 'Congratulamini mihi' and the work ends with a chorale 'Ressurrexit Hodie'. Other sections comprise trios, recitatives and arias. As one would expect this work is more mature in compositional writing and treatment of text than the exercise Dixon submitted for his Mus. Bac.

The examiners were Professor Kitson and Dr C W Pearce and they specially commended the eight-part Motet 'Congratulamini mihi'. Presentation of the Degree by the Vice-Chancellor of the University took place at the Royal Albert Hall in May 1925.

Dr Dixon was presented with his Doctorate Robes by the Mayor (Ald. G Jackson) at a concert held in the Ashton Hall, Lancaster on Saturday 16 May (the event was reported in the local press, source unknown). During the interval the Mayor accompanied by the Mayoress (Mrs A H Thurstan), escorted by Mr Charles Chadderton, the Very Rev Canon Blundell and members of the Organists' Association assembled on the platform for the presentation ceremony. The Organists'

---

7 *Lancaster Guardian*, 28 February 1925.

Association, the Corporation, people of the town and the surrounding area had all generously subscribed to purchase the robes.

After the presentation speeches were made by Mr Chadderton, Dr Dixon, Canon Blundell and Mr Frith. Mr Chadderton, a valued friend of Dr Dixon since he arrived in Lancaster, said, 'Dr Dixon has done more musically and charitably than any other man I know in the town.' Dr Dixon expressed his thanks to Mr Chadderton for arranging the event, to the Mayor and the Corporation for their promotion and support of the Municipal Concerts and Recitals, and was grateful to all those who had subscribed to the robes. He described the degree ceremony which had taken place at an earlier date in the Royal Albert Hall, London, and was honoured that the Mayor should present him with his robes on this occasion surrounded by all his friends. Dr Dixon made an offer that any lady in the audience who would like to try on the splendid robes could do so for a fee of 2*s*. 6*d*. which would be given to charity. Canon Blundell gave an appreciation of Dr Dixon's musicianship and character and remarked that a great musician had told the Bishop that Dixon was the greatest living authority on plainchant and polyphonic music of the Palestrina School. Speaking about the ministry of music and its effect on our lives in the world, Canon Blundell made reference to the fact that Dr Dixon could represent all the human emotions one could experience through his interpretation of music on the organ. Canon Blundell concluded by predicting that in years to come Dixon's name would be greater than it is today. Mr Firth gave an appreciation on behalf of the Organists' Association to the Mayor for being present and to Dr Dixon for his achievement which brought honour to the Association. The ceremony ended with the audience singing 'For he's a jolly good fellow' accompanied by Mr Chadderton on the organ.[8]

The concert programme was as follows:

Overture, 'William Tell' (By special request)	Rossini arr. Dixon
Andante with Variations from 'The Septuor'	Beethoven
Prelude in A	S. Wesley
Slow Air	Wm Russell
Overture in G minor (From Mysterium Resurrectionis)	Dixon
The Storm (By demand)	Arr. Dixon
Caprice, Vox Humana, Vox Organa and Fuga	Dixon
Organ Fantasia 'Sedbergh'	Dixon

The soloists for the evening were Mr Leonard F Pearson who sang 'Don Juan's Serenade' by Tschaikowsky, some Irish folk songs arranged Stanford and Songs of

---

8 *Lancaster Guardian*, 22 May 1925.

the Open Air – 'The Derby Ram' Hurlestone, and 'The Little Red Fox', arranged Somerville. Miss Lilian M Floyd sang 'Mad Bess' by Purcell, Handel's 'My Soul Awakes' and 'Lead, kindly Light' by Pughe-Evans.

The final piece in the programme by Dixon is based on the tune 'Sedbergh' composed by John Brook in 1916, and is in the form of an Introduction, Variations and Fugue. This could well have been the first performance of the work which is dedicated to Councillor John Brook of Southport and was published by Laudy & Co. in 1925.

It was a memorable evening in which everyone shared in the honour conferred upon a gifted musician.

The previous week on Sunday 10 May an orchestral concert was held in connection with shopping week. In order to avoid a clash with Sunday evening church services the concert began at 8.15 p.m. instead of the usual time of 7.30 p.m. This concert, attended by the Mayor, attracted one of the largest audiences ever seen at a similar event. Many people had to be turned away thus prompting a request for the concert to be repeated on 17 May, the day after the presentation. The orchestra under the direction of Mr Sackville Wiggins comprised approximately sixty of the finest musicians in the district. Madame Elsie Pym, Mr T Hurst Moffat and Master Harry Rawes were the vocal soloists, accompanied by Dr Dixon who also played some popular organ pieces. A varied programme was presented with the choice of some pieces being influenced by the fact that the concert was being given on a Sunday. The orchestral pieces included the 'Grand March' from *Le Prophète* by Meyerbeer, Mendelssohn's Overture *Fingal's Cave*, 'The Prize Song' from *Die Meistersinger* by Wagner, Tschaikovsky's *Andante Cantabile,* for strings and the 'Finale' from *The Miracle* by Humperdinck. Each vocalist sang two songs. Madame Pym sang 'The Lord is my Light' by Francis Allitson and Quilter's 'Fair House of Joy'. Mr Moffat gave a performance of Liddle's 'Abide with Me' and 'Love's Coronation' by Aylward. Master Rawes sang two pieces by Handel, 'Come, Ever Smiling Liberty' and 'Angels ever Bright and Fair'. Dr Dixon played a selection of pieces including the 'Londonderry Air', Handel's 'Largo' and excerpts from the *Occasional Oratorio*. The proceeds of the concert (which amounted to £50) were given to charity. It was suggested that the Corporation, having afforded facilities for organ recitals, should consider the possibility of establishing a Municipal Orchestra.

By July 1925, the Morecambe Annual West End Wesleyan Choir Festival, which sprang up from humble beginnings, had become a prodigious event featuring professional soloists from London. On this occasion the music was provided by an augmented choir under the direction of Mr H E Wilson ARCO. The soloists were Miss Mais Jones, the celebrated Welsh soprano of the Royal Eisteddfod, Mr Ernest Hargreaves, a popular tenor (both these singers well-known for their appearances at the Royal Albert Hall and the Queen's Hall Concerts) and Mr Harold Williams,

Principal Bass-baritone with the British National Opera Company. Dr Dixon was the organ soloist and acted as accompanist throughout the Festival. In addition to the Sunday services which included solos and anthems by the choir there was an afternoon concert featuring excerpts from Oratorios by Handel and Mendelssohn as well as works by Stainer and a performance of the organ piece *Sedbergh* by Dixon. On the following evening the same soloists and the choir gave a performance of *Hiawatha* by Coleridge Taylor and Mendelssohn's *Hymn of Praise*.

According to the local press it was reported that the services were fully attended and in the afternoon there was not enough room for all those who came. Some people expressed their appreciation of the music by clapping while others refrained from doing so. It was suggested that at a musical service in a sacred building on a Sabbath the congregation should refrain from clapping. The following observation was made by the reporter:

> One felt that such occasions as these gave the church new life, and that all the talk of the church losing its hold upon the people was quite unfounded. The impression gained at the West End Wesleyan Church was that if only the musical side of the service was developed and extended at the expense of the sermon the churches would be better attended than they are today.[9]

One of those little anecdotes which Dixon often told was of the occasion in 1925 when he went on a trip to Rome for 4*d*! Perhaps he stepped in to take the place of someone who for whatever reason dropped out at the last moment or maybe someone paid for him to go on the trip.

A certificate dated 6 April 1926 reveals that Dixon was appointed to act as a Special Constable for preservation of the public peace and for the protection of the inhabitants and security of the property within the Borough of Lancaster.[10] It is stated in several reports that Dixon was a Special Constable before the First World War but there is no evidence to substantiate this.

In May 1926 Dixon was again thinking of moving from Lancaster as he applied for the post of Musical Advisor under the Education Committee of the London County Council.

* * *

Dixon was an ardent collector of newspaper articles, cartoons, and jokes on a variety of subjects. He was also a prolific writer of letters and articles to various music publications, newspapers and friends. Some of his early published writings have already

---

9 *Morecambe Visitor, Heysham Chronicle and Lancaster Advertiser*, July 1925.
10 Certificate, Dixon archive.

been mentioned. Throughout the 1920s Dixon sent numerous letters to *The Tablet* and towards the end of the decade a series of articles appeared in the *Musical Opinion.*

Letters Dixon sent to the editor of *The Tablet* concerned a variety of topics. In a letter dated 5th April 1927 Dixon describes how a church near Lyon where he was stationed in 1918 celebrated Palm Sunday and compares it with the ceremony in England:

> In 1918 I assisted at the Blessing of Palms at St. Germain Mont d'Or, Nr Lyon – a fairly large village where Monsieur le Maire was a devout Catholic and where outdoor processions were freely permitted.
>
> We all assembled in the church for the first part of the ceremony, i.e. up to and including the first Gospel. Then we formed a procession, walking from the church to a wayside cross. The people brought with them boxes of plants. These were deposited in a large basket and were blessed. The procession then returned to the church, the people singing the usual antiphons, and the Gloria laus, and waving their palms. On re-entering the church the Responsory Ingrediente was sung.
>
> I wonder if this simple ceremony, performed amongst the glorious mountain scenery, has retained more elements of a primitive origin than has the more refined though perhaps somewhat abbreviated ceremony to which we in England have become accustomed.[11]

Another letter dated January 6th 1929 dealt with suggestions to architects of modern churches, the desirability of providing cloakroom accommodation, sanitary conveniences, a more suitable position for the organ and choir than the west end gallery, especially in churches with a long nave and where possible more parking for bicycles and cars.

> A pew makes a wretched cloakroom on a wet day and an awkward hat rack when crowded.
> And surely we can improve on the sanitary conveniences which disfigure so many of our churches.
> The organ being a comparatively modern instrument, the classical architecture never provided accommodation for it. Here then is an opportunity for enriching the design, bearing in mind the laws of acoustics and the modern liturgical requirements.
> Concerning cars and bicycles, a little consideration of the trend of the times would seem to show that in future some sort of provision will have to be made for their accommodation in the vicinity of churches.[12]

---

11 *The Tablet*, 16 April 1927.
12 *The Tablet*, 12 January 1929.

In modern churches many of the suggestions above have been taken into consideration and acted upon. Today those responsible for taking decisions on the growing trend of re-organisation of ancient churches have where possible made provision for amenities to suit the modern church-goer. With regard to the position of the organ the debate goes on. Very few are ever in the ideal position to suit all parties.

In a letter dated 11th September 1929 Dixon replies to correspondence concerning the length of the plainchant Graduals. He tabulates the relevant times it takes to sing the Kyrie and Gloria as set by some eighteenth and nineteenth century composers, those which are polyphonic settings and those set to Gregorian music. Comparisons are shown between these and the Graduals, Alleluias or Tracts. In addition times are given of the average length of the Epistle or Gospel and Sermons, Instructions and Notices.

It would appear that there was some confusion as to who was tired by the long plainchant Graduals. The editor explains that the parish priests are concerned about the congregation becoming tired whereas Dixon was under the impression that a previous correspondent had implied it was the choir who were tired. This was a misunderstanding, but the editor thought that Dixon's letter was of value.[13]

The three articles published in *Musical Opinion* under the title of 'Notes from an Organ Enthusiast's Diary' concern American organs which Dixon thought would be of interest to readers. He describes a tour of America, pipe and cinema organs seen, heard or played and his meeting with Professor Toogood, all of which reveal his witty nature and imaginary powers.

America is well-known for having some of the largest organs in the world, but the description of one such instrument given to Dixon on credible authority by the Professor is a gross exaggeration by any stretch of the imagination. The following quote refers to the organ in the Super XXX Cinema, 19th Avenue, Kansas:

> It is reputed to contain 549 stops grouped into seventeen departments, and including 24 tremulants. The great feature of this organ, as your readers doubtless are aware, consists in the tremendous pedal stop of 236ft. (true length to within a few inches) bearing the most diabolical name ever conceived for an organ stop, – i.e., *feu d'enfer* which is Spanish for 'roaring fires of hell'. There is I understand, a special tremulant to this stop alone. The pipes of the lower octaves are built of spotted concrete, lined with pitch and project far above the roof of the building. Being neither mitred nor hooded, they resemble nothing less than a huge stack of factory chimneys of varying sizes when viewed from the railway sidings.

---

13 *The Tablet*, 21 September 1929.

> The professor jokingly remarked that when the organist laid on the *feu d'enfer* ('give 'em hell', as he aptly put it in American slang), the whole of the city reverberated to its awful roar, and those gifted with second sight even saw red flames issue from the top of these elephantine pipes. He admitted however, that this was probably a slight exaggeration.[14]

In the second article a visit is made to Boston. The Grand Super Kinema on 27th Avenue is described as having two screens, showing two films simultaneously which patrons can watch either one or the other from a revolving chair. Musically there is a symphony orchestra, a jazz orchestra and a magnificent organ. An amusing story from the second article refers to an orchestral incident at this Kinema related to Dixon by the professor.

> At one time it appears, there had been friction between the orchestral pianist and some of the other players. So during a short interval the pianist went round stealthily to all the violinists desks and dropped some hard peas into their instruments, finally anointing the flute with a liberal supply of a particularly odouriferous variety of cheese. The sequel may be left to one's imagination.'

That prompted Dixon to tell the professor of an incident that happened many years ago at the Hovingham Musical Festival near York (not New York).

> The local amateur orchestra was reinforced by a number of professionals for the occasion; but at the final rehearsal in the afternoon the amateurs were found to be sadly lacking in efficiency, to the detriment of the orchestra as a whole. What could be done to save the situation? One could not insist on the amateurs absenting themselves at the evening concert, for many of them were the little-big-wigs who largely financed the festival. The conductor had a brainwave. Though no one knew who did the trick, when the amateur violinists and 'cellists took their accustomed places for the evening performance, they found – or possibly they did not notice – but at any rate their bows had been liberally rubbed with a tallow candle! The concert was, thanks to the happy band of 'pros.', a complete success.[15]

More details of the Boston Kinema Organ appear in the third article, plus a story about an opening recital to be given by Dixon in Indianapolis. Having prepared his programme on a large two manual instrument, he arrived on the day of the recital to find that the organ was not the same, the builder having

---

14 *Musical Opinion*, March 1929, Vol. 52, No. 618.
15 *Musical Opinion*, April 1929, Vol. 52, No. 619.

had a disagreement with the authorities decided to remove the instrument and so a replacement three manual was installed which was quite different from the original one.[16]

In addition to these writings a resumé of points from Lectures given to the Organists' Associations at Liverpool, Southport, Warrington and Lancaster on 'Continental Organs and their Music' was printed in the *Quarterly Record*.[17]

* * *

Pope Pius XI in his 'Apostolic Constitution' 'Divini cultus Sanctitatem' dated 28 December 1928, reaffirmed the principles concerning sacred music which had been laid down by Pope Pius X in his 'Motu Proprio' of 1903. In the intervening years between 1903 and 1928 priests, organists and choirmasters had been working to implement the ideals in liturgical music. Dixon through his articles in the *Musical Standard* (1915–16) sought to raise standards of music in churches, help musicians understand the relationship between liturgy and music by giving advice, sharing ideas and proposing solutions to practical problems. By 1928 there was still a lot of work to be done with regard to understanding the importance of music and liturgy in Catholic churches throughout the country, implementing the ideals and raising standards. It was thought that all those involved with liturgy and music would appreciate an opportunity to meet, discuss and exchange ideas on such matters. An initial meeting of about thirty people comprising prominent priests and musicians representing different parts of the country was organised by the Rev. J B McElligott OSB and held at Ealing Priory, London in November 1928. As a result of this and other meetings it was decided to form the 'Society of St Gregory' which was inaugurated on 12 March 1929.

The four main aims of the Society were, to maintain the dignity of the sacred liturgy as the supreme instrument of congregational worship, to carry out the wishes of the Church regarding church music, to provide a course of instruction in plainsong and polyphony and to help members find a solution to practical problems.[18]

Dr Dixon was one of ten Committee members with the Rev. J B McElligott OSB, elected as the first President and the Rev. J Burke BA Dean of University College, Dublin elected Vice President. The Society was supported by several patrons including His Emminence Cardinal Bourne, His Grace the Archbishop of Liverpool and Birmingham, the bishops of each Diocese and the Vicar Capitular of Edinburgh Monsignor C L Duchemin MA.

---

16 *Musical Opinion*, May 1929, Vol. 52, No. 620.
17 *Quarterly Record*, July 1929, Vol. XIV, No. 56 and January 1930, Vol. XV, No. 58.
18 *Music and Liturgy*, October 1929, Vol. I, No. 1.

SSG Oxford, Summer School 1931 (by kind permission of the Saint Gregory Society)

The annual subscription to the society was set at 7s. 6d. which included a copy of *Music and Liturgy* (a quarterly magazine) and entitled the member to attend courses.

Approximately two hundred members joined the Society in 1929, increasing to six hundred within the first year and the influence of the society extended to the public at large.

A Summer School attended by over a hundred members was held in August 1929 at Oxford and this was to become an annual event here until 1949. After this date Summer Schools were held in different venues throughout the country and continue to this day. The main aim of these early Summer Schools was to provide a course of instruction in plainsong for priests, choirmasters, teachers and choristers with an emphasis on the practical aspects.

An appeal was made for those with knowledge of chant who were capable of passing on the necessary skills to others to come forward as instructors. Canon Blundell of St Peter's Cathedral, Lancaster asked Dr Dixon to go on a tour of the Diocese, lecturing on the art of reading and performing Gregorian chant.

The official chant books of the church at this time were produced by the Monks of Solesmes and so it was their method that was adopted by the Society of St Gregory and taught on all courses. HMV recordings of plainsong sung by the Monks of Solesmes were loaned to members with an accompanying pamphlet enabling the audience to follow the music.

Written and oral exams were held and the Nuns of Stanbrook Abbey set up a correspondence course of personal tuition. Dr Dixon was an examiner for the Society and as such claimed that he never failed anyone.

A series of evening classes and study groups were set up in various towns and cities throughout the country. Those held in Liverpool also included special instruction in organ accompaniment where it was felt that some light support was necessary, although ideally chant should be unaccompanied.

The first Catholic Competitive Music Festival with classes in plainsong was held in Dublin in 1930. This was followed by the establishment of Plainsong Competitive Music Festivals, the first one of its type being held at Westminster Cathedral in October 1931 and these annual events along with local festivals proved a powerful means of instruction and produced excellent results.

Between January 1933 and April 1934 five articles entitled 'The Organ and Sacred Liturgy' were written by Dr Dixon for the journal *Music and Liturgy*. These articles deal with various matters applicable to organists in general and some which he believed were of primary importance to organists as Catholic musicians.

The first article begins with quotes referring to the organ, 'There let the pealing organ blow' from Milton's *Il Penseroso* and the verse from Dryden's *Song for St Cecilia's Day* beginning 'But Oh! What art can teach', followed by a basic definition of what an organ is.[19] Reference is made to the early type of organ forbidden in Christian worship and the development of large instruments in certain churches. He goes on to describe the role of the organ in other denominations compared with that which meets the requirements of the Catholic Church. Here music is subservient to the Liturgy and organ tones when used individually or in combination should provide suitable accompaniment to the Mass and other services such as Vespers and Benediction.

The other four articles deal with the qualities an organist should possess, study, repertoire, musical training, registration and suggestions for music before and after the service. Regarding the qualities of an organist, Dixon was of the opinion that the organist must not only be committed and efficient, but should reflect the spirit of the liturgy. In order to achieve this he felt it was necessary to have an understanding of the history, structure, ceremonies and the devotional significance of the Mass. The merits of an organ-loft apprenticeship were discussed, such

---

19 *Music and Liturgy*, January 1933, Vol. IV No. 1.

a scheme providing the Anglican Church with competent organists and Dixon advocated a similar system for the Catholic Church. While a list of repertoire pieces was mentioned including the early works of the Italian, German and French masters as well as some of the great composers, it was emphasised that suitable liturgical music does not have to be too difficult, but needs to be of distinct value. With regard to musical training, Dixon recommended that organists should keep up their piano technique and repertoire, as well as perfecting those techniques applicable to the organ such as pedalling, articulation and registration. As no two organs are alike and even stops with identical nomenclature differ in tone colour, the art of registration is an individual choice. This aspect of organ playing can be learnt from watching an experienced organist and reading books on the subject such as Dr Hull's 'Organ Playing'. Dixon also advised all organists to make a study of orchestration and apply the principles of instrumentation to the art of choosing and combining the various stops.

Regarding music before and after the service Dixon recommended that the voluntary should reflect the spirit of the service it precedes and likewise the concluding voluntary should continue in the same spirit as that evoked in the service. He lists some suggestions and concludes with ideas for improvisation.

J. H. REGINALD DIXON,
D. MUS. (Lond.), F.R C.O.,

ORGANIST, THE CATHEDRAL,
LANCASTER.

Desires to announce that he is prepared to advise the Clergy, Architects, Managers, and Organ Committees on all matters pertaining to the construction of Pipe Organs.

Organs specially designed to suit local requirements. Unit or straight system; electric or pneumatic action; American and Continental specialities—for Churches or Cinemas.

Specifications prepared, with estimates of cost.

Suggestions for modernizing old organs.

Direction and supervision of work.

"A boon to perplexed Committees!"

Consultations in all parts of the country.

CORRESPONDENCE INVITED.

MEADOWSIDE.   **LANCASTER.**

Organ Adviser & Consultant

From an early age Dixon had been interested in the construction of instruments and organs in particular. While on his travels around Europe he kept a notebook of organ specifications and sketches of designs.

His services were continually in demand as an expert adviser on organ construction and renovation, not only in England, but also in France and Germany.

The design put forward for a new Liverpool Metropolitan Cathedral in the 1920s prompted Dixon to write to the Right Rev. Bishop Dobson offering suggestions, complete with drawings regarding the most effective position of the Choir in relationship to the proposed Grand Organ and Choir Organ.[1] His ideas were discussed by Henry Willis and the architect Sir Edwin Lutyens, and while the former stated that Dixon's ideas were based on a misunderstanding of the general situation, he thought there was an idea behind them and the space suggested could be used to accommodate some sections of the organ.[2] Sadly neither the planned architectural design nor the organ came to fruition.

Dixon was in touch with many leading organ builders of the day and for many years he acted as adviser and consultant to the firm of Ainscough. He was a friend of John Compton and would often suggest some of his ideas to the Ainscough firm! Examples of small instruments built by Ainscough and designed by Dixon can be found at St Mary's RC Church, Wigan (1927) and St Mary and St Michael's RC Church, Garstang (1949), the latter being extensively restored by Pendlebury & Co. of Fleetwood in 1989. A large instrument was designed for St Michael's, Preston, and the most significant one was that for St Joseph's College Chapel, Upholland.

St Joseph's College, situated in Walthew Park, was founded in 1883 as a Roman Catholic Seminary, and is described in *The Tablet* 29 September of that year as 'an historic building of magnificent scale'. More building was undertaken over the

---

1 Letter, dated 12 September 1930, Liverpool Metropolitan Cathedral archive.
2 Letter, dated 14 November 1930, Ibid.

years as numbers of students and staff grew to become a community of approximately 350.

The Foundation Stone of the Chapel was laid on 26 July 1927 by Archbishop Keating and the Chapel built in the Gothic style, was designed by a local architect, James O'Byrne. Correspondence between Dixon and Messrs. Pugin & Pugin, architects of Liverpool, which dates from October/November 1927 deals with the size of the organ in relation to the space available and the position of the blower, pipes and console.[3] After much discussion regarding these matters, the problems encountered were eventually resolved by slight alteration to the architectural design between the Chapel and the Cloister. This provided space to accommodate the console and pipes on the north side of the chapel in a gallery which partially projected into the choir forming a kind of semi-transept. The Discus Blower was situated in a chamber below the organ gallery. Both the position and design proved to be acoustically successful, the tone being equally distributed throughout the Chapel. There is no exact date of completion of the organ, but it is almost certain that the first official/public playing would have been at the Consecration of the Chapel which took place on 6 May 1930.

St Joseph's College Chapel Upholland, Ainscough c. 1930
Original Specification

Great Organ

16 ft	Double Diapason	metal
8	Open Diapason	metal
8	Geigen Principal	metal
8	Stopped Diapason	wood
8	Flauto Dolce	metal
4	Principal	metal
4	Schöne Flöte	metal
$2^{2}/_{3}$	Twelfth Nazard	metal
2	Fifteenth	metal

Choir Organ

16 ft	Bourdon	wood and metal
8	Gamba	tin
8	Hohlflöte	wood
8	Echo Dulciana	metal
8	Unda Maris (Tenor C)	metal

---

3 Ibid.

4	Flauto Traverso	tin
2	Piccolo	tin
8	Oboe	metal
8	Clarinet	metal
8	Tromba (unenclosed)	metal (on heavy wind pressure)

Swell Organ

8 ft	Diapason Phonon	metal
8	Harmonic Flute	wood and tin
8	Viol d'Orchestre	spotted metal
8	Voix Celestes	spotted metal
8	Cor de nuit	spotted metal
4	Gemshorn	metal
4	Quintaton	tin
3 rks	Fourniture	spotted metal
8 ft	Vox Mystica	tin
16	Contra Fagotto	metal (on heavy wind pressure)
8	Horn	metal (on heavy wind pressure)
4	Clarion	metal (on heavy wind pressure)

Pedal Organ

32 ft	Sub-Bourdon	wood
16	Open Diapason	wood
16	Bourdon	wood
16	Montre	metal
16	Echo Bass	wood
8	Flute Bass	wood
8	Violoncello	metal
4	Viola	metal
16	Trombone	metal (on heavy wind pressure)

(Numbers 36, 38, and 39 are enclosed in the Choir Organ swell box)

Couplers, Etc.

Swell to Great
Choir to Great
Swell to Choir
Swell Octave
Choir Octave
Great to Pedals
Choir to Pedals

Swell to Pedals
Great Pistons to Pedal Comps.
Swell Tremulant
Choir Tremulant

Accessories
Balanced Crescendo Pedals to Swell and Choir Organs
Four thumb pistons to each of the Great, Swell and Choir Organ Stops
Four pedal pistons to Pedal Organ Stops
Four reversible pedal pistons, working stop numbers 50, 51, 46 and 32
Pedal piston reducing the entire organ to *pianissimo*
General Crescendo Pedal controlling all the stops

Wind Pressure (Electric Rotary Blower)

Great Organ	3¼ ins.
Choir Organ	3½ and 5 ins.
Swell Organ	3¾ and 5 ins.
Pedal Organ	3¼, 3½ and 5 ins.
Pneumatic action	5 ins.

Compass of Keyboards

Manuals CC to A	58 notes
Pedals CCC to F	30 notes (pedal board radiating and concave)

Metal used for the Pipes
Zinc for the large bass pipes.
Spotted metal for the treble pipes except where tin or heavy metal is specified.
Plain or *heavy*, or tin (75%) is used for the rest.

Dixon was of the opinion that when designing an organ primarily for service accompaniment and enhancement of the Catholic Liturgy, the instrument should have distinctive and characteristic features which differ from the usually accepted English (non-Catholic) organ building design.

Ainscough having secured the contract to build the organ for Upholland enabled Dixon to put his ideas into practice, making the instrument a rare example in England at the time. The unusual features which give the instrument its distinctive character and tone quality, are found in the design of the console, the relatively softer voicing of the pipes, an abundance of quiet-toned stops specially selected for accompaniment and eight stops of continental origin.

The instrument has a detached console fitted with tubular pneumatic action. It is low in height and of a semi-circular design with tinted stop-keys (pink, red, green and blue) to facilitate quick recognition of the various groups of stops. Another feature of the console is the disposition of the keyboards (Great I, Choir II and Swell III). This is useful when accompanying plainchant, antiphonal psalmody and playing quiet interludes, as well as being more convenient for playing the organ works of the great French and German composers. In addition the two upper manuals are slightly inclined and the new Ainscough Scale pedal board while radiating and concave is narrower than the standard RCO design, thus contributing to the comfort and ease of the player.

On a return trip from Lourdes in July 1929 Dixon stopped off in Paris to visit the famous firm of Cavaillé-Coll no doubt to discuss the two ranks of pipes being made for the Swell organ. These were the Harmonic Flute, a stop originally invented by Cavaillé-Coll whose tin pipes of huge diameter produce a gentle pure flute tone akin to the ocarina and the Vox Mystica (invariably misnamed Vox Humana).

Another well-known firm, Gebrüder Späth from Ennetach, Wurtemburg, Germany, all of whose employees at the time were Catholic, made the following six stops: Piccolo, Flauto Traverso and Gamba (Choir organ); Quintaton (Swell organ); Viola and Violoncello (Pedal organ). All these pipes (which are made of tin, except the large basses for which zinc is used) possess very distinctive and beautiful tones which differ in many respects from their English equivalents.

The piccolo is described by Dixon as 'an exaggerated form of a Spitz Flöte, being of very large scale and tapering to a narrow diameter at the top. It seems to combine the features of an Open Flute, with those of an old fashioned Stopped Diapason, plus a spice of Gemshorn quality. As a timbre creator it brings new colour to a department which so often lacks distinctive character.'[4]

There are two other stops worthy of note, the Schöne Flöte, an original stop which tonally Dixon describes as being 'midway between an English Harmonic Flute and a French Prestant' and the three-rank Fourniture, described as 'a unique mixture stop of curious original ranks giving a delightful bell-like effect when used as a solo stop and a remarkable cohesive blend when used in combination.'[5]

It is interesting to note that the small metal regulating slips in the Choir Hohlflöte voiced by Mr Ralph Mayor (a partner in the firm of Ainscough), were taken from the front pipes of the 1841 J C Bishop Organ which was originally built for the Catholic Chapel in Dalton Square, Lancaster. As mentioned earlier this instrument was moved in 1859 to the new church of St Peter where it was placed in the South Transept and continued in use until being replaced by the Ainscough Organ of 1889. From Lancaster the Bishop Organ went to St Sylvester's, Liverpool and then to St William's, Ince where according to Dixon it breathed its last and he played its dirge.

---

4 Notebook, Dixon archive.
5 Ibid.

Ainscough console St Joseph's Chapel Upholland (Bryan Hughes) 1999

Overall the tonal rich palette of colours range from the ethereal whisper of the Echo Dulciana, or the gently undulating Unda Maris, through sweet-toned Flutes, gentle yet firm and pervading Diapasons, to a thrilling climax when the Reeds and Mixtures are added, all supported by the Pedal department from the soft 32 ft Bourdon to the 16 ft Trombone.

Bishop Dobson described the instrument as Dixon's Bantling; an organ which Dixon thought was without a rival considering its size and purpose.[6] In an article written by Dixon in 1930 he referred to the organ as 'The most satisfying instrument I have ever played.'[7]

Details of the organ specification in an article by Mr Bryan Hughes[8] and that given on the National Pipe Organ Register (NPOR) vary slightly from that given by Dixon, the Piccolo being listed as a Flautina, and the colour blue is given as grey. Originally the action was tubular pneumatic throughout, but according to the NPOR the Great action is electro pneumatic. The NPOR lists the Tromba as being on the Great which Dixon originally placed on the Choir, and gives the disposition of keyboards as Great I, Swell II and Choir III which also differs from the original design. John Rowntree in his report on the instrument dated 1996 states that the pipework is of good quality and that survival of all the pipework without apparent significant change is an important feature of the organ. He

---

6   Upholland College Magazine, Liverpool Metropolitan Cathedral archive.
7   *The Universe*, 16 May 1930.
8   *The Organ*, October 1971, Vol. LI, No. 202.

observed that part of the leatherwork had been renewed at some point and that the keys had been poorly recovered. At this time the instrument was showing signs of wear and tear, wind leakage and some sections were not functioning.[9] In the specification given by Dr Rowntree the manual compass is listed as CC-c''', but it is in fact to A as Dixon clearly specified in his design.

The musical, historical and local aspects of the organ, together with the important part it played in the life of the College make it a rare surviving example of its type.

Sadly a decline in the number of students and amalgamations finally led to the announcement by Archbishop Patrick Kelly that the College would close on 30 November 1999. The final Mass of the Alumni Association to take place in the Chapel was held on the Feast of All Saints, Sunday 31 October 1999.

In Te Domine Speravi
(College motto)

---

9 Rowntree Report, Liverpool Metropolitan Cathedral archive.

LANCASTER MUSICAL FESTIVAL

FEBRUARY
Saturday, 1st, Children's Festival
Friday, 7th, Adults' Festival
Saturday, 8th, Adults' Festival

1930

TO BE HELD IN THE

ASHTON HALL

PROGRAMME & BOOK OF WORDS

ONE SHILLING

Music For All, 1930–40

> *'Of all the Arts, music exercises the widest appeal,*
> *for it knows no restrictions, it speaks in myriad tongues ...'*

> *'Music fulfils its most attractive and beautiful mission when*
> *the masses of people enjoy it as a recreation and a solace.'*[1]
> *Ruskin.*

THIS DECADE SAW THE establishment of the Lancaster Music Festival which encouraged more people to participate in music making and enabled others to gain an appreciation of music. It was also a period when Dixon became more widely known through the organ recitals which were regularly broadcast by the BBC from Dublin, London and Manchester. From about this time onwards the case of mistaken identity arose and it is still a topic of conversation today. Dixon continued to give recitals in the Ashton Hall, as well as other recitals to mark the opening of new or restored organs. In addition to writing, composing and teaching, he was still travelling each week to lecture in various villages, towns and cities throughout Lancashire. Towards the end of this decade there were special celebrations to mark the elevation of Lancaster to City status.

In 1929 Dr Dixon along with Mr J W Aldous, Mr T Arkwright and friends formed a Committee to launch the Lancaster Music Festival which became an annual event until 1939. Dr Dixon became Secretary, Mr Aldous Chairman, Mr Arkwright Treasurer and The Mayor (Councillor T Till) was President. Organisation of such a Festival was not an easy task and there were many initial difficulties to overcome. The Committee appealed to the public for support in two ways, either by becoming a guarantor, or a subscriber. They saw this venture as a cultural exercise to promote the appreciation of good music.

---

1 Foreword to the Lancaster Music Festival Programme, February 1930.

The first Festival took place at the Ashton Hall in February 1930, with morning, afternoon and evening sessions extended over a three-day period. So 'the little ship' began its voyage.[2]

This Festival attracted over 300 entries and numbered over 1,000 competitors, representing all walks of life. There were a large number of instrumental classes and the entries in the folk-dance section exceeded all expectations. The latter included Morris Dances, Country Dances, Maypole Dance and Sword Dance. In addition to the solo piano, instrumental and singing classes, there were school choirs (junior and senior), children's choirs and village choirs. There were three choirs comprising boys only from local schools with an age range up to 16, each choir consisting of between 12 and 20 pupils. Other classes included piano sight-reading, written aural, theory of music and elocution. Entry to the local classes was defined as living within a 16 mile radius of Lancaster. As well as competitors from Lancaster and the surrounding villages, some came from the Lake District in the north, others from several well-known Lancashire towns as far south as Manchester, some from the west coastal towns as far south as Wallasey and some from Yorkshire.

A class for works choirs was inaugurated at Lancaster which resulted in the formation of many small choirs that otherwise would never have come into existence. The choirs came from the well-known firm of Waring & Gillow, Greenfield & Bath Mills, Messrs. J Helme & Co., Halton Mills, Messrs. Reddrop & Co. and the County Mental Hospital. Special features of the Festival included The Children's Festival, Organ Solo classes, a Class for Original Composition and Classes for Works, Factory, and Business House Choirs. The pitch used in all vocal classes was Philharmonic A – 439 at 68 degrees F.

Competitors awarded 75% or 85% of marks were entitled to receive a Second Class or a First Class Certificate, respectively. As well as a certificate, prizes were given in the form of money up to the value of £2, books, volumes of music (some bound), a music stand, a piano stool, a violin case, a violin bow, a violin and interestingly camping equipment for the winner of the Scouts and Guides classes. The test piece for the Scouts and Guides in 1930 was 'The Kangaroo' by A Rowley and the programme stated that *Competitors must appear in regulation dress, and marks will be awarded for orderly entry and exit.*

The first adjudicators were Dr J Lyon, Dr P C Hull, Dr H L Read, Miss C Holbrow (Folk Dancing) and Miss Muriel Ferrie (Elocution). There were eight official accompanists: Miss E Bell LTCL, Miss E C Chadderton, Miss M Douthwaite, Miss N Leighton, Miss E A Linaker LISM, Miss H Pedley, Mr C Ball Mus. Bac. FRCO and Miss F Cockerill (for folk dances).

Two pianos were loaned to the Festival Committee, one by Horsefall, China

---

2 Ibid.

Street, Lancaster and one by Fisher & Son, Penny Street, Lancaster. Tomlinson's Music Warehouse had a plan of the hall and took bookings for seats.

Admission was by ticket for each session, or one could purchase a day ticket or even a season ticket. Prices for the morning and afternoon sessions ranged from 1*s.* for unreserved seats to 1*s.* 6*d.* for reserved seats. An evening session cost 1*s.* for unreserved seats in the gallery and back of the hall, 2*s.* for reserved seats in the area and 3*s.* for reserved seats in the centre gallery and stalls. Day tickets for all sessions in any one day cost 2*s.* 6*d.* including a reserved seat in the area for the evening concert, or 3*s.* 6*d.* including a reserved seat in the stalls or gallery for the evening concert. Season tickets for all sessions of the festival, with reserved seats for the evening concerts were 7*s.* in the area and 10*s.* in the stalls or centre gallery.

At the end of the foreword to the first programme Mr Aldous wrote:

> Music as an art tends to the refinement and civilization of a nation, and if the Lancaster Festival has encouraged in the district the love and practice of good music, its object will have been achieved.

In all but financial matters the first Festival was a success, with over 1,000 competitors taking part, representing all walks of life. Despite a deficit of £31 and some initial difficulties, the Committee had gained experience in organising the event and felt justified in undertaking a second Festival. They were convinced that the Festival had aroused local interest in good music, not merely amongst a few enthusiasts, but in a much wider field.

By the second Festival in February, 1931 the number of entries had increased, notably in the works choirs (10), with additional school choirs from the surrounding villages (9), and the folk dancing sections. The 350 entries representing 2,000 competitors was proof that the Festival Committee were contributing to spreading the love and practice of good music in the area. An extra afternoon and evening was required to accommodate the additional entries. The President for this festival was Viscount Clanfield.

The writer of the 'John O Gaunt' column in the local press recalls that:

> At one of the Festivals an eminent Doctor of Music who was adjudicating the organ class facetiously made the remark that F.R.C.O. stood for 'Fellows who Really Can't play the Organ'. Dr Dixon smiled broadly and at the end of the session demonstrated the fallacy of the statement with a splendid rendering of the National Anthem – syncopation included and proved that F.R.C.O. could also mean 'Fellows who Really Can play the Organ'.[3]

---

3 *Lancaster Guardian*, 23 December 1932.

In 1933 it was necessary to change the time of the Festival from February to November. The reason for this was that a series of concerts had to be held in order to offset the debt which had accumulated. These proved successful therefore it was not necessary to call on the guarantors to make a contribution. The number of competitors in most classes was felt to be satisfactory, but more were needed notably in the string classes and the vocal quartets. Perhaps the test pieces were too difficult. Due to the pressure of duties and indifferent health Mr Aldous resigned as Chairman and his position was taken up by Dr Dixon, who until now had been the Secretary. The first three Festivals involved the Committee in financial loss, but happily the fourth one ended with a small balance on the right side.

At the fifth Festival of 1934, which attracted a record number of entries the unexpected death of Mr Arkwright (initially Treasurer and latterly Secretary) was announced. A challenge shield in his memory was donated to be competed for by the Church and Chapel Choirs. This was felt appropriate as it was Mr Arkwright who instigated this class in the first Festival. In addition to Miss Muriel Roscoe and Mr Harold Dawber, there were two notable adjudicators at this Festival namely Sir Richard Terry and Dr Charles Moody.

A New Constitution was adopted at a meeting held on 10 October 1936.

> The object of the Lancaster Musical Festival shall be, by means of a Musical Competition, and in any other way that may be decided, to encourage the performance of good music, and the cultivation of musical talent (both vocal and instrumental) particularly in the town of Lancaster and the surrounding district.
>
> A Musical Competition shall be held at such times, and under such conditions, as the Council shall decide, and an Annual General Meeting of Patrons and Subscribers shall be held in the month of February in each year, when the Financial Statement shall be presented.
>
> The Musical Festival shall be managed by a Council, elected at the Annual General Meeting above referred to, and shall consist of 24 persons, one third of whom shall retire annually in rotation, but shall be eligible for re-election. The Council shall have the power, in addition, if they think fit, to co-opt a further number of persons thereof, but not exceeding in the aggregate a total number of six persons.
>
> Patrons shall be persons who subscribe a sum of One Guinea or upwards annually, and Subscribers shall be comprised of persons contributing not less than Five Shillings per annum, and the Council shall be elected from such two classes of financial supporters of the Festival.
>
> The Council shall elect a President, any number of Vice-Presidents, as well as a Chairman, Vice Chairman, Honorary Secretary and Honorary Treasurer, and such other Officers as they consider desirable to carry out the objects of the Festival.

> The Council shall have the power, if they think fit, to appoint a small Executive Committee, to whom shall be delegated such detailed work as may from time to time be decided.

One of the key changes was to give the subscribing public a voice in the management of the Festival in the hope that this would result in more subscribers coming forward and this in turn would help the Festival financially.

In the foreword to the 1936 Festival, Dr Dixon wrote:

> ... in asking ourselves whether we really have succeeded in making the Lancaster Musical Festival an outstanding event in the life of our County Town, we cannot give an entirely affirmative answer.

He felt that there was still a lot of work to be done before all prejudices could be eliminated and those who were pessimistic about such matters converted. Providing a large number of graded classes in progressive order gave young people an opportunity to perform in public while still in the early stages of their studies. Similarly, a variety of classes were provided for adults, both for solo performers, vocalists and instrumentalists, and for choirs. This provision formed a valuable contribution to the musical education of all those who participated and to all those who heard them. The Festival was a valuable training ground for talent, which in due course could bring further honours at more established Festivals, and in some cases launch a musician on the path to a highly successful musical career.

By 1936 a charge was made for the adjudicator's report, 6*d.* to individual competitors and 1*s.* to choirs.

As well as Mr Harold Dawber, a long standing adjudicator at previous Lancaster Festivals, the 1936 Festival Committee engaged Sir Hugh Roberton, conductor of the famous Glasgow Orpheus Choir; Mr Ivor Coombes MA and Mr W H Ellis FRCO.

With a noticeable decline in live music at the theatre and cinemas, the eighth Musical Festival of 1937 set out to encourage real flesh and blood musicians, to stimulate the making of music in the home and to lay the foundations of good taste in music. Mrs Watson donated silver medals to be competed for in the senior boys and girls singing classes. There were two new adjudicators at this Festival, Miss Sudel-Swarbrick and Dr Herman Brearley.

'Joy through music-making' was the motto of the 1938 Festival which was held in December, a little later than usual for reasons unknown. The Festival was to be thought of as not an end in itself, but another peak achieved on the path which the musical discoverers of the past years would continue to explore. Music making should give joy to all who participate in it, whether actively, as singers or instrumentalists, or passively, as listeners.

The death of Mr Henry Bickerstaff earlier in the year was a great loss, not only to the Festival, but to the town as a whole. He had been associated with the Festival since the very beginning and at one time was Honorary Secretary. Several choirs were formed under his direction and he became a well-known local choral conductor, who was passionately devoted to musical pursuits, and an enthusiastic supporter of the Festival. For many years he was Headmaster of the Boys' National School. The Committee decided to open a fund to which subscriptions were invited, for the purpose of founding a Prize in his memory to be competed for annually.

In 1938, the Right Reverend T W Pearson OSB, RC Bishop of Lancaster also passed away. He too was one of the earliest and most steadfast supporters of the Festival.

It would appear that popularity in the Folk Dance Classes had declined over the years as there were no entries in this field by 1937, but the number of entries overall continued to rise. By 1938 there were more Speech Classes. As well as Elocution and Unison Speaking the 1938 Festival included Duologues, Dramatic Speech and Dramatic Recitation. Piano Classes, Singing Classes, and Instrumental Classes remained as popular as ever, and there were still entries from School Choirs, Male Voice Choirs, Female Choirs and Mixed Choirs.

By 1938 the cost of tickets had hardly changed. Season tickets for the stalls and centre gallery remained the same at 10*s.* and the rest of the hall was 5*s.* Evening concerts compared with 1930 were just two prices, 2*s.* and 1*s.* for the stalls and centre gallery. The Day Sessions were reduced to 1*s.* for both morning and evening sessions. A programme and book of words remained at 1*s.* throughout all the festival years. The number of Patrons and Subscribers ranged from 20 in 1930 to 76 in 1937, but fell to 61 in 1938. Sadly the Festivals came to an end at the beginning of the Second World War.

* * *

Dixon first broadcast from Dublin in 1926, the year that Radio Eire was established and continued to broadcast regularly from there and London in the early days of broadcasting. In the 1930s and 1940s he gave several recitals on the famous Cavaillé-Coll organ in Manchester Town Hall.

It was at one of those recitals broadcast from Manchester Town Hall in October 1933 that Dixon was the first to broadcast the Elgar Organ Sonata which it is said Elgar himself heard.

The BBC contract for the above performance reveals that Dixon was paid five guineas for the actual performance and a Mechanical Reproduction fee of £1 6s 3d.

After the broadcast listeners were prompted to write to Dixon, two such letters are as follows:

12 Delaware Road, Blackpool
4.10.33

My Dear Dr Dixon
Why ever didn't Elgar write his organ Sonata to last an hour! Your broadcast tonight was a triumph for you. Personally, I have never heard a finer recital – you thrilled both my wife and self. Play us some more like it if you are asked to broadcast again!! (I hope that will be soon) You showed your listeners tonight that the organ is the 'King of Instruments' and that you were its master! Thank you very much and hearty Congratulations!

Yours sincerely
J. J. Breeze

* * *

25, Regent Street, Lancaster
Oct 5 1933

My Dear Dr
Manchester Town Broadcast – What a magnificent performance – I listened to every note and combination and the subjects given out with such taste and Brilliant execution. I shall never forget – Elgar was shown up at his best by the <u>foremost</u> organ expert in existence-
I hope he was listening-
Heartiest Congratulations

Your fondest 'fan'
Chris Chadderton

The following letters were sent after a broadcast in 1936:

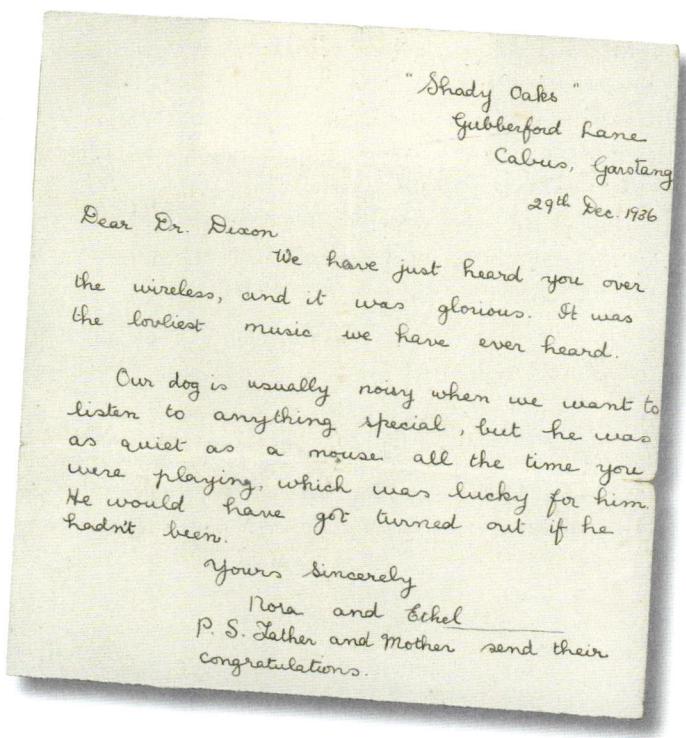

"Shady Oaks"
Gubberford Lane
Cabus, Garstang
29th Dec. 1936

Dear Dr. Dixon
We have just heard you over the wireless, and it was glorious. It was the lovliest music we have ever heard.

Our dog is usually noisy when we want to listen to anything special, but he was as quiet as a mouse all the time you were playing, which was lucky for him. He would have got turned out if he hadn't been.

Yours sincerely
Nora and Ethel
P.S. Father and Mother send their congratulations.

* * *

'Brooklands', 5 Welbeck Avenue, Fleetwood
31st December 1936

Dear Sir,

I once heard you remark at a lecture which you gave some years ago at Pilling Lane School, that you often received in mistake letters from radio fans, intended for your name sake who presides at the organ at the Tower Ballroom Blackpool.

Well I am taking the liberty of writing to you to say how very much I enjoyed your recital from Manchester Town Hall on Tuesday last.

The reception was extremely good and being somewhat of an organist myself, I listened with great interest to your programme.

The two items which I liked best were the 'Liebesträum' of Liszt, and your own Prelude & Fantasy Fugue (The Cunningham).

I am not particularly keen on transcriptions, and I have heard the 'Liebesträum' played by many cinema organists including your name sake at Blackpool, but I can honestly say I have never enjoyed a rendering better than yours on Tuesday night. I particularly liked your registration. It was very effective.

I had never heard your own Prelude & Fantasy Fugue before, and was much struck with it. As the tempo of the fugue was fairly fast, I am wondering if the subject of the fugue was based on G. D. C. the initials of Cunningham of Birmingham? It is rather difficult to pick out a subject at a first hearing especially on the wireless, so I may be wrong.

Anyhow I hope you will repeat these items again sometime when you are broadcasting.

It might interest you to know that the first time I heard you give a recital was about six years ago, at St Mary's Church Fleetwood, and I have since heard you more recently at Thornton Wignall Memorial Church.

With all best wishes for the New Year, and in the words of a chorus from one of Handel's oratorios may you have a long time before you, to enable you to play as a concluding voluntary 'Fixed in His Everlasting Seat'.

Yours truly
Roger M Cross

P.S. I think you ought to know that the Manchester announcer cut you off the air, three minutes before time and announced that the recital was over, when you were just about starting the Finale from Widor's Symphony no 2. Then we heard something classical.

* * *

Lancaster
Dec 31/36

Dear Dr
Many thanks for Great Organ Recital Tuesday night Manchester.
It was the finest recital I ever heard, execution & blending, a greatest performance I ever listened to — I could not refrain from writing you -
You are most wonderful Organist ever I heard in my long life. With hopes for you of a happy & successful New Year.

Yours as ever
V. sincerely
Chris Chadderton

A post card sent on 31 Dec 1936 reads as follows:

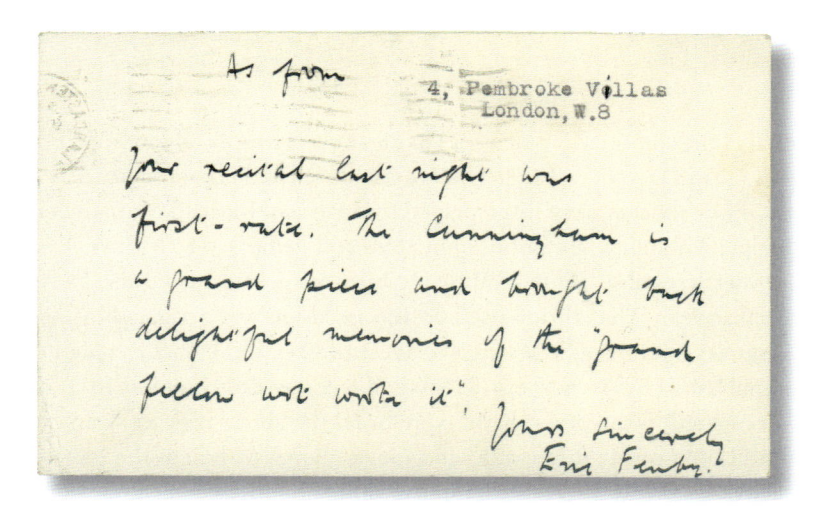

The *Prelude and Fantasy Fugue* (The Cunningham) for organ, composed in August/September 1935 is based on the initials of G D Cunningham (1878–1948), who was appointed Organist of Birmingham Town Hall in 1924 (the post Dixon applied for) a position he held until his death in 1948. This is the only work composed by Dixon in which he experiments with atonality and serial techniques, although aspects of the latter are not strictly adhered to. The Prelude in 3/4 time begins with a statement in the pedals of the three initials (G D C), transposed and in retrograde. As one would expect the theme gives rise to the predominant use of both melodic and harmonic intervals of seconds, fourths and fifths. The Fugue in 6/8 time has two contrasting sections in 4/4 and ends with a chord containing the notes C D G (all the notes being doubled except D).

Example 5, Prelude and Fantasy Fugue, bars 1–5

Example 6, Fugue subject, bars 62–68 'Prelude and Fantasy Fugue (The Cunningham)' by J.H. Reginald Dixon © Oxford University Press 1936. Extracts reproduced by permission. All rights reserved. Copies available to buy from Allegro Music, Tel: 01885 490375, Fax: 01885 490615, Email: sales@allegro.co.uk

A recital of the complete organ works of Elgar was given by Dixon in Manchester Town Hall on 15 December 1937. This was recorded and broadcast at a later date. The two Organ Sonatas were interspersed by a Suite of Pieces, originally entitled Eleven Vesper Voluntaries, composed in 1890 and dedicated to Mrs W A Raikes. The Suite was first published in 1891 by Orsborn & Tuckwood and also by Ascherberg later that year. The edition used on this occasion was arranged by Reginald Goss Custard (Organist of St Margaret's Westminster and later Liverpool Cathedral) and published by Ascherberg, Hopwood & Crew Ltd. London 1911.

It was reported in the press that Dixon found the above rare work among old, battered and torn music in second-hand music shop.[4] Although the existence of the work was known to Elgar's biographers, it had long since been out of print.

Another Cavaillé-Coll instrument on which Dixon gave several recitals was the one in Parr Hall, Warrington. A report on one such recital arranged by the Warrington & District Organists' and Choirmasters' Association reads:

> As in previous years Dr Dixon's playing was marked by aesthetic taste in regard to the choice of tone colour, which brought out, the characteristic features of the French organ. The programme submitted was a varied one drawn up with the object of appealing to the average listener rather than the organist fraternity in particular and was carried through with skill and judgement.[5]

---

4 *Daily Dispatch*, Tuesday 14 December 1937.
5 *Warrington Examiner*, 24 February 1934.

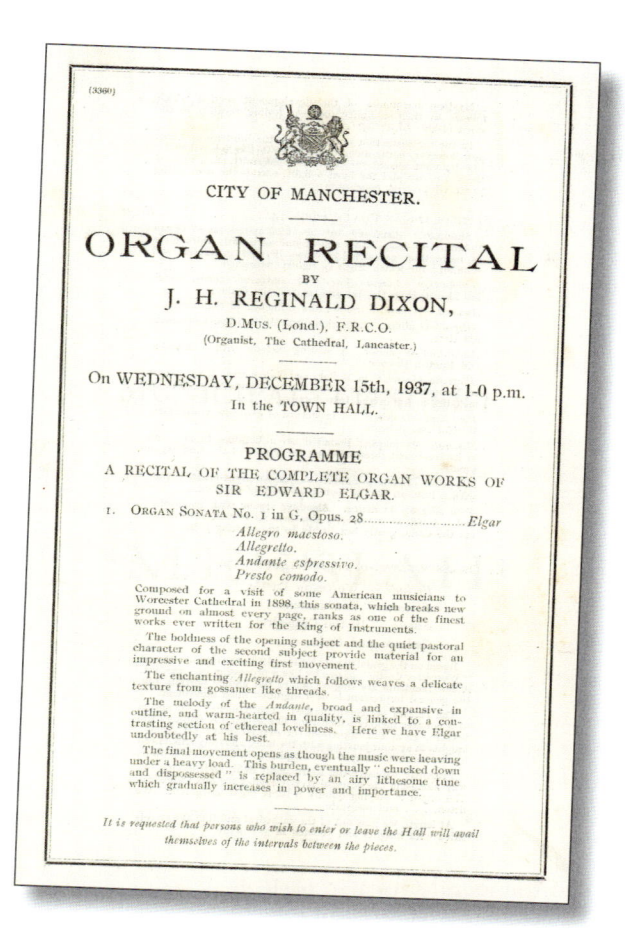

> (3360)
>
> CITY OF MANCHESTER.
>
> # ORGAN RECITAL
>
> BY
>
> ## J. H. REGINALD DIXON,
>
> D.Mus. (Lond.), F.R.C.O.
> (Organist, The Cathedral, Lancaster.)
>
> On WEDNESDAY, DECEMBER 15th, 1937, at 1-0 p.m.
> In the TOWN HALL.
>
> ### PROGRAMME
>
> A RECITAL OF THE COMPLETE ORGAN WORKS OF
> SIR EDWARD ELGAR.
>
> 1. ORGAN SONATA No. 1 in G, Opus. 28................Elgar
>   Allegro maestoso.
>   Allegretto.
>   Andante espressivo.
>   Presto comodo.
>
>   Composed for a visit of some American musicians to Worcester Cathedral in 1898, this sonata, which breaks new ground on almost every page, ranks as one of the finest works ever written for the King of Instruments.
>
>   The boldness of the opening subject and the quiet pastoral character of the second subject provide material for an impressive and exciting first movement.
>
>   The enchanting *Allegretto* which follows weaves a delicate texture from gossamer like threads.
>
>   The melody of the *Andante*, broad and expansive in outline, and warm-hearted in quality, is linked to a contrasting section of ethereal loveliness. Here we have Elgar undoubtedly at his best.
>
>   The final movement opens as though the music were heaving under a heavy load. This burden, eventually " chucked down and dispossessed " is replaced by an airy lithesome tune which gradually increases in power and importance.
>
> *It is requested that persons who wish to enter or leave the Hall will avail themselves of the intervals between the pieces.*

   In 1935 Dixon wrote a series of short dramatised stories for Children's Hour, but it is not known if these were ever broadcast. The synopsis of the first story entitled 'Dr Crotchet' begins with the Aunt playing a piano and Uncle commenting about how terrible the instrument sounds. Dr Crotchet arrives on the scene and is introduced to the Uncle as an old friend who at first mistakes him for a medical doctor come to visit their sick daughter. Dr Crotchet explains that he is a Doctor of Music not medicine. So he is then asked to repair the piano which is not only out of tune, but requires some adjustment to the action. The story ends with the couple asking the doctor to play a piece which leads to the second story entitled 'Dr Crotchet Plays the Piano'. In this episode Dr Crotchet plays Clementi's *Sonatina* in C Op. 36 and brings the piece to life, first by playing and describing all the motives as representing the actions of soldiers on parade playing their instruments. He suggests that the piece could be called 'A Game of Toy Soldiers' to suit the imaginary scene he has described and this story ends with a performance of the complete piece. Further pieces including the *Elfin Dance* by Jensen were selected for future programmes.

With regard to the case of mistaken identity, there was frequent confusion between Dr J H Reginald Dixon and Mr Reginald H Dixon of Blackpool, famous for his playing on the WurliTzer at the Tower Ballroom. They were not related in any way and sadly never met, but they did have many things in common. Both men saw the funny side of the mistaken identity, through receiving letters meant for the other, in conversations with people they met at various functions and reports in the local press when broadcasting on the radio.

Mr Dixon would receive letters complimenting him on his performances, or on giving the opening recital on a new instrument, and playing in places he had never visited. Some people thought they knew him as a child and some the regiment he served in during the war, but many of these comments were intended for Dr Dixon. Likewise Dr Dixon would receive letters from radio fans who were interested in the popular music played by his namesake. Sometimes people he met would compliment him on his broadcast from the Tower, and when he did not have time to explain the mistaken identity he would just say 'Sez you' 'Sez you' with a twinkle in his eye. It must have been very confusing to many listeners during the first week of October 1933 when both musicians broadcast on successive nights, Dr J H R Dixon giving one of his many organ recitals from Manchester Town Hall on Wednesday at 6.30 p.m. and Mr Reginald Dixon playing from the Tower Ballroom on Thursday also at 6.30 p.m.

Many years later CM, music critic of the Manchester Guardian, was confused after hearing a recital in Manchester Cathedral given by Ralph Downes. He wrote: 'The second curiosity was a Baroque Suite by Reginald Dixon, better known in another sphere of organ-playing.' Dr Dixon wrote to the editor pointing out that as Lancaster City and Cathedral Organist he had no connection with either his 'proper poorly' namesake, or with him whose deserved fame in another sphere of organ-playing emanates from somewhere 'beside the seaside.' CM replied 'The name Reginald Dixon, I learn to my cost, is as frequent among organists as is Oliver Edwards among literary critics. I apologise to both Mr Dixons for not being aware of this, and for assuming that they were one and the same person.'

In July 1954 the Tower Ballroom Organist Mr Reginald Dixon celebrated his Silver Wedding Anniversary. At the time Mr Ronald George Dixon brother of Dr J H R Dixon, who lived in Blackpool where he had taught Modern Languages for many years, recalled a story from some years earlier. In the 1920s Mr David Clegg (composer and organist) gave popular recitals on 'a very unorthodox organ' in the Empress Ballroom. After the death of Mr Clegg the instrument remained silent for many years. Mr R G Dixon thought that the instrument should be brought back into regular use, so he contacted the secretary of the Winter Gardens Company then a Mr Harry Clegg and suggested that if anyone could play that contraption it was his brother Dr Reginald Dixon. Mr H Clegg liked the idea and made a note of Dr Dixon's name and address. The Company manager was also employed by the Blackpool Tower Company who were about to look for someone to play the new WurliTzer which was shortly to be installed in the Tower Ballroom. Some time passed before Mr R G Dixon read in the *Herald & Gazette* that Mr Dixon had been appointed. However he soon discovered that it was not Reginald his brother, but Sheffield-born Reginald Herbert Dixon.

Reginald Herbert Dixon, a church organist at fifteen and at one time a concert pianist, played music for the silent films in the cinema. He was based at the New Victoria, Preston before his appointment at the Tower Ballroom. As a young man of twenty-one he hated jazz but grew to enjoy it while still preferring serious music. His position as organist at the Tower was unique, and the instrument he played at the time was probably the only unit organ to be used on a regular basis for both recitals and providing music for dancing.

The original Tower organ installed in 1929 had two manuals and ten units, and although flexible and effective in some ways it had a rather thin tone partly due to its character and the acoustic of the ballroom.

In 1935 a new superior instrument designed by Reginald Dixon was installed comprising three manuals, thirteen units (English Horn, Harmonic Tuba, Diaphonic Diapason, Tibia Clausa, Tibia Clausa No 2, Saxophone, Krumet, Orchestral Oboe, Viole d'orchestre, Viole Celeste, Kinura, Concert Flute, Vox Humana), eighty-eight stops plus couplers and percussion stops, twelve percussion attachments, including a piano placed in a special chamber, and approximately thirty combination pistons. The organ was enclosed in two chambers and had a movable console. It was capable of producing the characteristic effects and tone-colours of the old instrument as well as new effects, colours and a rich church organ sound.

Reginald Dixon affectionately known as 'Mr Blackpool' popularised the song 'I do like to be beside the seaside' by using it as his signature tune. He was organist at the Tower Ballroom for forty years, earned a world-wide reputation through his broadcasting and recordings, as well as his arrangements of dance numbers which were a speciality, appreciated by thousands of people.

There was another link between the two Dixons, Blackpool, a cinema organ and the Church of the Sacred Heart. In 1933 Father James Oldham SJ took up an appointment at the Church. With the advent of the 'talkies' which superseded the silent films and spelt the end of the cinema organ, many of these instruments came on the market for disposal. In early November 1935 Father Oldham heard that the organ in the Waterloo cinema was for sale and he had an idea that parts of this instrument could be used to enlarge and modernise the present church organ which dated from 1876. He was an accomplished organist and after playing the instrument he put in a bid of £150 which was accepted. This cinema organ when new had cost £3,000.

Father Oldham commissioned Messrs. Jardine & Co. of Manchester who had built the church organ, to dismantle his newly acquired bargain and store it

SPECIFICATION OF THE ORGAN.

Three Manuals (CC to C) - - 61 Notes
Pedal Organ (CCC to F) - - 30 Notes

SWELL ORGAN.

1. Lieblich Bourdon - - 16 feet
2. Geigen Principal - - 8 feet
3. Viole d'Orchestre - - 8 feet
4. Viole Celeste - - 8 feet
5. Flauto Amabile - - 8 feet
6. Gemshorn - - - 4 feet
7. Mixture (Two Ranks).
8. Horn - - - 8 feet
9. Oboe - - - 8 feet
   Tremulant.
i. Octave.
ii. Sub-Octave.

GREAT ORGAN.

1. Contra Flute - - 16 feet
2. Open Diapason (Large) - 8 feet
3. Open Diapason (Medium) - 8 feet
4. Vox Angelica - - 8 feet
5. Clarabella - - 8 feet
6. Principal - - 4 feet
7. Harmonic Flute - - 4 feet
8. Fifteenth - - 2 feet
9. Tromba - - 8 feet
iii. Swell to Great.
iv. Choir to Great.

CHOIR ORGAN.

1. Open Diapason - - 8 feet
2. Viola - - - 8 feet
3. Lieblich Gedact - - 8 feet
4. Flute Douce - - 4 feet
5. Piccolo - - 2 feet
6. Corno di Bassetto - - 8 feet
7. Vox Humana - - 8 feet
   Tremulant.
v. Choir Octave.
vi. Choir Sub-Octave.
vii. Swell to Choir.

PEDAL ORGAN.

1. Harmonic Bass - - 32 feet
2. Open Diapason - - 16 feet
3. Bourdon - - 16 feet
4. Octave Diapason - - 8 feet
5. Flute Bass - - 8 feet
viii. Swell to Pedal.
ix. Great to Pedal.
x. Choir to Pedal.

ACCESSORIES.

4 Thumb Pistons to Swell Organ.
4 Thumb Pistons to Great and Pedal Organs.
4 Pedal Pistons to Swell Organ.
4 Pedal Pistons to Great and Pedal Organs.
1 Reversible Pedal Piston to Swell to Great Coupler.
1 Reversible Pedal Piston to Great to Pedal Coupler.
1 Reversible Thumb Piston to Great to Pedal Coupler.
7 small Adjustable Pistons to Choir Organ controlled by 2 Pistons under Choir Keys.
Balanced Swell Pedal.
Balanced Choir Pedal.
Detached Console.
Tubular Pneumatic Action.
Dermid Rotary Blower.

with a view to incorporating any suitable parts into rebuilding the pipe organ. To successfully fuse two such diverse instruments into one, called for expertise and experienced practical skills. Although the plan of reconstruction necessitated structural alterations to the organ loft to accommodate the enlarged instrument, Father Oldham's dynamic energy and Jardine's capability resulted in the entire project being completed within three months at a cost of £680.

The specification for the new instrument with tubular pneumatic action was drawn up by Mr W. Vann, organist at the time. Much of the original organ was retained with regard to the pipe work, which was re-voiced. A third manual was added, as well as a new large Open Diapason on the Great, together with an Acoustic Harmonic Pedal Stop (32 ft), and a new Octave Diapason (8 ft) on the Pedal Organ.

I.—DEDICATION AND BLESSING OF ORGAN

By Rev. J. H. OLDHAM, S.J.

II.—RECITAL.

1. Prelude and Fugue in D .... *J. S. Bach*
2. " Ave Maria " .... *Bach-Gounod*
3. Motet .... " O Sacrum Convivium " .... *Palestrina*
   (1516-1594)
   THE CHOIR.
4. Légende .... " St. Francis preaching to the birds " .... *Liszt*
5. Allegretto .... *W. Wolstenholme*
6. Prelude and Fantasy Fugue .... " The Cunningham " .... *J. H. Reginald Dixon*
7. Motets .... (1) " Panis Angelicus " .... *C. H. Kitson*
              (2) " Venite ad Me " .... *Zulueta*
   THE CHOIR.
8. Scherzo .... *P. W. Whitlock*
9. Transcription .... " To Music " .... *Schubert*
10. Finale .... Organ Symphony in C minor .... *F. W. Holloway*

" Faith of Our Fathers."

The dedication and blessing of the 'new organ' took place on Sunday 26 April 1936 and the opening recital was given by Dr J H R Dixon. The programme was carefully selected to demonstrate the quality and range of the instrument. Among the large congregation assembled for the occasion were a number of 'regulars' from the Waterloo cinema and a few bewildered and disappointed devotees who, seeing the name Reginald Dixon billed in bold type on the poster outside the church had come expecting to hear a recital by the wizard of the Tower WurliTzer!

The case of mistaken identity still lives on. Quite recently in a University Concert Brochure notes on the composer of the *Baroque Suite* referred to Reginald Dixon of Blackpool.

Dr Dixon was fascinated by cinema organs, and it was not unusual to find him seated at such instruments entertaining whoever was around. One day he was found in the Theatre Royal, Fishergate, Preston, seated at the organ, exploring the scope the instrument had to offer. His friend Mr Barrie, manager of the theatre whom he had come to visit, described him as 'One of the most charming men it has been my lot to meet.' [6]

The Annual Congress Meetings of the Incorporated Association of Organists often provided an opportunity for Dr Dixon to indulge in his passion for playing organs of a different variety than he was accustomed to week by week. More details of these events will be mentioned later.

**

On the morning of 12 May 1937, Coronation Day of George VI, it was announced that the Borough of Lancaster would be elevated to the dignity and status of a City. Confirmation of this announcement was issued by Letters Patent on 14 May and celebrations to mark the event were planned for later in the year.

Dixon composed a Grand Civic March especially for the occasion. There exists a draft letter from Dixon to His Majesty King George VI requesting permission to dedicate the work to him.[7] It is not known whether the letter was ever sent:

> To His Most Gracious Majesty King George VI
>
> May it please your Majesty
> In connection with the elevation by your Majesty of Lancaster to the dignity and status of a City the Mayor & Corporation of Lancaster have accepted as an official March in honour of the occasion a Grand Civic March entitled 'Lancastria' which I have composed – and which will be played by the Band of the 5th King's Own Regiment after the National Anthem has been sung by the Massed Children of the Lancaster Schools on Thursday September the 30th.
>
> In view of Your Majesty's close connection with the City of Lancaster, I am writing humbly to ask that permission be given me to dedicate this Civic March 'Lancastria' —to His most Gracious Majesty The Duke of Lancaster.
>
> I have the honour to remain
> Your Majesty's most obedient & faithful subject
> J H Reginald Dixon[8]

---

6   Postcard, Dixon archive.
7   Draft copy of letter, Dixon archive.
8   Letter, Dixon archive.

During the week beginning 27 September Souvenir Spoons were given to the school children of Lancaster. At 10.00 a.m. on 30 September members and officials of the Lancaster City Corporation robed ready for the official celebrations. The party assembled on the steps of the Town Hall, with invited guests and the senior school children of the City in front of a large gathering of citizens from Lancaster and the surrounding area. After the singing of the National Anthem the 5th King's Own Royal Regiment Band conducted by the composer gave the first performance of *Lancastria*.

The Civic Procession followed by the school children and citizens made their way through the town to the Priory and Parish Church, where a State Service was held attended by representatives from the ecclesiastical, military and civic life of the city. The Service began with the hymn 'All people that on earth do dwell', followed by the Letters Patent being presented to the Bishop the Right Rev. B Pollard, who laid them on the Altar. The sermon given by the Bishop was based on the text 'And there was great joy in that city'. During the service the choir under the direction of Mr Paul Rochard sang the anthem *Zadok the Priest* by Handel.

On returning to the Town Hall the Mayor, members of the Council and invited officials, gathered to observe the unveiling of a Commemoration Plaque by Earl Winterton, MP, Chancellor of the Duchy and County Palatine of Lancaster. This was followed by a Luncheon at 1.00 p.m. at which Dr Dixon was one of the guests. The celebrations on this day ended with a football match on the Giant Axe Field, Lancaster City v Morecambe.

A great pageant of 21 episodes representing historical scenes associated with Lancaster took place on Saturday 2 October. These included the Ancient Britons, Roman Occupation, Other Invading Forces, Religious Events, The passing of Charters, Royal Visits of former Kings and Queens, Historical Battles, Education and Literary connections, The King's Own Royal Regiment and World Trade, presented by students, staff and pupils from the schools, employees from local firms, various organisations and professional bodies.

Episode 5 entitled 'The Founding of Cockersand Abbey' representing the life and times of the Canons and Lay Brethren, was presented by St Peter's Cathedral Choir and the Catholic Confraternity. Dr Dixon set to music a text which had been written by Canon R N Billington some years earlier. Members of the Women's Evening Institutes were responsible for the costumes, the white habits being made by the Skerton ladies and the Queen Street ladies made the birettas and mitre.

The colourful Historic Cavalcade including a large model of a trading vessel assembled between Ashton Road Bridge and Ripley Hospital at 2.45 p.m. ready to process through the town at 3.00 p.m. As the procession made its way through the town to the Giant Axe Field over 60,000 people lined the streets.

On 24 September the Town Clerk on behalf of the Corporation had written to

Episode 5, 'The Founding of Cockersand Abbey' (Dixon archive)

Dixon asking him to compose a Fanfare of approximately eight to sixteen bars for two trumpets, which would be played as the Mayor's carriage entered the Giant Axe Field for the Finale of the Historical Procession.[9] This unique pageant ended with the singing of the hymn 'O God our help in ages past' and the National Anthem.

Other celebrations included Mayoral 'At Homes' on Friday 1 October and a Grand Ball on the following Friday, both these events being held in the Ashton Hall.

---

9 Letter, Dixon archive.

DIXON THE INVENTOR

DIXON WAS NOT ONLY a musician but also an inventor. His inventions included an improved organ or like musical instrument, another instrument which could be regarded as a forerunner of the electronic organ, a self-help aural method, a game and various products under the trade name 'Elro'. It was often mentioned in conversation with local musicians that he also marketed a brand of nuts called 'Dixie Nuts', but no evidence has been found to support this.

James Hugh Reginald Dixon and George John Harris Bearman, a Pianoforte Dealer in Lancaster, applied for a Patent for their invention of An Improved Organ or like Musical Instrument. The provisional specification dated 28 May 1912 was followed by a complete specification dated 4 January 1913 and the application was accepted on 19 September 1913 (Patent No. 13262).

According to the Patent this invention has for its object a musical instrument having the sound-producing features of an American organ combined with those of a harmonium, and embodies an improved method of blowing whereby pressure and suction wind are simultaneously produced in an easy manner, together with improvements in the touch, quality and variety of tone, stop actuating mechanism and general compactness.

This information fits the description of an instrument called a 'Diapella' which was mentioned in an article by Father Lockwood.[1]

When writing a series of articles in 1929 on American organs and a Professsor referred to earlier, Dixon gives a description of a little chamber organ:

> The console occupies no more room than does an upright piano with pedal attachment, but from its appearance one would never think that it is really an organ, for there are neither stops nor stop-keys, their places being taken by an elaborate system of rheostat levers, grid leak controls and circular discs controlling the condensers, potentiometers, anode tunings and valves. Briefly the system is this. The keys work a series of electronic contacts which

---

1 'Profile' Church Music, August 1971, Vol. 3, No. 10, p 15.

cause a set of dulciana pipes to sound. These pipes are located in a sound-proof box in the wine cellar. Inside the box are placed three microphones adjusted specially for low, medium and high pitched sounds respectively. The usual transmitting apparatus is connected to a small frame aerial placed in the cellar; and in the music room a similar small frame aerial receives the wireless waves which pass into an elaborate seven-valve set placed in the console. The various controlling devices, which take the place of stops in this instrument, marry to a wonderful extent both the volume of sound and also its quality and *timbre*. So that incredible as it would seem, from this single set of dulciana pipes placed in the cellar it is possible to have, by suitable combination of valves, condensers, &c., an exact reproduction in the music-room of the various orchestral instruments, or of a gorgeous organ replete with diapasons, sparkling mixtures and brilliant reeds, and in all possible degrees of dynamic power. A turn of the knob and the dulciana has become a liquid-toned flute: another turn of the knob and – lo! – the gentle dulciana is transformed into a fiery trumpet; another twist or two and anætherial viol, a roaring 32ft. contra bombarde or a piercing piccolo greets your ear from the exquisitely carved loudspeaker surrounding the console.

At present the organ boasts of only one clavier, but the professor is so delighted with the success of the innovation that he intends to erect a more elaborate instrument with independent keyboards and a simplified system of controls, after the manner of the ordinary pipe organ. As it is the instrument is rather sensitive; hand capacity not being entirely eliminated, so that occasionally when one has 'tuned-in', as it were, a delicate echo viol type of stop, on removing the hand from the controlling lever, a terrific howling is instantly set up, which as your readers will agree, rather gets on one's nerves. Already the professor has made considerable improvements by means of a number of gadgets; and in a letter I received from him this month he says that he hopes soon to be able to introduce an organ on these lines – as a commercial proposition manufactured in mass production – which will revolutionise the organ building world and bring a magnificent four-manual organ effect into the homes of any who can, at least, afford the equivalent of a four valve wireless set.[2]

Although the imaginary tales concerning the visit to Professor Toogood in America were at times very much exaggerated, they also contained some elements of truth.

The late Miss Ethel Taylor, a pupil and life long friend of Dr Dixon, confirmed to me in conversation that he had invented an early example of an electronic instrument and one similar to that described above did exist. A reference to such

---

2 'Notes from an Organ Enthusiast's Diary', *Musical Opinion*, March 1929, Vol. 52, No 618, p 560.

an instrument appeared in the *Yorkshire Evening Post* Wednesday 23 August 1950 when it was reported that Dixon had built an electronic organ ten years earlier which he had in his home and still played. This could well have been an improved version of the instrument mentioned above.

An original and unique system of self-preparation in aural training under the title **Auscultics** was a correspondence course. The idea of this course stemmed from the fact that students attending Colleges of Music had the advantage of lessons every week in aural training, musical dictation, musical appreciation and general musicianship, whereas the private student did not. Dixon felt that the only way the latter could develop such important skills was to enrol for one of his courses under the auspices of the School of Auscultics. This would enable students to benefit from regular and systematic preparation, in the privacy of their own homes without being dependent on another person to play the tests. Students could either take a short three-month course divided into six fortnightly lessons, or a full course of twelve lessons. Alternatively the lessons could be spread over a longer period of time convenient to the student. The short course was intended for those candidates whose general standard of preparation was satisfactory, but may just have failed in the last exam to obtain a pass mark and required some help with specific questions. The full course was recommended for students taking the exam for the first time. A fee of £1 11*s.* 6*d.* was charged for the short course and three guineas for the full course.

The course comprises scientifically graded instruction in ear training. After completing the course the student would be well prepared in all the aural tests required for the various Diploma examinations. The exercises were designed to promote proficiency in accurate listening, stimulate musical imagination and improve general musicianship. Each student required a piano tuned to Philharmonic pitch (C520–C522), a metronome and a gramophone/wireless set.

SCHOOL OF AUSCULTICS

An ingenious and unique
SYSTEM OF SELF-PREPARATION IN AURAL TRAINING
Invented by Dr. DIXON
D.Mus., Lond., F.R.C.O.

AUSCULTICS

SURMOUNTS the difficulties of those who have no one to play so-called *ear tests* to them.

ENABLES anyone to practise Aural Training privately at home, with complete success.

ELIMINATES guesswork.

ENSURES your gaining high marks in all Aural Tests required for the R.C.M., R.A.M., and R.C.O. Diplomas.

An explanatory leaflet on *Auscultics* will be sent, post free, on application to
**THE SECRETARY, SCHOOL OF AUSCULTICS,
252-260, REGENT STREET, LONDON, W.1**

Each lesson consists of:-

1) Notes and explanations embodying the fundamental principles of ear training, transposing, memorising, sight singing, recognition of chords, musical dictation and rhythm etc.
2) Exercises for self preparation.
   Over one hundred interesting and fascinating exercises provided with upwards of a thousand musical examples.
3) A self examination paper.
   This when duly worked is returned to the tutor, who is thus kept informed of the student's progress. Where special weakness is shown, suitable additional exercises are prescribed.
4) General study on composers and their music. Playing, listening and reading relevant articles.

Dr Dixon personally supervised the work of each student. They were expected to study each lesson carefully, practise the exercises daily, be honest with themselves and answer the self-examination test papers faithfully, according to the instructions given and to discuss their difficulties when sending in their answers.

If a student failed to reach the pass standard in the aural tests after having completed the full course of 12 lessons, the School provided a special additional revision course of 6 lessons free of charge.

The game known as 'Soccatome' was invented in 1938. It is a round-table game for any number of players, based largely on the principles of and terms used in Association Football. There are three variations of game;

1) Ordinary Match Play
2) The Progessive Soccatome Drive
3) The Soccatome Pool-Forecasts Game

The game consists of a board, a pack of playing cards, 8 wooden pieces in the shape of a jersey in team colours, coloured counters, score cards and a set of forecast coupons. There is a booklet describing the game, method of playing a match and rules of the game. Clubs featured are: Arsenal, Aston Villa, Everton, Huddersfield, Leeds United, Preston North End, Sunderland and Wolverhampton. It was advertised as being:

> Suitable for both young people and grown-ups, a great favourite and increasing in popularity. The game can be obtained from Dr Dixon price 6s. 11d. post free or from Lawson's Toy Shop, New Street, Lancaster

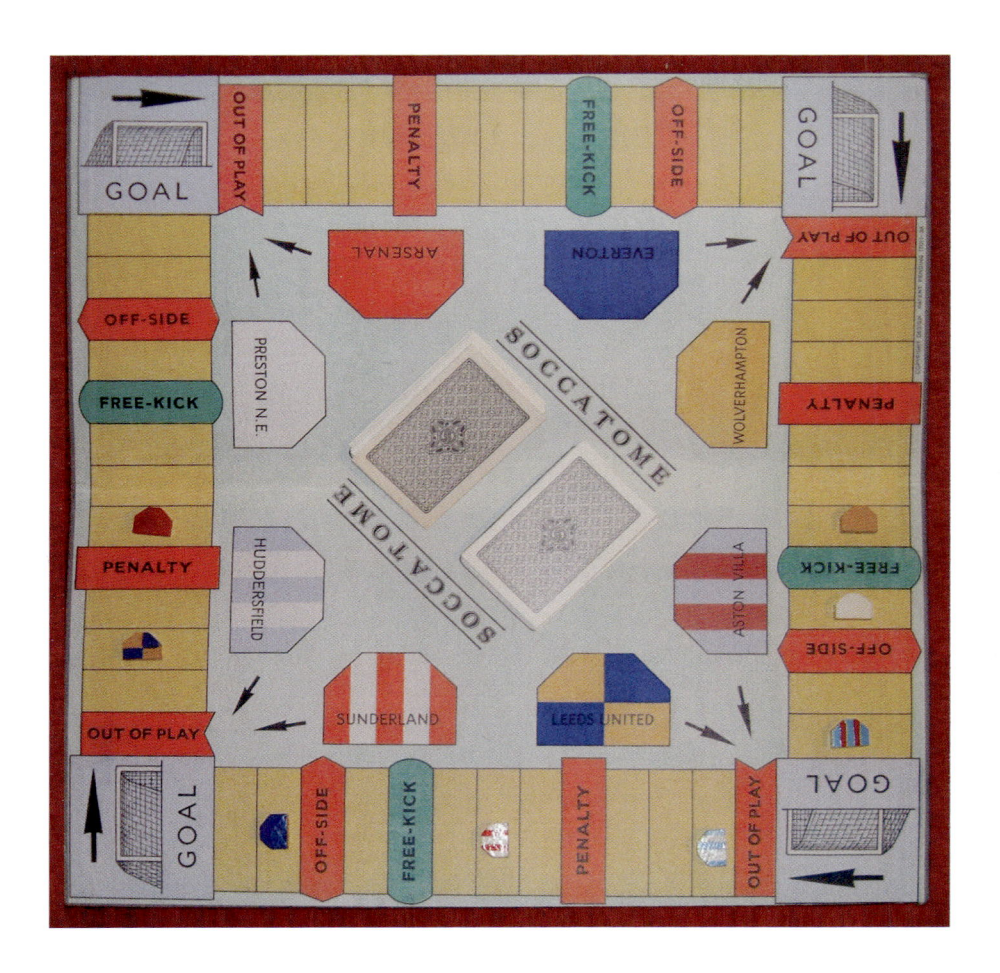

Reginald Dixon's

Great Friendship Novelty
SOCCATOME

A game for any Number of Players

AN ACCEPTED PASTIME

FOR LEISURE EVENINGS

Patent Pending — 17011–38

J. H. R. DIXON   **LANCASTER**

	CREDIT NOTE.		
C''STOMER'S ORDER NO..........		INVOICE NO..........	

J. H. REGINALD DIXON
GAMES MANUFACTURER.

Tel.: LANCASTER 841.   51, MEADOWSIDE, LANCASTER,   21st Jan. 1947

	GAMES, "SOCCATOME" @ 74/- DOZEN.	PURCHASE TAX	PRICE
Jan. 1947.	By returns :- 2 dozen "SOCCATOME". To :- Messrs Davis & Davis, The Argosy, High Street, Lyndhurst. Hants.	£2. 8. 0.	£7. 8. 0. £9. 16. 0.

2/- per dozen Discount, 7 Days, Otherwise Strictly Nett.

Sadly the toy shop, known to many as the 'Rocking Horse Shop' closed in 2009, but the model nursery size rocking horse above the shop entrance is still there today.

In the 1940s Dixon was a Director of the firm Elro Products (Lancaster) Ltd, specialists in Rodent & Insect Pest Control. Walter Rogerson, also a Director of the firm, John Brennan and James Hugh Reginald Dixon applied for a Patent regarding Improvements in and relating to Compositions having Insecticidal Properties. The provisional specification dating from 17 August 1945 was followed by the complete specification dated 1 August 1946 and was accepted 7 April 1948 (Patent No. 600362).

According to the Patent the object of the invention was to enable insecticides of a type described to be applied to glass, mirrors and polished surfaces of furniture, fittings and loose objects without impairing their aesthetic and other qualities while rendering the surfaces lethal to most forms of insect life and particularly flies contacting with them.

The description fits the product known as 'Pol-Kill' which was advertised as follows:

'POL – KILL'

The New Wonder Polish containing D.D.T./Geigy.

POLISHES YOUR WINDOWS   KILLS YOUR FLIES

Lightens Housework   Does Two Jobs in One

THE DUAL PURPOSE CLEANER   AN 'ELRO' PRODUCT

Realising the long-felt want of the modern housewife to obtain a clear brilliant finish on windows, mirrors and similar glassware, we have now produced a cleaning material which not only does this, but of which, one application in accordance with the directions, renders the treated surface for a period toxic to flies and other insect pests which come into contact with it.

The knock-out is not sudden and spectacular, but it is non-the-less real and effective, particularly on surfaces which are not subjected to heat or strong sunshine.

How is this done? You may ask.

The answer is, by the introduction of the wonderful new insecticide D.D.T., suspended in our cleaner by our own special process.

AS A **CLEANER** : UNBEATABLE

AS A **WINDOW POLISH** : SUPERB

Try it once and you will use no other.

It is ideally suitable for use in the home where a good cleaner and reviver of polish surfaces is required.

'**POL-KIL**' can be used most successfully for cleaning and whitening pianoforte keys; for polishing motor car windscreens and chromium fittings, etc.

REMEMBER THE NAME – '**POL-KIL**'[3]

---

3   Advertisement leaflet, Dixon archive.

There were two other 'Elro' products for dealing with the elimination of mice and rats which were advertised as follows:

'MYRO'

FOR MICE

THE LITTLE TIN WITH THE BIG PUNCH
IT'S A KNOCK-OUT

Mice foul food stuffs with their droppings and nibbling and we cannot afford to have any food wasted thus. Mice also spoil flooring and skirting boards, and have even been known to have caused outbreaks of fire by eating away the insulation from electric wires. Like rats, mice are prolific breeders. One pair of mice in ten weeks will rear 30 or more, so that in a very short time instead of the odd mouse or two you have been accustomed to seeing, you may find your premises are overrun with them.

Don't wait for this to happen. The remedy is so simple.

Just get a small tin of 'Myro' Mouse poison from your chemist. Put the powder in little heaps where mice are known to run. Leave for a few days, then clean up what is left, collect your victims and burn.

'Myro' is clean to use, and does not soil or stain articles on which it is placed.

Caution – Insist on 'MYRO' – The only preparation of its kind on the market. Satisfaction guaranteed.[4]

The firm of **Elro Products (Lancaster) Ltd**, an organisation built up during the last few years on the rock of public service, is marketing a product which, following experiments under varying conditions has been found to be a most satisfactory medium for the swift and clean eradication of all rat infestation, the process involved being the simplest to perform, whilst obtaining the maximum clearance.

---

4 Ibid.

'ELROSTAR' RAT EXTERMINATOR

DON'T **SCARE** THOSE RATS AWAY

KILL THEM THE **ELRO** WAY

In these strenuous days when it is of supreme national importance that we obtain full value from every ounce of food produced, it is a matter of the gravest concern to us all that millions of pounds worth of food supplies are consumed or otherwise ruined each year by the ravages of rodents.

Rats are most prolific breeders. When it is realised that from one pair it is possible to breed 800 young rats in a year, the immensity of the problem will be better appreciated.

Various methods of dealing with this problem have been tried with varying results, but the fact remains that the rat menace is becoming daily more serious in view of the world shortage of food stuffs and our own dwindling reserves. It is therefore essential that immediate steps should be taken to eradicate this enemy in our midst, not only by taking reasonable precautions, but also by utilising methods found by practical experience, to be the most effective for the speedy and wholesale clearance of these pests.

It is with confidence therefore that we recommend **'ElroStar'** Rat Exterminator to the Local Authority, the Warehouseman, the Miller, Baker, Confectioner, Grocer and others who suffer material damage to stock and risk damage to prestige through rodent infestation.

For the Farmer, Stockbreeder, Nurseryman and other bulk users we have introduced a special pack which if unable to procure through your usual dealer will be forwarded direct (postage extra). Agriculturalists speak highly of this special pack as being ideally suitable for their needs.[5]

---

5   Ibid.

ASHTON HALL, Lancaster

MAY 4th, 5th, 6th, 7th & 8th,
at 7-30 p.m.

THE CATHEDRAL GIRLS' ASSOCIATION
presents

THE DREAM OF GERONTIUS

A Dramatic Version of the Famous Poem
by Cardinal Newman

IN TWO ACTS

Vocal, Incidental and Ballet Music by
J. H. REGINALD DIXON, Mus. Doc., F.R.C.O.

Dancing under the direction of
MISS ARNOTT

IN AID OF
Local Charities and the City War Purposes Fund

PROGRAMME 3d.

Frank N. Shires, Ltd., Mary Street, Lancaster.

Sacred & Secular

This was once more a period when Dixon was involved in entertainment both practically and through composition. On a serious note in 1943 he collaborated with the Rev. B Lockwood of St Joseph's Church, Skerton, Lancaster, in a dramatised version of Newman's poem *The Dream of Gerontius* and in a more light-hearted vein collaborated with Monsignor Lawrence Smith of Carlisle in a series of Operettas, as well as composing several secular songs on a variety of subjects.

Cardinal John Henry Newman (1801–90), wrote his poem *The Dream of Gerontius* in 1865. It first appeared in print later that year, in two separate parts, published in the May and June issue of a periodical known as the 'Month'. The publication was first owned and edited by Miss Frances Taylor, who later became Mother Magdalen Taylor, foundress of the Institute of the Poor Servants of the Mother of God. In 1866 the poem with minor revisions by Newman was published separately and bears a dedication to his dear friend Father Joseph Gordon.

The 900-line poem portrays the final hours of life on earth for Gerontius, the mysterious journey of his soul guided by the Angel to judgement, time in purgatory and ends with the words of the Angel, 'And I will come and wake thee on the morrow.' It is a work intensely mystical in thought and one which expresses religious feeling and moral teaching in such a sensitive way.

Critics differ in their opinion of its merits as poetry. Some regard it as a masterpiece comparable to the writings of Dante and Shakespeare. For many people *The Dream of Gerontius* is more than poetry. It is a spiritually powerful work of universal appeal which can bring solace to those who are near the end of their earthly journey through life. General Charles Gordon, who faced danger and subsequent death in the siege of Khartoum (1885), had in his possession a copy of the poem in which he marked out certain lines and passages that were important to him at the time.

Although the poem was popular in Newman's lifetime both at home and abroad, it may well not have remained so, were it not for Elgar's setting of the text in Oratorio form composed in 1900 which is still regularly performed. The original draft of the poem, along with a fair copy in Newman's handwriting and Elgar's score, signed by the artists who took part in the first performance, are preserved in the Birmingham Oratory Library.

Elgar chose to set 430 lines of the poem (omitting a considerable portion of the text from the second part), as well as rearranging some lines and making other alterations thus presenting a different interpretation of the poem. While Dixon also omits some text mainly from the second part and rearranges some lines of the Chorus of Angelicals, he sets 760 lines of the poem retaining the original meaning of Newman's writing.

Numerous editions of the poem have been published which differ in minute detail, mainly regarding punctuation. The edition used by Dixon is one published in 1938 by the Catholic Truth Society.

Dixon's choice of setting *The Dream of Gerontius* in a dramatised version was partly influenced by Father Lockwood and began as an idea for entertainment of women's organisations in Lancaster during the War. This form with its solo and chorus spoken word, solo and choral singing, ballet and mime, as well as a full range of incidental music, plus action, costumes, lighting and effects offers much more scope for the realisation of the poem than that of other forms such as Oratorio.

Completed in April 1943, the original score in two acts (Act 1 'The passing of Gerontius' and Act 2 'The journey to eternity'), consists of parts for a small orchestra (Violin, Violoncello, Double Bass, Flute, Clarinet, Trumpet), Organ and Piano. Some of the text spoken by the Angel, the Angel of the Agony and the Greek Chorus, interspersed with music for the Soprano solo (The voice of the Angel), the Singing Chorus, Organ and Piano is written out in two separate manuscript books. The part of Gerontius is a spoken one throughout.

The text, which is treated with great sympathy and imaginative insight, displays a deeply personal expression of empathy with the mystical ideal of the poet.

In the speaking parts the words are interpreted by using different levels of pitch, dynamics and varying speeds. Occasionally the text is highlighted by other effects; at the words 'List to their cry', for example, the demon chorus give three yells, and immediately before the words 'Chucked down, by sheer might of a despot's will' there are three orchestral chords with a scream on each followed by a demon laugh at the words 'To psalm-droners and chanting groaners.'

The idea of a Greek Chorus was to improve 'the theatre', appropriate words from the text being given to them. According to the director's score the Greek Chorus should not be interpreted too strictly in the classic form. They are seen as living people who react to the whole piece as an apparition, serving to communicate as performers to the audience the atmosphere and emotions they are intended to experience. The same may be said of the Singing Chorus. Their singing of 'Praise to the Holiest' off stage is the angelic choir. When they assemble to sing it on stage they are mortals joining voices with the Angelic-Hosts.

Musical features of this work include use of the dorian and hyperdorian modes as well major and minor keys; modal and conventional harmony with some dissonance and use of chromaticism; a wide range of dynamics and changes of tempo between movements and changes of time signatures within a movement; melodic lines vary from short fragments to long sustained phrases; textures range from a single instrumental part to homophonic and contrapuntal writing. All these features reflect the nature of the text whether the music is setting the mood for the scene, serving as an accompaniment to the action or providing background music to the spoken word.

While use is made of themes found in the 'Dies irae' from the plainsong Requiem Mass, it remains an original composition. An analysis of the work can be found in the Appendix.

The first performance took place on 4 May 1943, in the Ashton Hall, Lancaster and ran for five nights. It was produced by Father Lockwood, conducted by Dr Dixon with the dancing under the direction of Miss Arnott. The dancers, soloists and those in both the speaking and singing chorus were from the Cathedral Girls' Association. Miss Nora Taylor, a pupil of Dr Dixon played the organ/piano and the other twelve musicians came from Lancaster and the surrounding area. This first stage realization, cast entirely for women was presented by a total of 49 performers including 13 musicians and the conductor. Lighting equipment was loaned by the Lancaster Amateur Dramatic & Operatic Society and by arrangement with the Strand Electric Company, under the supervision of Messrs. Calvert and Heald, Lancaster. This performance was an important event in the cultural life of the city and the proceeds raised were given to local charities and the City War Purposes Fund.

In a short article entitled 'My most thrilling musical experience', Winifride Porter who sang the part of the Angel in the first performance said of the 'Angel's Song'

> It breathed forth that celestial, blissful charm which earth cannot claim. It was as though the members of the orchestra had reached to Heaven for suitable instruments. The piano, doing duty for the harp was purposely off the beat – time meant less than eternity. The arduous development of the subject with telling and deliberate crescendo gave emphasis to the lofty theme.

She went on to describe what the Praise Chorus meant to her

> The greatest thrill came in the 'Praise to the Holiest in the Height'. A tune had been written which fitted perfectly to the words. It would almost enable one to utter them without knowing them. I plunged headlong into the spirit of it all, and was carried on wings of song into a blissful realization of all it

meant to me. Earth was far behind and the sublime purpose of giving glory to the Lord of Creation stood large and impressive before me. Never before and maybe never again will such an experience be mine.

Winifride Porter's thoughts on the final movement the 'Angel's Farewell' was that

> The insistent rhythm in the bass instruments marked the departure of Gerontius in no uncertain measure, and then fading into the distance the music descended with skilful use of accidentals to press home the mood and feeling of the words.[1]

Mr E A Dowbiggin music critic for the *Lancaster Guardian* thought that it was the best amateur performance of a piece with any serious intent that he had seen for many years. In a later report he confirmed his first impressions of the work:

> Dr. Dixon's incidental and vocal music blended propriety with strength and romantic feeling. His approach to the subject and texture of his composition were orthodox. There were no uningratiating harmonies, and we were spared the arid tedium of some contemporary music. There was no revelling in devices and effect for its own sake – that is to wilfully misconceive the function of incidental music. The composer's imagination here was obviously traversing the same territory as that of the poet, and the language, shape and colour of the music were determined from first to last by the mood of the poem. He achieved nobility of theme without resorting to any gingerly solemnity, and the music thus became, not incidental in the literal meaning of the word, but an integral part of the production. At their best, intrusions from another art can bring real enrichment to a verbal text; and that is just what Dr. Dixon's music did.[2]

Dowbiggin was surprised, impressed and deeply moved by the first performance of 1943 and after attending the final performance of the week, he summed it up as 'a considerable work of art by all involved in the production.'[3]

Information on the cover of the instrumental score indicates that a second performance took place on 21 October 1943 at Skerton, Lancaster. There are no other details at this time as to where the event was held, but is likely to have been performed at S. Joseph's Church Hall. Was this a rehearsal for the forthcoming performances to be given in Preston?

According to the programme three performances were given on 25, 26 and 27 October in the Queen's Hall, Preston, by The Lancaster Miracle Players, a new

---

1 'My most thrilling musical experience', Dixon archive.
2 *Lancaster Guardian,* 14 May 1943.
3 Ibid.

name for the group who first performed the work (still an all female cast). Most of the performers in this production were the same as before, with one change of principal character, two changes in the chorus and some extra dancers in the demons' chorus. The orchestra for the Preston performance comprised, first and second violins (one change of performer), viola (added part), 'cello (an extra 'cellist), double bass, flute, clarinet (an extra clarinettist), bassoon (added part), trumpet (change of performer), trombone (added part) and piano/organ. The additional instrumental parts were written into the original score in red ink. Also at some time the organ solo movements 20–23 appear to have been omitted and the following movements 24–26 are renumbered as 20–22. The reason for this is unclear. As before the production was directed by Father Lockwood, conducted by Dr Dixon, with the dancing under the direction of Miss Arnott.

The following report on the Preston performance was written by WP in the *Lancashire Daily Post*:

> Their performance reflected their devotion and intensive study. Male voices would have improved the general effect, but on the whole voices and music blended well in an exalted key and realised the play's devout mood and lofty ideals.
>
> The orchestra of 18, conducted by the composer, and led by Miss Anne Hornby, of Preston Chamber Music Society, were also recruited locally. Their playing was in complete sympathy. Ballet, organ, colour and costume effects heightened the spiritual atmosphere. In gesture and declamation the performance was also free from jarring notes.
>
> The singing, solo and choral satisfied the critical listener, and the speaking chorus impressed with its unison and clarity. Dorothy Davies was most happily chosen as Gerontius – her diction, smooth delivery and notable mien would make her a perfect Portia. Winifride Porter gave strength and dignity to the singing; Margaret McKinney revealed a poetic sense as the angel; and all the other principals showed an earnest grasp of what was required of them artistically.[4]

After 1943 the work did not surface again until 1955, when the Lancaster Amateur Dramatic and Operatic Society presented three performances at the Grand Theatre Lancaster on 8, 9, and 10 November, with further performances being given the following week at the Royal Hippodrome Preston. What prompted a revival of the work is not known. It could be that a member of this society had taken part in one of the 1943 performances and suggested a revival. A new music score was created which was now enlarged and rescored regarding new vocal parts and additional orchestral resources.

---

4 *Lancashire Daily Post*, Tuesday 26 October 1943.

It is interesting to note that there are slight differences in the titles of Act 1 and 2 between what appeared on the programme and what is written in the Lockwood score. The programme is almost the same as before, Act 1 'The passing of Gerontius' and Act 2 'The soul's journey to eternity'. In the Lockwood score Act 1 is entitled 'The death of Gerontius' and Act 2 'The journey to judgment and the reception into purgatory'. These differences may have been thought necessary in order to appeal to a wider audience outside the Catholic Church.

Apart from the work now requiring a much larger orchestra (Flute, Oboe, Clarinet, Bassoon, Horn, Trumpet, Trombone, Violin, Viola, 'Cello, Double Bass, Organ, Harp, Timpani and Percussion including Drums, Cymbal, Triangle and Bell), the chorus parts were scored for Soprano, Contralto, Tenor and Bass, a new Praise Chorus with vocal trios was added and the ballet was reconstructed. In the 1955 Preston performance the singing chorus comprised 11 sopranos, 5 contraltos, 6 tenors, and 4 basses compared with 20 ladies in the first performance of 1943 and 18 in the Preston performance of that year. The members of the speaking chorus remained at 6 as in the 1943 performances. In contrast to the 7 ladies who took part in the 1943 chorus of demons there were now 3 ladies, 2 men and 4 children. There were a few additional dancers in the Corps de Ballet, including a male dancer and some of these doubled for the two mimes ('Shifting parti-coloured Scene' and the Holy Souls Mime). While Gerontius remained a spoken part there were both spoken and sung parts for the Priest. On this occasion the part of Gerontius was played by Joseph Lockwood, the brother of Father Lockwood and that of the Priest was Philip Byrne (Tenor), a friend of the late Kathleen Ferrier who sang with her on many occasions. Other dramatis personae were Margaret Fazackerly and Pauline Harrison who shared the part of The Angel, Monica Smith (Soprano), Voice of the Angel, Teresa Duckworth (Contralto), The Angel of Agony, Winifride Porter (Soprano) and Daisy Spence (Mezzo-soprano), first and second Devout Mortal respectively. Some of the singers taking part had professional operatic experience and others while not professional had received training. The organist on this occasion was Stanley Thewlis (Music Master at the Royal Grammar School, Lancaster), with choreography by John Grounsell and the Stage Director was Kenneth Gardner. Like all previous performances it was produced by Father Lockwood and conducted by Dr Dixon.

A reporter writing in the *Preston Herald* refers to one of the performances given at the Grand Theatre Lancaster as:

> A unique presentation, which truly merits support and points out that even those theatre-goers who normally shy away from anything savouring religion, will do well to see this skilful blending of many arts.[5]

---

5   *Preston Herald*, 11 November 1955.

Cast of the 1955 Preston performance

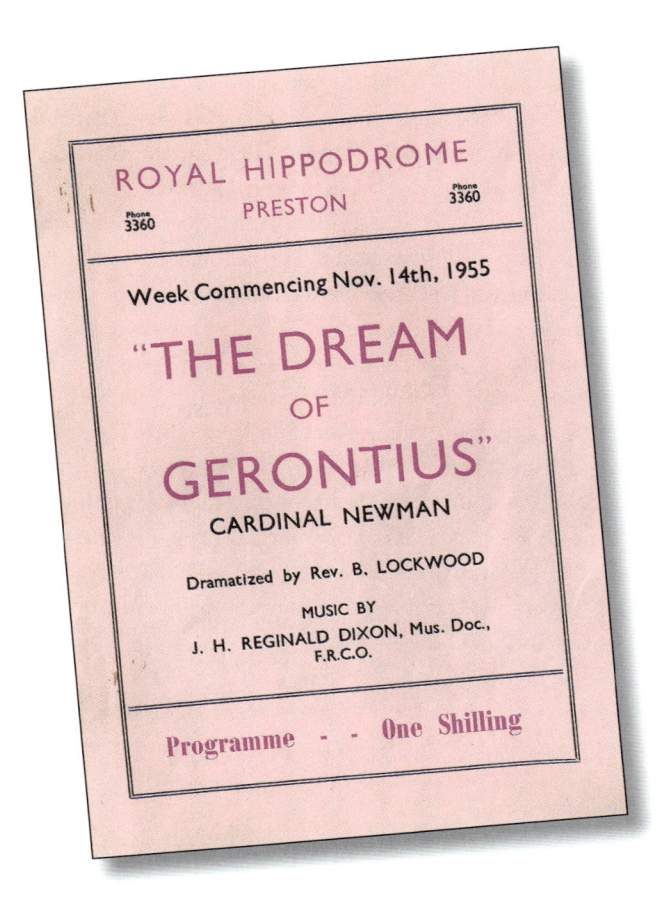

> ROYAL HIPPODROME
> PRESTON
> Phone 3360
>
> Week Commencing Nov. 14th, 1955
>
> "THE DREAM OF GERONTIUS"
> CARDINAL NEWMAN
>
> Dramatized by Rev. B. LOCKWOOD
>
> MUSIC BY
> J. H. REGINALD DIXON, Mus. Doc., F.R.C.O.
>
> Programme - - One Shilling

Ernest Bradbury, writing in the *Yorkshire Post*, on a Preston performance sums up the work as follows:

> All in all, this is a gracious work of modest dimension wholly without ambition except such as must find favour in the sight of Heaven, and something of a tribute to the enthusiasm and loyalty of the many performers, dancers and singers who travel each night from Lancaster, Morecambe and elsewhere to perform it. [5]

Completion of the work on the score is dated September 1955. However, there are several pages where parts are incomplete, but these can be filled in by referring to the organ score or the two manuscript books mentioned earlier.

***

---

6 *Yorkshire Post*, 17 November 1955.

In 1941 a young soprano, Lillian Gates, came from Wakefield to live in Lancaster. She had been a member of West Parade Choir and a Wakefield Concert Party which visited Pinder Fields Emergency Hospital to entertain wounded soldiers. Miss Gates became a popular young lady, entertaining troops and audiences at local concerts in association with the war effort and regularly appeared at the Lancaster Soldiers Club. While on a visit to Wakefield in 1943, she once again took the opportunity to assist the Pinder Fields Hospital by appearing at the Opera House for one week. It was here that she popularised Dr Dixon's 'Cigarette Song' by performing it in her programme each evening. The audience were invited to show their appreciation of the song by contributing cigarettes for the wounded soldiers. In the course of the week no fewer than 3,500 cigarettes were collected.

Dixon composed several secular songs in the early 1940s. Some were part-songs scored for male voices and others for female voices. There were also a number of solo songs for different voices including a few for countertenor, probably written for friends who were available to participate in the various concerts arranged by Dixon to entertain the people during the war.

Between 1944 and 1951 Dixon collaborated with Monsignor Richard Lawrence Smith of Carlisle in several light musical works.

Smith was born in Lancaster near the Cathedral and as a young boy would certainly have known Dixon and may well have been one of his choristers or pupils. Educated at Stonyhurst and Balliol College, Oxford he studied for the priesthood in Rome, becoming Vice-Rector of the English College Rome (1932–42) and Privy Chamberlain to the Pope (1935). In January 1943 Mgr Smith was inducted as parish priest to Our Lady and St Joseph's, Carlisle by the Bishop of Lancaster, the Right Reverend Thomas Edward Flynn. As an enthusiastic amateur musician he became noted for writing librettos, composing music and producing Operettas/Musical Comedies which were performed by members of the Catholic Youth Movement in the Waterton Hall, Carlisle.

The Catholic Youth Movement, founded in 1941, aimed to provide a well-balanced weekly programme of spiritual, educational and physical training to Catholic boys and girls between the ages of fourteen and twenty resident in Carlisle and the surrounding district. By 1943 the group had a membership of 80 boys and 65 girls.

Canon George Waterton, appointed priest of Our Lady and St Joseph's Church, Carlisle in 1879 was responsible for the construction of the present church and the building of the Waterton Hall (the largest hall of its type in Carlisle) to commemorate 25 years of his pastorate in Carlisle. Sadly this building was demolished in 2007.

There is a brief reference in the *Carlisle Journal* to a performance of a work by Mgr Smith having taken place in June 1944, but no further details are given. The second work entitled *Girls will be Grown-ups* is an early Victorian Comic Opera dating from November 1944, which was first performed in April 1945 and again in March/April 1949, the music being orchestrated by Dixon. While there were many new members in the second performance, a number of the principal parts were played by the original cast.

The plot features an acidic Principal of a Girl's Academy, a comic Assistant Mistress, Pupils, a stately Duchess, a Light Infantry Division, and the Devil plus a male and female chorus. Pupils of the Academy were unhappy and longed to escape the strict regime. Both pupils and staff are tempted by the Devil, but eventually repent. Order is restored and the pupils vow to work hard and be cheerful.

Kathie (or *Maid of the Mountains*), a musical comedy in two acts, was written and composed in July/August 1945. Dixon not only orchestrated this work, but composed an Overture, incidental music and music for some additional numbers.

The work is set in a picturesque alpine village and a Ducal Palace. Kathie, a young girl with white skin, flaxen hair and long eyelashes, has been in the village for two years, but very little is known about her or where she came from. Some villagers believe she is a witch, but others think that she is beautiful, gentle and wise. Making friends with a visitor to the village, Kathie tells him that she has enemies who must not find her. Shortly after this the Duke and Duchess of Oberania visit the village and recognise Kathie as the daughter of the late Duke and Duchess whom they had eliminated. Kathie is kidnapped and taken back to the Palace. The friend from the village and his companion secretly enter the Palace, organise a plot against the Duke and Duchess and with the help of unhappy servants, imprison them. Kathie (a name derived from Katherina at confirmation), originally named Hansi, is rightfully restored to the throne.

Performed for six nights 7–12 January 1946, the production involved a cast of thirty teenage boys and girls some of whom had never appeared on stage before, eleven musicians, a back stage crew and assistance from parents and friends. A well-known Catholic artist, Mr Gascoigne painted the scenery. Members of the cast in ordinary life were shop assistants, clerks, typists, telegraph boys, errand boys, tradesmen and workshop apprentices. They met in the evening after a hard and often long working day to rehearse twice a week for four months. Testimony to the success of the production was the fact that the BBC were considering recording excerpts from *Kathie* and Mr J C Clarke, Director of the BBC, Newcastle commented in an interview:

> It was the most enterprising youth venture he had ever come across, in fact it was unique and he was particularly impressed by the choral singing and the voice of Alice Grice, the leading lady. Although Mr Clarke could not guarantee that a recording would be made, he expressed great admiration for the show.[7]

---

7 *Carlisle Journal,* 11 January 1946.

Kathie was recorded and excerpts were broadcast on the Radio Home Service, on Friday 3 May 1946.[8]

The Jolly Roger, an operetta in three acts written in October/November 1949 and orchestrated by Dixon, was performed in January 1950. It tells a romantic story of a ship that is a school for pirates. Its pupils, desiring practical experience of their profession, board a passing West Indian ship and take prisoner her passengers, a host of lovely ladies. The females then seize the ship from the pirates, but realize that they are unable to sail the vessel to port so the crew are released.

According to the *Carlisle Journal* critics were full of praise for the lyrics, music and presentation of this Operetta. The lyrics were considered to bear the hallmark of a master craftsman and a perfect match for the music which displayed a variety of moods – tuneful, romantic, enchanting and bewitching – in a glittering cascade of choruses, solos, duets and trios. It was a production noted for its originality, imagination, expression, timing and attention to details. The singing, dancing and mime were all commendable.

The final work in which Dixon and Mgr Smith collaborated was *Kingdom for Cash*, a Comic Opera in two acts written in December 1950/January 1951 and orchestrated by Dixon in May 1951.

Set in Medieval times the action takes place in the Palace of King Ethelred and Queen Ermentrude who have fallen on hard times and decide that the only solution is to find a rich suitor for their daughter. Meanwhile the rich Monarch of a neighbouring kingdom, wishing to unite the two kingdoms, sends his son disguised as an envoy to visit the King, with the threat of an invasion if the King does not pay all his dues by midday. This gives the Prince an opportunity to see the Princess before agreeing to the marriage. After other false plots, various disguises and impersonations, the real Prince and Princess meet face to face and fall in love.

This work is a revised version of a one-act Operetta, *Princess Pauper,* first written by Mgr Smith in 1940. Three different programmes exist as proof of performances. One for the Feast of St George 1940 in which the work is described as not being entirely original! Where the performance took place or by whom is not known. A second programme indicates that a performance was given by the Catholic Youth Movement, Carlisle and it is likely that this was the first Operetta presented in June 1944 referred to earlier. Another programme relates to a performance given by the Pro-Cathedral Youth Club, but there is no indication of date, time or place.

With the exception of *Princess Pauper* (which had a piano accompaniment), Dixon orchestrated all the works for strings, flute, clarinet, trumpet, trombone, timpani and piano, writing out a full score and individual parts for each instrument in separate manuscript books. The tuneful melodies, simple harmonies, light textures, conventional formal patterns and the orchestral arrangements resemble

---

8   *Radio Times*, Friday 3 May 1946.

the works of Sullivan, a composer whom both Smith and Dixon admired. They also shared a keen sense of humour. The popularity of these Operettas/Musicals proved to be a successful collaboration in providing light relief from the harsh social and economic realities of the times.

As well as writing the libretto, composing the music and producing the works, Mgr Smith conducted all the performances. Not only was he a priest and an accomplished musician, but he also wrote several books and was well-known for his radio broadcasts on a variety of topics.

* * *

In 1945 Lancaster City Council made a decision to rectify some of the deficiencies of the Ashton Hall Organ which had been mentioned by Reginald Whitworth and Lawrence Elvin in articles about the instrument.

Reginald Whitworth, writing about the instrument in his article entitled 'Popular Recitalists and their Organs', made the following comments:

> Everything about the organ is good and solid: in fact to quote Dr Dixon, 'the instrument possesses the faults of its virtues.' It would have a better chance in a large cathedral.
>
> Here is a colossal diapason chorus, the 16ft. member of which has a fine bearded string bass, which forms the pedal violone: and truth to tell, this is the more correct name for the stop than double open diapason. The medium open diapason is almost the exact octave of this stop, whilst the large specimen is truly big and masterful. The delightful geigen principal is the least stringy of the family: the 4ft. principal, too, is fairly free from bite. Of the flute toned stops, the 4ft. is the louder: both are pleasant.
>
> The two reeds, together with the upper work of the great *plus* the sub-octave reeds, gives a real thrill. The fiery trumpet has a somewhat smoother companion in the clarion. The mixture is the usual 15th, 19th, and 22nd. It tells out very well in the full great, which is infinitely better *minus* some of the diapasons!
>
> A large open diapason on heavy wind – not unlike the Hope-Jones leathered variety – dominates the swell flue work. It is a fine stop but too big for accompanimental work. The contra gamba, too, is large, with a glorious full length bass. It is a pity this is not duplexed as a pedal stop. The 8ft. viols are keen, but not unduly so: and the lovely rohr flöte is of a kindly disposition, with excellent blending qualities. The full swell cries out for a mixture, the pleasant little flageolet being quite unable to cope with the rather smooth and powerful reed chorus. I think the contra fagotto might have been more correctly named double horn. The oboe and vox humana are both good stops of their type.
>
> One cannot but wish that the little choir organ was enclosed: it would have more than doubled its utility. A full, keen, rather aggressive gamba, a nice gedackt

with pierced stoppers, a fairly bright flauto traverso and a calm dulciana need a swell box to enable them to be used for the accompaniment of the solo stops.

The flutes of the solo organ gain immensely by their enclosure, and the two imitative stops blend with them when required. Both the clarinet and the orchestral oboe are distinctly good, the latter (so Dr Dixon informs us) has true cor anglais resonators for the two lower octaves. The tuba on 12in. wind is tremendous. It is a capital stop and easily strikes through the rest of the organ, but the full organ is almost overpowering.

Consisting as it does of but three ranks of pipes,—viz., open diapason, bourdon and trombone (with their extensions), it is wonderful how well this pedal organ supports the immense power of the manual departments. All the stops are really good, and the reed is on 12in. wind. It is very telling. The 32ft. octave of the contra bourdon is very fine indeed in combination.

Despite its deficiencies, this instrument is a truly grand organ and one of which the city of Lancaster may be justly proud.[9]

Lawrence Elvin said of the instrument:

It contains many fine features, as well as several weaknesses in tonal structure. The scheme of the Great and Pedal Organs is the most comprehensive, and it is somewhat strange to find that an otherwise complete Swell Organ should lack the very essential mixture. The diapason foundation is exceedingly fine; it is on very bold lines and typical of Norman & Beard tone of the period. The upper work, however, is what may be termed 'milk and water', and possesses neither the requisite brilliance nor the boldness of tone to cope adequately with the unisons. Consequently, the build-up is not nearly so fine as it might be were the octave, super octave and mutation ranks developed in the correct proportion, while the absence of a Swell mixture does not help matters. Apart from the exquisite quiet work and the orchestral registers, all of them bearing the hall mark of the firm's skill in that direction, the outstanding feature of the instrument is the magnificent series of chorus reeds. Even after some twenty-six years' of service and an accumulation of dirt inside the organ, these are still of impeccable finish and regularity – a great testimony to the care bestowed upon them in the final finishing. It is difficult to pick out a single reed that is finer than its brother; all of them show the greatest skill in reed voicing, for at this period of their work Messrs. Norman & Beard were producing reed work of the very highest order. Perhaps the stop that impressed the writer most was the Swell contra fagotto, the timbre and quality of which is a sheer delight, while the firmness and regularity of its magnificent bass is most marked. The crescendo of the Swell reed chorus is terrific and most thrilling, but how much

---

9   *The Organ*, July 1931, Vol. XI, No. 41.

more so, were a four-rank mixture present to add to its quota of sparkle to the brilliance of the reeds. Among the quieter stops may be mentioned the keen Swell viol d'orchestre, and its milder brother, the 16ft. contra gamba, which is of great beauty and firmness of tone right down to CC. There are no less than seven varieties of flute tone, particularly colourful being the Solo harmonic flute and concert flute. The two orchestral reeds are of true orchestral timbre.

The pedal organ boasts a 32 ft. extension of the bourdon, which is an outstanding example of 32 ft. tone produced from stopped pipes, as a substitute for the real thing. The value of the Swell contra gamba as a quiet string bass would be great, but unfortunately this is not available. The pedal reeds are grand specimens, and are of the same superb quality as the manual reeds.

The acoustics of the hall give every assistance to the instrument, and despite the defects in the flue chorus previously commented on, as a concert organ it is eminently successful and capable of any demands made upon it.[10]

Having made a decision to renovate the instrument another three years were to pass before a major overhaul was undertaken in September 1948 by the original builders (now Messrs. Hill, Norman and Beard Ltd) no doubt in consultation with Dr Dixon.

The instrument was given a thorough cleaning to remove the dust and dirt which had accumulated over the years since its installation in 1909 and various improvements were made. It was decided to interchange the great organ geigen and the choir gamba, as well as creating a geigen bass pedal stop by extension and a three rank mixture was added to the swell. The choir organ became enclosed thus providing a wider choice of softer toned stops which are invaluable for accompanying. Although the excessive power was reduced to wind pressures varying from 3½ to 10 inches, more brilliance and variety of tone were created by the other alterations and additions. Until this date the pitch had been C. 517 so it was decided to raise the pitch to C. 522 thus enabling the organ to be 'more in tune', so to speak, with the orchestra.

This alteration in pitch provides an opportunity to relate a story often told by Dr Dixon about a magnificent performance of the *Messiah* some years earlier.

Because of the organ being low in pitch the organist was obliged to transpose the score to be in harmony with the orchestra. Dixon admired the way in which Balfour and Bridge in the performances of Handel's *Messiah* from the Royal Albert Hall interpreted the chorus 'For unto us a child is born'. Every time the phrase 'and his name shall be called wonderful' was sung the organ volume increased.

---

10 'Organ Notes', *The Choir*, Vol. 37. 1946.

Ashton Hall Organ (Cecil Thomas)

On this occasion in the Ashton Hall, as the chorus advanced the organ increased accordingly and the last appearance of the phrase was truly 'WONDERFUL' because Dixon forgot to transpose, playing the notes as written!

Although the work on the organ was not complete by Christmas 1948, enough had been done to enable the instrument to be used for the annual performance of the 'Messiah', thus Dixon did not have to transpose this or any other score again.

Throughout the 1940s Dixon continued to broadcast organ recitals from Manchester Town Hall and to give other recitals, some for charity, a few to open new or re-built instruments and others to mark a special occasion. In addition to giving recitals, teaching and performing in various choral society concerts he also continued lecturing in his role of extra-mural tutor in music to Liverpool University. As part of the Christmas Lectures 1949 held at the Arts Theatre, Brownlow Hill, he gave a lecture entitled 'Chopin: The Poet of the Piano'.

The National Union of Organists' Associations

Visit to The

CATHEDRAL, LANCASTER

TUESDAY, AUGUST 28th, 1928.

Programme of Choral and Organ Music by the Cathedral Choir, and

Dr. J. H. REGINALD DIXON,

Organist and Choirmaster.

1. TWO VERSETS, from "Heures Mystiques." — *Boellmann*
2. GREGORIAN MELODIES.
   - Introit - "Gaudeamus." — Mode I.
   - Gradual - "Propter veritatem." — Mode V.
   - Antiphon - "Asperges me." — Mode IV.
   - Respousory - "Velum Templi." — Mode II.
   - Hymn - "Verbum Supernum." — Mode VIII.
     with Strophes by Guilmant.
3. SUITE LATINE, for Organ — *Widor*
   Prelude—Beatus vir—Lauda Sion.
4. FIGURED MUSIC.
   - KYRIE & GLORIA, from the Mass "Iste Confessor." — *Palestrina*
   - MOTET, "Sacerdotes Domini." — *Byrd*
   - Selected "FALSI BORDONI" by Viadana.
   - SANCTUS
   - BENEDICTUS } From the Four Part Mass — *Byrd*
   - AGNUS DEI
5. MEDITATION. "Ascendit Deus." — *Reginald Dixon*
6. KYRIE—SANCTUS—BENEDICTUS—AGNUS DEI
   From the Mass of St. Wulstan. — *Reginald Dixon*
7. SONATA, for the Organ. — *Sir E. Elgar*
   Allegro Maestoso—Allegretto—Andante expressivo—Presto (comodo.)
8. ANTIPHON. "Salve Regina." — *Gregorian*
   Mode I.
   Accompaniment written by Rev. Fr. Hérbert Desrocquettes, O.S.B., of
   Quarr Abbey, Isle-of-Wight.

A retiring collection will be taken at the doors in aid of the Organists' Benevolent Fund.

Kelletts (T. Bulcock, Prop.) 15 King St., Lancaster.

The Incorporated Association of Organists

'An Organists' Fellowship'

D IXON WAS A FOUNDER member of the Incorporated Association of Organists, originally known as the National Union of Organists' Associations which was officially established in 1915. The object of forming the Union was to create a brotherhood of musicians interested in organ music, not a trade union, but a body designed to further the interests of music in general and organ music in particular.

The Lancaster Association was established in January 1922 and was accepted as being affiliated to the National Union at the Bradford meeting of the Union in May of that year. In 1922 each member was required to pay an annual capitation fee of 6d. and to take the *Quarterly Record*, the association magazine costing 1s. 4d. At this time John Brook of Southport, a founder member and first secretary of the National Association, was editor of the *Quarterly Record*. Each Association was allowed to elect a Delegate to the Governing Body in accordance with the Constitution. The first Annual General Meeting of the Lancaster Association was held on Wednesday, 31 January 1923 at the Paladium Café, Market Street, Lancaster. After the meeting a social evening for members and friends had been arranged which included a concert, a game of whist, supper and parlour games.

With the exception of the years from 1940–45 a Congress has been held annually in towns and cities throughout the British Isles and abroad, attracting professional and amateur organists and choirmasters, as well as organ builders, music publishers and those interested in the organ and its music.

Dixon rarely missed a Congress in his lifetime and he felt that in some respects one Congress was much like any other, but in other ways they differed. There were the official receptions, mayoral or presidential, annual general meetings, corporate meals, the group photograph, meeting old friends, making new acquaintances, lectures, recitals, church services and visits to places of local interest. Wherever the Congress was held Dixon frequently attracted the interest of the local press and was well-known for waking up a meeting by saying something controversial or singing an apt phrase. At the Congress in later years he would often be seen with a lady on each arm; these were the Taylor sisters, Nora and Ethel, former pupils and life long friends. It is not the intention here to describe each Congress, but to recall a selection of interesting events and comments associated with Dixon who was always willing to contribute to the numerous discussions which took place on these occasions.

At the Exeter Congress of 1925 a discourse was given by Alderman Widgery on 'Music and its Influence' and in the discussion as to what constituted the good or bad in music, Dixon said that the criterion was whether it had power and charm.

The Congress of 1928 was held at Lancaster week beginning Monday 27 August and attracted approximately 150 members including family and friends. A reception was given in the Town Hall by the Mayor and Mayoress, Councillor and Mrs Parr, followed by a concert performed by local musicians. On the evening of Tuesday 28 August two programmes of choral and organ music were heard, the first at the Parish Church performed by the Choir and Organist Mr N S Wallbank, and the second given by Dr Dixon and the Choir of St Peter's at the Cathedral. Those attending the recital acknowledged the excellence of the organ, but few had heard of the builder. On a visit to Morecambe a second reception was held at the Grafton Hotel given by the Mayor and Mayoress, Councillor and Mrs Gardener. In addition to recitals and meetings visitors enjoyed a visit to the historic Castle, a tour of the Shrigley & Hunt stained-glass works and an excursion to the Lake District. The annual dinner was held at the Royal King's Arms Hotel and the after dinner speeches were interspersed with vocal and instrumental items provided by local musicians. Sir John Hamilton Harty, the well-known conductor and a founder member of the Organists' Association, was President at this time.

Two important proposals were discussed at this Congress, namely an application for a Charter of Incorporation, which would give the Association legal status, and the foundation of a Benevolent Fund to help members in need. The new title was to be 'The Incorporated Association of Organists' with a sub title 'An Organists' Fellowship' which was adopted in 1929. It was also at this Congress that Dr Dixon suggested including a weekend thus providing members with an opportunity to attend a Sunday service and this was adopted.

On a visit to Buckfast Abbey during the 1930 Congress held at Torquay, Dr Dixon gave a short recital before Vespers on the new three-manual Hill organ. His programme included the *B minor Chorale* by Franck and one of his own compositions.

Speaking at the Huddersfield Congress in 1931 on the 'Organ Console', Dixon said:

> Many organists today have gadgets to the right of them, gadgets to the left of them, gadgets in front of them and by gad, through his gadgets he blunders.[1]

He was of the opinion that organists do not need all the 'gadgets' provided by modern organ builders and advocated a return to greater simplicity in this respect.

At the Portsmouth Congress of 1934, one of the topics for discussion was the broadcasting of services on the radio reported in the *Daily Mail* dated 27 August. Dr Dixon held very strong views on the subject and is quoted as saying, 'You cannot broadcast a soul, neither can you broadcast a soul's aspirations. And this is prayer.' In his opinion broadcasting techniques were an intrusion on the communication between the individual and God. Regarding talks and sermons, he thought that they ought to be more instructive and heard in full, with each of the principal religious bodies being given equal time every Sunday and minority religious bodies also having an opportunity to be heard. He felt that the current system of broadcasting was unbalanced. Another quote by Dixon from the discussion was 'Do not let us regard a broadcast service as a substitute for the real thing. The real thing cannot be broadcast.' He held the view that the object should be to provide spiritual preparation for the time when participation in the actual service could be made. He said 'Passive BBC broadcast religion will empty churches, as so much passive listening has emptied our concert halls and teaching studios.' On a final note it was pointed out that while the listener did not make a financial contribution to the service, they did contribute to the BBC through a licence fee and therefore churches and church officials involved in preparation and participation of the broadcast should receive adequate payment for their work. It was at the this Congress that Dixon first met Percy Whitlock, then Organist at St Stephen's Bournemouth and later appointed Organist at Bournemouth Pavilion (1935).

In 1937 at the Plymouth Congress while on a visit to Buckfast Abbey Whitlock and Dixon played the organ there. Just before the Congress Whitlock had begun composing his Plymouth Suite and discussed the piece with Dixon. Of particular interest was the third movement 'Chanty' which is dedicated to Dixon and is reminiscent of a traditional hornpipe. Dixon told Whitlock about his 'Organ Shanty' composed in 1927 which is in the style of a traditional sea shanty consisting of a bold tune interspersed with short interludes. This piece was included in Dixon's recital which was broadcast from Manchester Town Hall, 4 June 1935.

Dixon was described by Whitlock as 'generally the naughty boy at any party', perhaps referring to his sense of humour and being a well-known practical joker.

---

1 *Musical Times*, 1 October 1931.

Example 7, Organ Shanty tune, bars 8–26

At the Leicester Congress of 1948, just as the official photo was about to be taken Dixon suddenly appeared, ran in front of the assembled members and laid at an angle on his side in the centre.

In conversation with me, Miss Ethel Taylor recalled that at one Congress Dixon played 'I do like to be beside the seaside' on an electronic organ in a public house. This was no ordinary rendition of the song. He began the piece and gradually modulated descending through several keys, the tempo becoming slower and slower, rather like a gramophone record slowing down. When the music had almost come to a standstill, he brought the piece all the way back up through the keys faster and faster until he reached the key he had started in.

During the Leeds Congress of 1950, customers having a lunchtime drink at a public house in the city were surprised to hear strains of a different kind of music instead of the usual popular songs and dance music provided by the resident organist Mr Newill. Guess who was seated at the organ? Dr Dixon was never one to let an opportunity pass by to educate the masses and raise the public taste in appreciating good music. So the white-haired organist wearing a blue suit and black high heeled shoes, smoking a large cigar and with a glass of sherry to hand entertained those present. After a programme of classical pieces including Handel's *Largo* and a Chopin *Nocturne*, customers called for some popular songs, but Dixon declined. As a compromise he concluded with 'Moonlight and Roses'. Little did the audience know that the original title of this piece is *Andantino in D flat* composed by Edwin H Lemare. The Hammond Organ estimated to be worth £2,000–£3,000 was purchased in 1938. It is believed that this public house was the first in the country to have such an instrument. Dixon became so absorbed in playing this instrument that he was nine minutes late for the official lunch.

Later that day Dixon told a reporter that he intended to visit a Leeds cinema to play the WurliTzer organ of nineteen ranks.[2]

Speaking at the Congress he shocked his fellow musicians by saying he did not believe that organ playing should be confined to sacred music and churches. He declared, 'I believe in giving the public what they want… People come into public houses for relaxation. They want light music and I see no reason why they should not have it.' He did not believe in playing down to the public but saw organ music in public houses as a way of introducing music to people who would not ordinarily hear it.

There were several topics up for discussion at the Leeds Congress including Organists' pay and conditions, how to attract more theatre organists into the Association and that of singing hymns to popular tunes which could be heard on the radio.

It was reported in the *News Chronicle* that one vicar had set the old hymn 'Rest of the Weary' to Henry Hall's signature tune 'Here's to the next time'. Dr Dixon commented 'I think it is degrading. It is like the parson turning up for morning service dressed in a football kit. The practice should be stopped immediately.'[3] If he were here today what would he have to say about the numerous traditional texts of hymns, psalms and parts of the Mass that have been set to popular tunes?

During this Congress Dixon along with other delegates was presented to the Princess Royal. On this special occasion he was wearing his gold earrings set with a blood red stone, one of his favourite pairs valued at twenty five guineas.

The wearing of earrings by Dixon and his theory on the subject was a frequent topic of conversation, and even attracted correspondence from around the world as well as giving the local and national press something to write about. According to a report in the *Daily Mirror*, members attending the Congress were fascinated by Dixon's magnificent antique jewelled pendants and the pair he wore when being presented to the Princess Royal.[4]

Regarding the topic of wearing earrings Dixon related an incident from his schooldays, when a glass containing some liquid blew up in an experiment and shattered the teacher's glasses which resulted in him losing his sight. During the First World War someone told Dixon that wearing earrings helped one's eyesight, so fearful of his glasses being broken through enemy action, he dispensed with them and began wearing earrings. Later he had his ears pierced and discovered that wearing earrings did indeed improve his eyesight. His personal experience, as well as an interest from his schooldays in electricity and magnetism probably led him to expound the theory that the movement of the earrings sets up alternating currents in the magnetic field surrounding us which clears the vision, thus improving one's eyesight.

---

2   *Yorkshire Evening Post*, 23 August 1950.
3   *News Chronicle*, 22 August 1950.
4   *Daily Mirror*, 22 August 1950.

Dixon's advice to anyone regarding eyesight was 'If your eyesight gets worse, don't overburden the Health Service by ordering new spectacles – wear a pair of earrings instead.'[5] He demonstrated to colleagues that he could read small print at a distance of three yards. A Leeds optician did not believe that having one's ears pierced and wearing earrings could improve vision, but thought it more likely that Dixon suffered eyesight problems in his younger days and like many other people his eyesight improved of their own accord as he got older.

No doubt the topic of wearing earrings by men and women had appeared in the press before 1949, but from then until 1952 there appeared a flurry of correspondence to various newspapers. Several letters were received seeking advice on the method of piercing one's own ears to which readers replied giving a detailed description of the correct tool (a silver piercer obtainable from the jewellers), sterilization and the use of sleepers. Other people wrote letters confirming that having pierced ears and wearing earrings did indeed improve one's eyesight. As well as improving one's eyesight some correspondents thought that wearing long pendants helped deportment, enabled girls who had a tendency to act like tomboys to became more ladylike and could transform a dull teenager into a vivacious girl. Some letters concerned the wearing of earrings by men. One writer recalled the family gardener (formerly an old sailor) wearing brass earrings and thought it would be fashionable for men to do so again, believing that it would add glamour to the sporting youth and a touch of distinction to elderly diplomats.[6] In another case a young man took up the idea of wearing earrings and created such a stir with the girls at the youth club that several male teenagers followed suit.

Dixon was known to have a collection of twenty pairs of earrings ranging from plain gold ones to some which were decorative and jewelled, worth over £100. He admitted to a *Daily Express* reporter that he was a bit self-conscious when he first started wearing earrings, but was now quite used to it,[7] and to a *Daily Mirror* reporter he said 'People do stare a bit, but it causes me no embarrassment.'[8]

One reporter at the Congress described Dixon as a 'Pickwick-like' character[9] and another (earrings apart) as resembling Winston Churchill,[10] perhaps the latter description coming from his appearance in the public house smoking a large cigar.

The following extract comes from Dixon's report to the Lancaster Association in October 1956 of the Congress held earlier that year in Glasgow (August 13–17):

---

5 *Daily Mail*, 22 August 1950.
6 *Daily Mail,* 29 May 1950.
7 *Daily Express*, 22 August 1950.
8 *Daily Mirror,* 22 August 1950.
9 *Daily Express*, 23 August 1950.
10 *Yorkshire Evening Post*, 23 August 1950.

> Up to this date the weather had not been kind – plenty of rain – But on Friday for the steamer trip to the 'Kyles of Bute' due amends were made & we had a glorious sail in sunny weather – with lunch and tea served on the Steamer 'Queen Mary II'.
>
> It was on this sail 'Doon the Watter' that I invited Sir William Harris to come to Lancaster and give a recital on the restored Cathedral organ – which you are aware he did last Wednesday October 3rd – delighting all who heard him with his masterly handling of this fine instrument.[11]

Also at the Glasgow Congress there was a performance of Dixon's *Prelude and Fantasy Fugue* (The Cunningham) given by William Coulthard FRCO (Director of Music, Glasgow Academy) on the new Hill Norman & Beard organ built for Giffnock South Parish Church. Stainton de B Taylor in his Congress Report mentioned this performance and referred to Dixon as 'that ever delightful and puckish figure without whom no Congress of the past thirty years has been complete.'[12]

The Exeter Congress of 1958 was considered by Dixon at the time to be one of the best, not just because there were four civic receptions given by the Mayor of Exeter, Plymouth, Paignton and Torquay. His impressions of Exeter were that it was a lovely city, with its Cathedral, abundance of small churches and friendly inviting public houses. He noted that the churches though low in height structurally, were high regarding their style of theology. Dixon observed that this Catholic atmosphere seems to be more prevalent in the South of England than in the North. The main drink in these parts is cider, rough or sweet which some people claim is a cure for rheumatism. Not Dixon's usual drink, nor was the famous Devonshire cream tea for him as he never took cream or milk. On a visit to St Andrew's Parish Church, Plymouth he made the following comments:

> A fine recital by Dr Webber, but in the soft passages the organ could scarcely be heard and in the loud passages the sound was overwhelming, which reminded one of Elijah's advice to the prophets of Baal 'Call him louder, call him louder.'[13]

The general opinion was that Almighty God was deaf in these parts – the necessity for organs which would raise the roof, so as to enable Almighty God to hear what was going on. The closing meeting was an unusual one in that it took the form of a private cinema show – the original silent film of 'Charlie Chaplin

---

11 Congress report, Dixon archive.
12 *Musical Times,* October 1956 Vol. 97 No. 1364.
13 Congress report, Dixon archive.

at the Circus.' After the event Dixon unwittingly changed his hat for one which belonged to someone else and got the better bargain![14]

In the Brighton Congress Programme Booklet of Recitals and Services 1960 Dixon posed and answered the following question:

> What do you understand by the Church of England? A church with hard seats and a loud organ to wake up God who is rather deaf

In the same booklet by a piece of which both title and composer will remain anonymous he wrote; 90% rubbbische!

At the York Congress in 1961, a report in the *Yorkshire Evening Press* mentions Dr Dixon as being the last surviving founder member of the Association and his connections with York. Reference is also made to his oratorio *Panis Vitae* ending with the following quote:

> Those who have heard Dr Dixon's music agree that he has found new beauties in the white notes rather than in the weird chromatic harmonies of contemporary composition. The harsh modern formless music without any melody makes you long for the chord of C major declared the Grand Old Man of Lancaster and York.[15]

After serving on the Executive Committee for many years Dr Dixon was elected a Vice-President of the Association at this Congress. At this time he had only missed the Annual Congress twice since the first one was held.

Dr Francis Jackson in his Presidential Address sparked off a controversy when he stated that the Mendelssohn Wedding March from 'A Midsummer Night's Dream' is theatre music and as such is intrinsically inappropriate for use at a marriage service in church.[16] He felt that theatre music should be performed in the theatre, music written for church used in church and music written for the organ played on the organ. Many musicians sympathised with Jackson to whom controversy is nothing new. Whatever one's view of this piece, it has been traditionally used for many years and is popular with brides. When interviewed the majority of brides felt that the choice of music was a personal thing and to some brides a Marriage Service without the Mendelssohn would not seem right. With regard to choice of music, it was reported that one vicar refused permission for a bride to have 'Moonlight and Roses' played at her Wedding. The organist volunteered Lemare's *Andantino in D flat* as a substitute. This was accepted, the vicar like the customers in the public house mentioned earlier not knowing the two pieces are one and the same.[17]

---

14 Ibid.
15 *Yorkshire Evening Press*, 30 August 1961.
16 *Yorkshire Post*, 31 August 1961.
17 Ibid.

When the Congress was held at Bristol in 1962 Dr Dixon in his report again considered that organs were invariably loud and noisy, with the exception of Gloucester Cathedral. He asked, 'Is God deaf down Bristol way?'[18] He commented that a lot of modernisation had been going on in organ building with the result that much of the nobility and dignity of the organ had gone, being replaced by an excessive amount of upper work and mixtures which certainly made a great deal of sound, but not always a pleasant one. Fashions change in organs as in organ music. He had no doubt that in a few years some of these organs would be rebuilt on more conservative lines, to the benefit of players and hearers alike.

Taking time off from musical activities members visited some famous firms including Fry's Chocolate, Harvey's the makers of Bristol Cream Sherry and Wills Tobacco and Cigarettes, the latter two would be popular with our friend. Later in the week an interesting conducted coach trip of Bristol took place and Dixon reported that they ate lollipops on the Clifton Suspension Bridge. The type of lollipops is unknown. They could have been ice lollipops if it was hot, or whatever type they were, maybe this was an occasion when a group of adults were just being young at heart again.

At the Edinburgh Congress of 1963 Dr Dixon felt honoured to be a guest at the top table on the occasion of the local Association's Jubilee Dinner.

The 1972 Congress was once again held in Lancaster, marking the local Association's Jubilee year and appropriately began with an evening devoted to the works of James Hugh Reginald Dixon in honour of him being the oldest living founder member of the Association. It was an event at which the composer proudly presented a varied selection of his compositions including *Introduction, Variations and Fugue* on the hymn tune 'Sedbergh', excerpts from *The Dream of Gerontius,* the *Organ Concerto*, Violin and Piano solos the latter played by the composer himself and the concert ended with excerpts from the *Suite Carolorégienne*. The evening was certainly one to remember as a tribute to a remarkable man who over eight decades through composition, performance, lecturing and teaching had made a valuable contribution to the world of music. No one minded that the concert lasted about three hours!

A feature of this Congress was the performance practices, keyboard techniques and interpretation of the music of J S Bach. Visits were made to Blackburn Cathedral, Cartmel Priory and the Railway Museum at Carnforth (a star attraction for many organists who are also railway enthusiasts).

Events held by the Lancaster Association were typical of those held by most Associations throughout the country. These included composite recitals, lectures, visiting recitalists, visits to local organs, an annual outing and a dinner. After being Secretary of the Association for eleven years Dr Dixon became President in 1932. According to the Secretary's Report in 1948 there were 41 members of the Association. Although

---

18 Congress report, Dixon archive.

> **THE INCORPORATED ASSOCIATION OF ORGANISTS**
> **LANCASTER CONGRESS, 1972**
>
> # CONCERT of MUSIC
>
> by Dr. J. H. REGINALD DIXON
>
> in the ASHTON HALL
>
> MONDAY, AUGUST 7th at 8 p.m. Doors open 7.30 p.m.
>
> **ADMISSION BY PROGRAMME**
>
> *Manchester Mozart Orchestra:* Guest Conductor, JOHN ASHWORTH
> *St. Joseph's Operatic Society:* Director, Rev. B. LOCKWOOD
>
> 1. NATIONAL ANTHEM
> 2. ORGAN SOLO: "Sedbergh" .... Joan Carter
>   To the memory of JOHN BROOK who was a founder and first Secretary of the I.A.O.
> 3. SELECTIONS FROM "THE DREAM OF GERONTIUS."
>
>   PRELUDE .... The Orchestra
>   KYRIE .... Chorus
>   PROFICISCERE (Go on thy journey) .... THOMAS SHERLOCK AND CHORUS
>   ANGEL'S SONG .... Valerie Edwards
>   Speaker: Cynthia McPherson
>   2nd BALLET MUSIC .... The Orchestra
>   Praise to the Holiest .... Chorus and Trio
>   Valerie Edwards, Marjorie Britton, Thomas Sherlock.
> 4. PIANOFORTE SOLOS .... J. H. R. Dixon
>   Two ETUDES: Fugue: (from Homage to J. S. Bach)
>   Nocturne "Sunset over Morecambe Bay."
> 5. VIOLIN SOLOS. .... EDGAR DACRE BIRTLE
>   LEGENDE—Meditation "Meadowside."
> 6. ORGAN CONCERTO ..... J. B. WISHART-HODGSON AND ORCHESTRA
>   Allegro Moderato: Larghetto: Allegro comodo
> 7. LE DEPART .... THE ORCHESTRA
>   British Troops leave Charleroi from Suite CAROLOREGIENNE
>
> *Retiring Collection towards Expenses*
>
> John B. Barber & Son, Printers, New Street, Lancaster.

the cost of the *Quarterly Record* (which had been subsidised at 1½d per copy) and the size of the publication increased, the subscription remained at 6s. It was in this year that J W Aldous was made an Honorary Life member in appreciation of his long and valued service to the association. In 1949 the annual dinner was revived after a lapse of twenty years. Other activities in this year included two illustrated lantern lectures, recitals and visits to members' instruments, an outing to St Bees and five members attended the Edinburgh Congress. As frequently occurs today it was recorded that several members had not paid their subscription. Whenever a visit was made to play various organs in the area, Dr Dixon never ever made any critical comments on members' performances. He was always there to offer encouragement and advice. Sadly the Lancaster Association no longer exists, but happy memories of friendships and shared activities will always be treasured.

A Golden Decade

This was a decade in which several memorable events occurred including royal visits, centenary celebrations, presentation of an honour from the Pope and renovation of the Cathedral organ. It was also an active period of composition culminating in the Oratorio *Panis Vitae*.

Lancaster was a local centre for the Trinity College of Music, London graded examinations. Dr Dixon was Chairman of a Committee responsible for all the necessary administration in connection with the exams. Other members of the Committee included Miss N E Taylor ARCO, LRAM (Secretary), Mr G M Bland, the Rev. B Lockwood, Councillor R T Barnard and Miss L C Burkitt LRAM, LTCL.

In January 1951 Dr W Greenhouse Allt FRCO, LTCL, Principal of the College, presented certificates to sixty successful candidates from Lancaster, Morecambe, Carnforth and the surrounding area. This event which took place in a room at the Centenary Congregational Church was the first of its kind to be held in Lancaster. Despite an outbreak of influenza the attendance numbered over one hundred people. After the presentation Dr Allt gave a speech in which he is quoted as saying:

> These young musicians of the future may not become great players or singers, but they will have some knowledge of music which will be a joy for the rest of their lives.[1]

From this date onwards the Presentation of Certificates was to become an annual event for many years. Several pupils of Dr Dixon became music teachers and remained in the area entering candidates for both Trinity College and the Associated Board of the Royal Schools of Music examinations.

On 6 March 1951 a second visit to the city of Lancaster was made by King George VI and the Queen, this time accompanied by HRH Princess Margaret. This visit was arranged to coincide with the 600th Anniversary of the creation of the County Palatine of Lancaster. As on previous Royal visits Dr Dixon presided at

---

1 *Lancaster Guardian,* January 1951.

1. Andante (Sonata in B Flat) .... Mendelssohn
2. Chant sans Paroles .... Tschaikowsky
3. Intermezzo .... Hollins
4. Meditation .... Massenet
5. Adagio Cantabile (Sonata Pathetique) Beethoven
6. The Rivulet .... J. H. Reginald Dixon
7. Allegretto in B Minor .... Guilmant
8. Solemn Melody .... Walford Davies
and, immediately the Royal Party have left the Reception:—
9. Land of Hope and Glory .... Elgar

CITY OF LANCASTER

VISIT OF
THEIR MAJESTIES THE KING AND QUEEN
AND
H.R.H. THE PRINCESS MARGARET
on
TUESDAY, 6th MARCH, 1951

GEORGE CHIRMSIDE,
Mayor.

R. M. MIDDLETON,
Town Clerk.

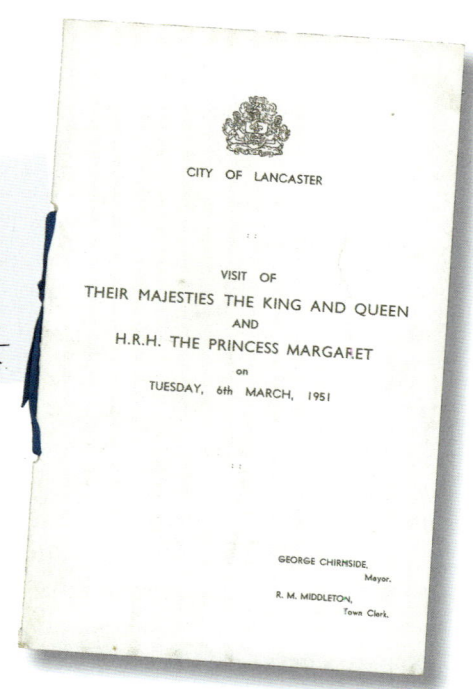

HOLY TRINITY CHURCH
STOCKTON-ON-THE-FOREST

*

RE-OPENING OF ORGAN
AFTER RENOVATION
AND ADDITIONS

SUNDAY, 2nd SEPTEMBER, 1951 AT 6-30 p.m.

*

Programme of
ORGAN RECITAL
by
Dr. REGINALD DIXON, F.R.C.O.
(Organist, the Cathedral, Lancaster)

---

1. HYMN TUNE
   "Lift the strain of high thanksgiving"
   This was the first hymn tune ever played on the Organ in this Church.

2. GRAND OFFERTOIRE in G   Lefebure-Wely

3. TRANSCRIPTION
   "If with all your hearts"
   Mendelssohn
   These two items were performed the first Organist here, Mr. Kingsley, a blind musician; the occasion being a Recital to demonstrate the capabilities of the new Organ.

4. SOLEMN PRELUDE
   "Gloria Domini"   T. T. Noble
   Dr. Noble was at one time Organist of York Minster

5. SCHERZO IN G MINOR   Bossi

6. MELODIE
   "The Rivulet"   J. H. R. Dixon

7. TOCCATA & FUGUE IN D MINOR   Bach

the Ashton Hall organ and entertained the guests with the programme opposite.

Several events were held in 1951 to celebrate the centenary of the Cathedral Primary School. The first of these was a concert of singing, dancing and acting presented by the pupils on 12 and 13 June in St Joseph's Hall, Skerton. Three groups of songs sung by the fourth form choir, were interspersed with country dancing by the juniors and fairy-tale sketches performed by pupils of the transitional, junior and infant forms. Over one hundred children whose ages ranged from four and a half to eleven years sang a centenary song 'Here's to the school of a hundred years' specially written for the occasion by Father Lockwood and set to music by Dr Dixon. Embodied in the song was the school motto, 'Do duty to God, the country and the city.'

On Sunday 2 September 1951 Dixon gave a recital at Holy Trinity Church, Stockton-on-the-Forest to celebrate the re-opening of the organ. Work on the instrument was carried out by Messrs. Summers and Barnes of York. The cost of the renovation, which included the addition of the salicet and tremulant stops, was paid for by Dr Dixon, his brother Ronald and his sister Beatrice as a memorial to their parents. A tablet on the organ case bears the words:

> In Loving memory of
> GEORGE DIXON 1864–1941
> Churchwarden and Schoolmaster
> And of JANE, His Dear Wife, 1864–1929
> This Organ was Renovated and the Salicet and
> Tremulant Stops installed in the year 1951 by their
> Daughter and Two Sons, as an Act of Thanksgiving
> to Almighty God, for their Parents' many good works
> and Godly Examples of Life.

The salicet stop replaced the original voix celeste.

An historical Pageant 'Beneath Hadrian's Tower' by T Alderson was performed at the Ashton Hall on 28, 29 and 30 May 1953 as part of the Coronation celebrations. The last Pageant, an historical procession through the streets featuring the history of Lancaster, was held in 1937 to celebrate the town's elevation to city status. A combined effort by the local Amateur Dramatic Societies in staging the 1953 Pageant was thought to be the first occasion when local history was re-enacted in terms of the theatre. Each of the seven Episodes recounting an event which occurred between 1588 and 1953 was complemented by dancing and appropriate vocal or orchestral music. The orchestra was under the direction of Mr J Sackville Wiggins with Dr Dixon at the organ and Herbert Horrocks conducted the Lancaster and District Musical Society.

On 13 April 1955 Lancaster was host to another Royal visit, that of Queen Elizabeth II. Once again Dixon presented a programme of organ music which he played during the civic reception.

Shortly after Christmas 1956 Dr Dixon suffered ill health for several months and being too weak to shave he grew a beard. Later in the year, a reference to the beard was made in a message written on a letter card to the Taylor sisters, sent from the Glasgow Congress

> My 'Beard' has provoked interesting comments. No longer am I 'Mr Churchill' – but now I'm Bernard Shaw!!![2]

From now on his beard was either neatly trimmed, when performing or attending an official function, or it would be rather long and shaggy on other occasions.

In May 1956 Dr Dixon was in hospital awaiting an operation when he was visited by the Right Rev. Bishop T E Flynn, who was there to present him with the Golden Cross pro Ecclesia et Pontifice bestowed on him by the Pope for his faithful service to church music.

During the summer of 1956 it became necessary for some renovation work to be done on the Cathedral organ and this provided an opportunity to make some improvements and additions to the instrument. The work was carried out by Ainscough in consultation with Dr Dixon at a cost of approximately £1,080. In addition to parts of the action being renewed, a new electric blower was installed and a starting switch was placed at the console. After many years of waiting Dr Dixon must have been delighted that the Choir Organ was now enclosed with a lever expression pedal similar to that of the Swell. Other additions to the instrument included a Choir Tremulant and an Octave Coupler, as well as a Swell Sub-Octave Coupler to the high pressure Reeds.

As mentioned earlier to mark the re-opening of the restored organ, Sir William Harris, Organist of St George's Chapel Royal, Windsor, gave a recital on Wednesday 3 October 1956. The programme included works by J S Bach, W A Mozart, César Franck, Louis Vierne, Frank Bridge and three pieces by Harris. A report on the recital reads as follows:

> The restored organ greatly improved in tonal quality and action, responded beautifully to the masterly touch of Sir William who delighted the congregation with a programme in which one of the highlights was a selection of his own compositions. Sir William who was paying his first visit to Lancaster began with an impressive performance of Mozart's Fantasia in F minor and fully captured the mood of the work with its powerful opening followed by the more delicate movements.'[3]

---

2 Letter card, Dixon archive.
3 *Lancaster Guardian*, 5 October 1956.

> **The Cathedral, Lancaster.**
>
> RE-OPENING of the RESTORED ORGAN
>
> ## ORGAN RECITAL
> BY
> **SIR WILLIAM HARRIS,**
> K.C.V.O., M.A., D. Mus., F.R.C.O., F.R.C.M., Hon. R.A.M.
> (Organist, St. George's Chapel Royal, Windsor.)
>
> WEDNESDAY, 3rd OCTOBER, 1956,
> at 7-30 p.m.
>
> ### Programme
>
> 1. Fantasia in F minor. ..... Mozart
> 2. Adagio. ..... Frank Bridge
> 3. a Trio
>   b Toccata & Fugue in C. } ..... J. S. Bach
>
> Collection for the Organ Restoration Fund
>
> 4. Madrigal ..... Louis Vierne
> 5. a Prelude
>   b Romance and Scherzetto
>   c A Fancy } William Harris
> 6. Choral in A minor ..... Cesar Franck
>
> The Castle Press, King Street, Lancaster.

It was in 1957, probably while on a pilgrimage to Lourdes that Dr Dixon made a return visit to Lyon and St Germain au Mont d'Or. He had last been here over forty years ago, but he was duly recognised and received with open arms by those who remembered him. On his journey home via Paris he visited the church of Sainte-Clotilde.

High Mass was televised from St Joseph's Church, Lancaster, on 15 June 1958. Father Lockwood had asked Dr Dixon to play the organ and suggested that he compose a setting of the prayer 'Domine Salvum Fac' for the occasion. The composition is scored for four mixed voices and organ accompaniment. A two bar introduction is based on the first line of the National Anthem but with four beats in a bar instead of three, although the way it is written it has a feel of the original. The idea of using this motive was that people unfamiliar with Catholic Liturgy would make the connection of the piece being in honour of Her Majesty the Queen.

Throughout the 1950s Dixon composed several new works, made minor alterations to some earlier pieces and those Mass settings which were originally written for male voices were re-scored for mixed voices.

In 1952 Dixon began work on an *Organ Concerto* scored for Organ and Orchestra which was completed by 30 August. The first performance was given by Dr Dixon and the Lancaster Orchestral Society at their annual concert held in the Ashton Hall on 26 November 1952 in the presence of Earl Peel, grandson of Lord Ashton to whom the work is dedicated. It is interesting to note some special features of the work. A Concerto usually has three movements, but this work has four: Allegro Moderato (D minor), Tempo di Minuetto Scherzando (D major), Larghetto (G minor), and Allegro Comodo (D major). The pedal cadenza, a feature of the first movement includes three-part chord writing which tests the pedal technique of the performer. While the second movement is a typical Minuet there are two trios, the first in B minor which has a fanfare-like theme for horns and trumpet, with alternating phrases for either organ or orchestra and the second in G major which has a playful waltz-like theme scored for strings and woodwind, with the triangle making an appearance. After a repeat of the Minuet and a lively coda the movement has a soft almost abrupt ending. The Larghetto begins with a reflective melody for 'cellos, accompanied on the organ with a motive taken from the melody. After a short duet in canon between the organ and oboe on a new theme, a chorale-like melody is announced on the organ accompanied by muted strings. The final movement is in fugal form, and after statements of the subject and counter-subject the episodes are based on the chorale-like theme from the previous movement, alternating with entries of the fugue subject in various keys. Both themes are then combined and the work ends in majestic style.

Themes from the *Organ Concerto*:

Example 8, First movement, bars 1–5

Example 9, Second movement, bars 1–4

Example 10, Second movement, first trio

Example 11, Second movement, second trio

Example 12, Third movement, bars 1–6

Example 13, Third movement, duet in canon

Example 14, Third movement, chorale-like theme

Example 15, Fourth movement, fugue subject

Originally the organist played from a short score, but a separate organ part was written out for the second performance which was given by the Lancaster and District Musical Society at their spring concert on 29 March 1958. In a letter to the Taylor sisters Dixon suggested that they could perform the work by one playing the solo part on the organ and the other playing the orchestral part from short score on the piano!⁴

The manuscript of the *Berceuse* for organ is dated December 1953, but a piece with this title coupled with a Toccata appears in two recital programmes given by Dixon 1927. This may or may not be the same work in a revised form. A gentle rhythmic motif representing the rocking of the cradle, persists throughout the piece until a pause four bars from the end suggests the child has fallen asleep. This motif acts as an accompaniment to a graceful refined melody, and as a contrast in the middle section treatment of the material appears in a contrapuntal and antiphonal style.

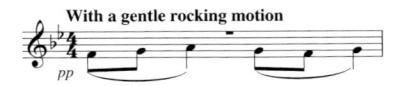

Example 16, Berceuse, bar 1 rhythmic motif (by kind permission of Peters Edition Ltd)

A petit Oratorio *Anglèse de Sagazan* with both French and English text was composed in August 1955 and is scored for Tenor or Baritone solo, a two-part chorus for Soprano and Alto, a Reader and organ accompaniment. The work is dedicated to Père Vergé, priest of the Lourdes Sanctuaries, and recounts the miracle which took place in 1515 at Garaison (a village near Lourdes in the Haute-Pyrénées, France). At this time the people of Garaison were poor and food was scarce due to failed harvests. The Blessed Virgin Mary, known on this occasion as Our Lady of Good Counsel, appeared to a twelve-year-old shepherdess, Anglèse de Sagazan, near the spring at Garaison and requested that a church be built there. As proof of her appearance the black bread which Anglèse had in her bag was turned into white bread and as a result of this miracle an oratory was built. The first church was replaced in 1541 and Notre Dame de Garaison remains a pilgrimage place today where many miracle cures have occurred, but the appearance of Our Lady was originally associated with provision of food for the family of Anglèse and the villagers. Four pieces from the Oratorio (Prelude, Meditation, Idylle Pastorale and Chorale) were arranged by Dixon as a Suite for Organ.

After the 1955 revision of *The Dream of Gerontius* the ladies who took part in the performances joined the Cathedral Choir. This resulted in Dixon re-scoring the Mass of St Peter, St Wulstan and St Cecilia for mixed voices.

In addition to composing Dixon was still actively performing, teaching and lecturing. It was at a lecture in December 1955 in response to a question 'How do you compose?' that he spontaneously wrote a hymn tune which he named *Inspiration*.

After being discharged from hospital in May 1956 Dr Dixon went to Bridlington in June and while convalescing there he began three new compositions, a unison

---

4   Letter, Dixon archive.

setting of an *Ave Maria,* a four-part setting with soprano solo of the same text and a Mass dedicated to *Our Lady of Syon* [sic]. These compositions were completed a week later when he returned home to Lancaster. The Mass was originally written in three parts (SAB) but at a later date Dixon added a tenor part, probably with a view to having the work published.

Sometime in 1956 Monsignor Brimley (Administrator of St Peter's Cathedral, Lancaster), discussed with Dr Dixon the desirability of having some suitable hymns for use at Evening Masses and other occasions. The result was a series of eight hymns entitled 'Carmina Missae' which interpret in simple language the various parts of the Mass. With the congregation in mind Dixon pitched the melodies within easy compass of the average voice, varied the rhythms and tempo, wrote harmonies which reflected the nature of the text and carefully selected the sequence of keys for smooth transition from one hymn to the next. Although not acknowledged in the published score Dixon also wrote the words as well as composing the music.

It was in the late 1950s that Dixon met the music publisher Max Hinrichsen and formed a friendship which was to last a lifetime. Hinrichsen visited Lancaster on more than one occasion, and his discovery of a provincial composer living in what one might describe as a 'back-water' at the time resulted in the publication of several works.

The first of these publications which appeared in 1959 was the *Baroque Suite* for organ composed in September 1957. It is a modern work, but one in which each of the four movements are written in modes, Toccata (Aeolian), Pastorale (Lydian), Verset (Dorian) and Finale in Modo Festivo (Ionian) and dedicated respectively to Sir William Harris, Lady Susi Jeans, Ralph Downes and Dr Leo Sowerby. In this composition Dixon's intention was to demonstrate some of the possibilities of the Baroque style of registration. The work can be performed as a whole or in individual movements and for many organists it remains the most popular of all the published organ pieces.

This was followed by the *Berceuse* mentioned earlier and the *Mass in E flat* in honour of St Paulinus, the first Archbishop of York, which was composed in 1958. In addition to the Kyrie, Gloria, Sanctus, Benedictus and Agnus Dei, a Credo for use with the Mass was published separately. With reference to this Mass, the following quote is taken from the writings of Max Hinrichsen about his musical impressions of 1959:

> On a cold wet and cheerless day in November I was wonderfully warmed on hearing at St John's Church, Islington Mr de Rivera's fine choir giving the first London performance of Reginald Dixon's St Paulinus Mass. The impression of this simple yet beautiful music will last long in my memory.[5]

Another work published in 1959 was *Transfiguration* (subtitled *Only a Town by the River*) which dates from 1943/4 and is scored for unaccompanied mixed voices.

---

5 Dixon archive.

Dixon first set the poem as a baritone solo. The work is a setting of a poem by Will Foster who was a local Methodist preacher and with his brother owned the Flax Mill and the Mustard Mill in Selby. The author described his inspiration for the poem to Dixon when they first met at the time of Dixon's appointment as organist and choirmaster at Selby Wesleyan Chapel, 1906–08. Foster related that one day he went for a walk through the town into the countryside. He was struck by the grubbiness of the old streets and the drabness of the muddy tidal riverside, but on turning round to come homewards the sun was setting, and he saw Selby silhouetted against a wonderful golden sunset. There was the Tower of Selby Abbey, the Spires of St James' Church and the Catholic Church together with the two dome-capped turrets of the Methodist Chapel all bathed in the fiery glow of a glorious sunset. His impressions of this transformation became the poem 'Transfiguration'. Due to the redevelopment of Selby, the view described by Foster no longer exists.

Example 17, Transfiguration, bars 1–4 (by kind permission of Peters Edition Ltd)

The purposely expressionless opening depicts the drab aspect of many a town 'with hopeless aspect', but when viewed from a distance in the glow of a glorious sunset, a magical transformation takes place in a town dim and golden with many a dome and spire which seems stretching far and golden into the sunset fire. As in a symphonic poem the work evolves from a single thematic germ. There is a logical development of the themes with a realisation of the universal and human appeal of the many pictures suggested by the poem. The music aptly captures the mood and description of each scene through melody, harmony, tonality, dynamics and changes of tempo.

Example 18, Transfiguration, bars 36–41 (by kind permission of Peters Edition Ltd)

Dixon at the Cathedral organ c. 1955
(Peter Anthony)

Dixon was known to have made a financial contribution to the publication of all the works mentioned above. Hinrichsen intended to publish the *Organ Concerto* with three movements omitting the Scherzo and *The Dream of Gerontius* but neither work was published. Other works with a view to publication were submitted including the *Mass of St Peter* and a revised version of the *Passacaglia* on a theme by Purcell for organ, but these remain in manuscript.

Missa Ferialis in C was composed in August 1958 as a competition entry for a Parish Mass and later became known as the *Mass in honour of St Beatrice* (manuscript dated January 1959). This Mass is a simple unison setting for Cantor/Choir and Congregation with organ accompaniment. Originally the Mass had four movements, Kyrie, Sanctus, Benedictus and Agnus Dei, but Dixon added a Gloria which he composed in June 1959.

In this decade 1959 was a special year not only because several works were published and work was begun on *Panis Vitae*, but also because there was a Jubilee and a Centenary to celebrate.

The first special celebration of the year on 20 May was the Jubilee of Dixon's appointment as Organist. At this time there were three surviving members of the 1909 choir who were still associated with the Cathedral, Mr Edward Suart (then a boy chorister, aged 10) and Mr Joe Greenbow, members of the present choir, and Mr W Darwen, now retired, having not been able to attend services for several years through ill health.

On Sunday 4 October celebrations were held at the Cathedral to mark the Centenary of the Church Dedication. Pontifical High Mass was sung by the Right Rev. Bishop T E Flynn and the sermon was given by the Most Rev. J C Heenan, Archbishop of Liverpool. Music on this occasion included Haydn's Imperial Mass and excerpts from Dixon's *Panis Vitae* sung by the combined choirs of St Peter's Cathedral and St Joseph's Church, Lancaster conducted by the Rev. B Lockwood.

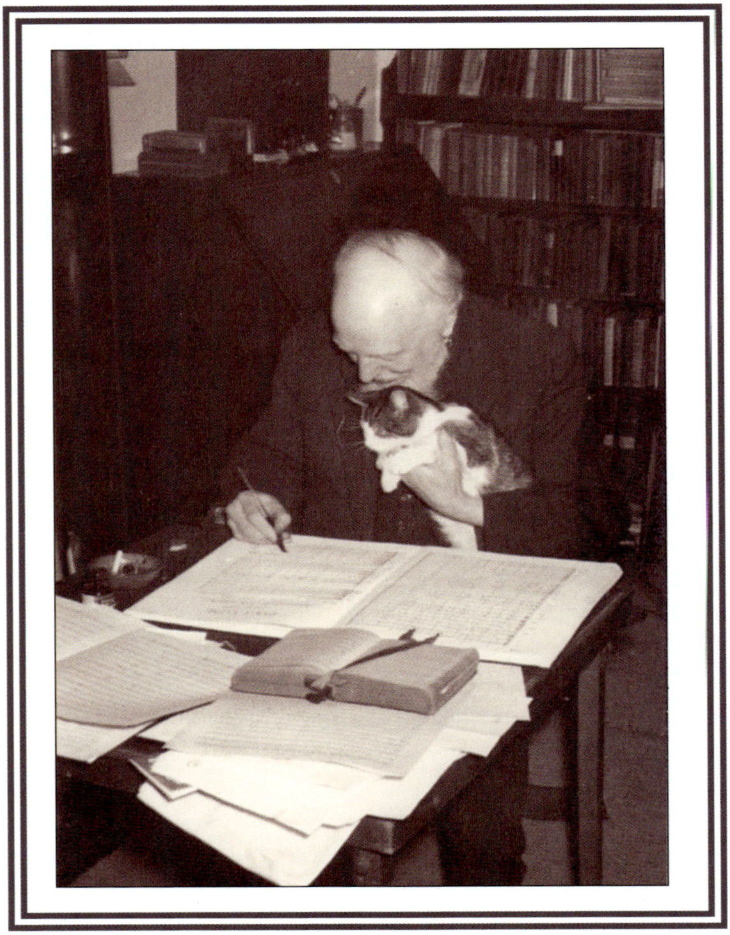

Panis Vitae

The Congress Committee responsible for organising the International Eucharistic Congress to be held at Munich in August 1960 were looking for a Eucharistic Oratorio to be performed for the occasion.

In a letter dated 13 July 1959, Max Hinrichsen asks Dixon if he has such a work.[1] It would appear that sometime just before this date Hinrichsen had met Dr Alfons Ott (City Librarian under Herr Hieber and principal organiser on the Congress committee) at an event in Cambridge and as well as discussing the idea of a Eucharistic Oratorio the works of Dixon had been mentioned.

A reply to the letter was sent within twenty-four hours enclosing a sketch plan of a Eucharistic Oratorio. At this stage the plan consisted of seven movements, ending with a Magnificat and including an orchestral prelude. The text of each section within a movement was given, with an indication of style which included Gregorian chant, polyphonic and contrapuntal writing, vocal scoring, and type of accompaniment i.e. organ or orchestra. For Dixon to respond so rapidly one might wonder if he already had an outline plan of such a work in his mind.

The next letter from Hinrichsen to Dixon dated 16 July begins:

> Thank you for your letter of 14th July. I must say that you are a wonderful person to work with. You are the fastest and most excellent worker who has ever come into my orbit, and to show you that I appreciate this, I am writing to-day to Munich and am enclosing herewith a copy of my letter so that you will know I have written.
>
> The sketch plan for the suggested Oratorio seems to me to be excellent.[2]

In the copy of the letter Hinrichsen sent to Munich he mentions the Choir of St John the Evangelist, Islington and the director Edward de Rivera.

---

1 Letter, Dixon archive.
2 Ibid.

Opposite: Working on the Panis Vitae score (F L Common Lancaster)

Sketch Plan for Oratorio Eucharistica

Latin text selected from the various offices (or services) connected with the Eucharist. Accompaniment will be for full orchestra – organ, chorus mainly In 4 parts and 3 soloists.

1. **Orchestral Prelude**

2. **'O Quam Suavis est' Motet for choir (unaccompanied)**

3. **'Verbum Supernum' (Hymnum). Accompanied**

Verbum supernum	Chorus (Gregorian)
In mortem	Chorus (Polyphonic)
Quibus) Se nascens)	Trio. Soprano, Tenor and Bass Soloists
O Salutaris	Chorus (Gregorian) in which the audience could join in singing.
Uni trinoque	Chorus (Polyphonic)

4. **Sequence. 'Lauda Sion'.**

Lauda Sion	Chorus
Laudis thema	Duet Tenor and Soprano
Sit laus plena	Chorus
In hac mensa	Solo Bass
Dogma datur	Chorus
A sumente	Solo Soprano
Ecce Panis	Chorus
In figuris	Solo Tenor
Bone Pastor	Chorus, with Bass Solo
Tu Qui Cuncta) Alleluia)	Chorus

5. **Hymnum. 'Pange Lingua'**

Pange lingua	Chorus (Gregorian)
Nobis Datus	Soprano Solo
In Supremæ	Chorus
Verbum caro	Tenor and Bass Duet
Tantum ergo	Chorus (Gregorian) in which the audience could join.
Genitori	Chorus (based on Gregorian melody)

6. **Motet. 'O Sacrum Convivium' Chorus unaccompanied**

7. **Magnificat**

Magnificat	Chorus
Quia respexit	Soprano Solo
Et misericordia	Chorus with Soprano Solo
Fecit potentiam	Tenor and Bass Duet
Esurientes	Chorus
Suscepit	Trio (Soprano, Tenor, Bass)
Gloria	Chorus

Earlier in the year the Choir of St John the Evangelist, Islington, London under the direction of Edward de Rivera had received an invitation to sing two Masses at the Congress. In correspondence which passed between de Rivera and Dr Ott the idea of commissioning a Eucharistic Oratorio was mentioned. Edward de Rivera had links with Dr Dixon through performing some of his works with the Choir of St John's and in conversation with me he recalled a visit to Lancaster in April 1959. At this meeting with Dr Dixon it would appear that a Eucharistic Oratorio was mentioned; therefore it is possible that Dixon gave some thought to the idea and this could account for the rapid response to Hinrichsen's first letter.

While awaiting confirmation of approval for the work from the committee Dixon decided to press ahead with composing the music.

A letter from the Music Committee received in August found the liturgical structure to be very good. However, they were a little concerned at the length of the work and therefore suggested omitting the Magnificat, as the strictly Eucharist connection is not as obvious any more compared to the hymns and sequences. It was also suggested that a link be made between the different sections of the work in the form of recitatives or by using a narrator, taking the texts from the Messianic Prophecies in the Old Testament or Christ's words relating to the Eucharist in the New Testament.

In a letter dated 20 August Dr Ott thanks Dr Dixon for complying with the requested changes and accepts that the structure of the revised version is exactly what the Committee were looking for. Again Dixon is advised that the actual performance time should not exceed one hour thirty minutes. The committee were due to meet again in October when a final decision regarding the Oratorio would be made.

The final version of the work differed from the original sketch plan in several ways: the Magnificat was taken out which resulted in changing the position of the 'Pange Lingua', recitatives were added and thus new texts were introduced, some sections were scored for different voices and an orchestral interlude was inserted after the 'Lauda Sion'.

The revised form became symmetrical comprising five main sections, with the great sequence 'Lauda Sion' forming the central section, which is preceded and followed by an orchestral piece, a motet and a hymn all linked together with recitatives.

Sections of the Sequence from 'In hac mensa' to 'A sumente non concisus' were now all scored for tenor or bass solo interspersed with chorus sections. 'Ecce Panis' was rescored for soprano solo and chorus. In the Pange Lingua 'Nobis datus' originally intended for soprano solo was set for double chorus and 'Verbum caro' was scored for soprano and tenor instead of tenor and bass. The motet 'O quam suavis est' is now accompanied.

Revised Outline Plan for Panis Vitae

Prœmium	Orchestra
Praecurrentia	Recitative – Choraliter 'Dominus mandavit nubibus'
	Motet – 'O quam suavis'
Sacrificium	Recitatives for Bass and Tenor
	'Immolabit hœdum', 'Pascha nostrum'
	Hymnum – 'Verbum supernum prodiens'
Promissum et Laudatio	Recitatives for Bass and Tenor
	'In illo tempore', 'Convenit itaque'
	Lauda Sion
Preludium	Orchestra
Invitatio	Recitatives for Bass and Tenor
	'In illo tempore', 'Venite comedite'
	Motet – 'O sacrum convivium'
Institutum	Recitatives for Bass and Tenor
	'Fratres, ego' (Paulus), 'Accipite et manducate'
	Hymnum – 'Pange Lingua'

Dixon in his Eucharistic Oratorio reverts back to the 'Laudi Spirituali' of G. Animuccia (c.1500–1571), Maestro di Cappella St Peter's Rome (1555–1571) and a friend of St Philip Neri, for whose Oratory he composed such works. The original purpose of 'Laudi Spirituali' – mystical exposition of doctrine was to aid and encourage devotional observances, through Psalms, Motets, Hymns and Songs of Praise.

Several texts in the work are taken from the writings of St Thomas Aquinas, the most important being that of the central section 'Lauda Sion' in which a complete exposition of the significance of the Blessed Sacrament and Catholic doctrine is summed up. The concise nature of the writing in a didactic and lyrical style which has rhythmic flow is considered to be a masterpiece of theological doctrine, devotion and literary taste.

> Devotion to the Blessed Sacrament must not consist only in prayers and actions, but primarily in acquiring and preserving within us the grace and efficacy of this Victim of our redemption.
>
> 'Liber Sacramentorum' Schuster

Other texts are selected from the Psalms, the Gospel of St Luke, the Gospel of St John and St Paul's first letter to the Corinthians.

In the Recitatives reference is made to, the giving of manna, the sacrifice of goats, the promise of a living bread, praising the power of God who in the sacrament has worked in a wonderful manner and the invitation to partake of the heavenly banquet, with an account of its solemn institution.

Short melodic motives are contrasted with longer lyrical phrases to emphasise or illustrate the text. Dixon's harmonic vocabulary, mainly diatonic with some chromaticism and use of modes, was considered old fashioned at the time, but in some ways was refreshingly new. Modern harmony would have been unsuitable for the spiritual and devotional nature of the text. Dixon mentioned the fact that the work includes over thirty different forms of cadence.

From one movement to the next the key scheme has a tendency to rise transporting the listener to a higher place before returning to where it began.

Dixon's orchestration ranges from delicate accompaniment with use of the organ, harp and oboe obligato to tutti. The organ is used as a contrasting accompaniment to the orchestra in a traditional sense, not as a continuo, and use of the harp accompanying the plainsong hymns is linked to the Psalms of David. Throughout the work there are examples of homophonic, contrapuntal and antiphonal writing.

Provision is made for audience participation in the 'O Salutaris' and 'Tantum Ergo', which is similar to the audience singing the chorales in the works of J S Bach.

The opening Orchestral Prœmium, contains several themes and motifs which are developed in the vocal sections and the Orchestral Prelude (Interludium) to Part II, entitled 'Pax Domini' (The peace of the Lord) – evokes a peaceful feeling sentiment – which is one of the fruits of reception of the *Panis Vitae*. This Prelude is based on a new theme and its inversion, which is orchestrated to suit the mood.

In the Recitatives use is made of *Leitmotive* with the organ or orchestra being used to accompany alternating phrases. The opening recitative is based on the fifth psalm tone with Faburden and gives rise to the material (theme) for the Motet 'O Quam Suavis.'

Traditional melodies form the basis of the two Hymns. The first and fifth stanzas of 'Verbum Supernum' are sung to the official Gregorian melody. In the second stanza 'In mortem' the melody appears in the tenor part, harmonised by the other voices in free rhythm. Another choral version of the theme treated freely in contrapuntal imitation is used for the third stanza 'Quibus', leading into the fourth stanza 'Se nascens' scored for three soloists which is more dramatic in character. The final stanza 'Uni trinoque' is scored for full chorus and orchestra ending with an 'Amen'.

The Hymn 'Pange Lingua' begins with a 24-bar orchestral introduction based on motives from the traditional plainsong melody. This is followed by the complete melody which is used for the first stanza (unaccompanied) and the fifth stanza (with organ accompaniment), with short orchestral interpolations between each line. The second stanza 'Nobis datus' is scored for six-part unaccompanied choir (SSATBB) with antiphonal phrases between the three upper and three lower voices. An orchestral section of 15 bars introduces the third stanza 'In supremæ nocte' scored for SATB which is mainly accompanied by the organ, interspersed with orchestral phrases and ends with a coda. After a 12-bar orchestral section the fourth stanza 'Verbum caro' is set as a duet for soprano and tenor with imitative entries. Each phrase is repeated by the choir and is accompanied by the orchestra throughout. A 14-bar orchestral section introduces the fifth stanza 'Tantum ergo'.

For the final stanza 'Genitori genitoque' Dixon uses both orchestral and vocal resources to the full, ending with an impressive fugal 'Amen', the theme of which is developed by inversion from that of the chorus 'Tu qui cunta' at the end of the 'Lauda Sion'.

The Sequence 'Lauda Sion' opens with a magnificent paean of praise which includes a duet 'Laudis thema specialis' for soprano and tenor in canonic style. This is followed by 'Dies enim solemnis agitur' sung by the chorus in a solemn style. The didactic parts of this glorious sequence are shared between the tenor and the bass interspersed with the occasional choral passage. Towards the end of this central section there are two solos, the first 'Nulla rei fit scissura' scored for tenor with an obligato for two oboes, reminiscent of the style of J S Bach, and second 'Ecce panis Angelorum' for soprano with harp accompaniment reminiscent of the Angels Song in Dixon's *Dream of Gerontius*. The Sequence ends with the Chorus 'Tu qui cuncta scis et vales' in which rich distinctive harmonies are woven round a ground bass (a similar descending motive can be found in the opening movement of the *Baroque Suite*).

In general the mood throughout the work is serene and meditative, with some joyful passages and the occasional dramatic moment.

There is evidence that the composer has assimilated aspects of the music of Palestrina, Mozart, Haydn, Brahms and Elgar, but nevertheless it is an original inspiring work of great emotional intensity.

With over a million people of all nationalities taking part in the Congress, a discussion took place as to the language in which the work should be sung. The solution was to use Latin, this being the official language of the Catholic Church at the time.

Later there was a discussion regarding the addition of English words for the Lauda Sion (and if so which translation to use), and also the two Motets 'O Quam Suavis' and 'O Sacrum Convivium'.

Both Hinrichsen and Dixon were at the IAO Congress held in Newcastle in August 1959 and Dixon took along some manuscript parts of the Oratorio to play to the delegates who gave the extracts their seal of approval.

By 25 September 1959 Dixon was ready to take his MSS of the vocal score to Max Hinrichsen's home where a small group of Catholic Church musicians met to listen to the work and offer their comments. This group included Mr H Swarsenski (promotional director of the Catholic Department at Peters), Edward de Rivera (Music Director of St John the Evangelist Islington), Gordon Phillips (well-known for his lunchtime organ recitals at All Hallows by the Tower), Robert E Munns and Donald Osgood. After the meeting the group went to Remos, a nearby restaurant for a meal.

Mr Swarsenski wrote to Dixon saying how much he enjoyed listening to the work and that it was an unforgettable experience. He also sent Dixon a bottle of Indian ink, pen, nibs and guidance notes on copying out the score so as not to compromise the photographic reproduction. Gordon Phillips wrote to thank Hinrichsen saying 'I enjoyed last evening immensely'.

An anonymous opinion of the work sent to Hinrichsen and copied to Dixon reads:

> In respect of the works previously used for this occasion which, according to Mr di Rivera [sic], were by Perosi and Refice, Dr. Dixon's composition appears to be particularly conservative in idiom and texture and although it may be well suited for the function for which it has been written in place of a less determined taste, the Munich public is used to the most advanced manifestations in all kinds of music. By the mere fact that so much music has been heard in that town, people may find literal analogies between Dr. Dixon's work and other very well known pieces and this perhaps even, though only style and texture is so utterly familiar to them and, on the whole, so much considered a thing of the past. Whereas Dr Dixon only intended to produce a composition to fulfil the functionary requirements of a beautiful service, in just that town which for many years has prided itself in being one of the most advanced in music, his honest desire to sacrifice his own personality to the purpose for which he has written, may be taken for a lack of originality and the passages in his work which are certainly legitimate inspirations justified by the style of the piece, may be taken for literal infiltrations derived from other sources and derided.[3]

Sometime later in a letter sent to Dixon and copied to Hinrichsen, Dr Alfons Ott writes

> Let me assure you that in our opinion the religious message of your work is more important than the purely aesthetic concerns of ultra-modern thinking musical experts. After all, your work is supposed to appeal to the people and not just to a small group of experts.[4]

At their meeting on Friday 9 October 1959 the Congress Committee decided to permit the Eucharistic Oratorio to form part of the Eucharistic Congress, subject to the acceptance of a covering reserve of DM 10,000 through the Congress Financial Committee.

---

3   Copy of letter, Dixon archive.
4   Letter, Dixon archive.

In a letter from Dr Ott to Hinrichsen the following three points were mentioned;
   a) The Music Commission is in agreement with the second scheme
   b) Time of the performance should fill the whole evening
   c) The Commission requests another effective Title such as 'The Bread of the People', 'The Bread of Life'

Designation 'Oratorium Eucharistica' should appear as a sub-title.[5]

The letter reveals further information. There was a query over whether an English Choir could study and perform the Oratorio with the German Orchestra. It was suggested that Dean Dixon conduct the work as he would be a colour witness to the World Union, but would the resemblance of the same surname as the composer lead to confusion? Hinrichsen is asked for his suggestion of a conductor. Another question was, 'Can the material be printed in time?' From an earlier letter there is evidence that a recording of Dixon's *Dream of Gerontius* (now lost) had been sent to Germany and it had created an extremely favourable impression.

Hinrichsen replies to Dr Ott informing him that apart from Edward de Rivera and the Choir of St John the Evangelist he knew of no other English people taking part in the Congress. Should he lend his choir to Dean Dixon? Hinrichsen goes on to suggest that Rivera could conduct the work. He had studied church music in Rome for three years and also studied with Nadia Boulanger.

From a letter Hinrichsen wrote to Dixon on 24 December 1959 it would appear that he had not heard from Munich.[6] In a Christmas card which Hinrichsen had received from Herr Adolf Hieber (Bürgermeister of Munich) it was stated that the musical matter had not been settled and caution was recommended. Hinrichsen found this rather puzzling since he assumed that the performance was going ahead. He concluded that if for whatever reason Munich did not now want the work it could be performed elsewhere.

Finally, on 26 January 1960 it was good news from Munich. Dr Ott in a letter to Dixon confirms that a guarantee of DM 10,000 has been granted by the Financial Committee. He concludes that while there are still decisions to be made regarding the participation of a German choir, the orchestra and the conductor, the Music Committee are happy that their negotiations have resulted in a positive outcome.[7]

In the meantime since Dixon's visit to London in September 1959 he had begun the final draft of the vocal score which was completed by 3 December. Dixon then wrote out the full orchestral score by hand and completed this by April 1960. Photostat copies of the full score having been made, the orchestral parts had to be written, the 'master part' for each instrument being proof read and corrected

---

5 Translation of letter, Dixon archive.
6 Letter, Dixon archive.
7 Letter, Dixon archive.

> EUCHARISTISCHER WELTKONGRESS
> MÜNCHEN 1960
>
> Kongreß-Saal im Deutschen Museum
> Sonntag, den 7. August 1960, 20 Uhr
>
> ## Panis vitae
>
> Eucharistisches Oratorium
> für Sopran, Tenor und Baß,
> gemischten Chor, Orchester und Orgel
> von
>
> **J. H. Reginald Dixon**
>
> (Uraufführung)
>
> AUSFÜHRENDE:
>
> **Noelle Barker (Sopran)**
> **Alfred Hallet (Tenor)**
> **John Frost (Baß)**
> **Shaun MacCarthy (Orgel)**
> **Der Chor der Church of St. John the Evangelist, London**
> **und Liedertafel Freising**
> **Einstudierung: Hanns Haas**
> **Das Bayerische Rundfunkorchester**
>
> LEITUNG:
> **Edward G. de Rivera (London)**
>
> Konzertvorbereitung:
> Bayerische Konzertdirektion Karl Gensberger

before printing. Dixon had some help from two first-class copyists employed by Hinrichsen who worked day and night to prepare the parts! At one stage there was a discussion regarding compressing the choir parts into two staves, but there was the question of what would happen in the few cases where the parts divided. By 2 June everything was ready and rehearsals were taking place in Munich and London.

Dr Ott writes to Dr Dixon saying 'German singers have great pleasure in singing your beautiful music.'[8] The wife of Herr Hieber was the owner of a Bavarian Music Shop and Hinrichsen agreed that scores of *Panis Vitae* and other works by Dixon could be distributed from the shop.

A bound copy of *Panis Vitae* was sent to Pope John XXIII and an acknowledgment was received from the Vatican.

---

8   Letter, Dixon archive.

The performance was to be transmitted by the Bavarian Broadcasting System and perhaps by others also. The Peters Office at Frankfurt asked for two full scores for the 'Tonmeister' as *Panis Vitae* would definitely be broadcast and a further full score went to Berlin. By 22 July all the parts had gone to Germany except the organ part which was with Shaun MacCarthy. It was intended that the whole Oratorio would be performed without an interval.

At the beginning of August 1960 Munich was ready for the 37th Eucharistic World Congress. This was the second time the Congress had been held in Germany, the previous one being held in 1909 at Cologne. The first World Congress took place in Lille in 1881 when approximately 3,000 Christians gathered for the event. Over the years the form has changed and for this Congress a million Christians assembled in Munich.

The World Première of *Panis Vitae* was given in the Concert Hall of the Museum on Sunday 7 August at 8 p.m. with Noelle Barker (Soprano), Alfred Hallet (Tenor), John Frost (Bass), Shaun MacCarthy (Organ), the Choir of St John the Evangelist, London, the Liedertafel Freising Choir (Choral Director Hanns Haas) and the Bavarian Broadcasting Orchestra. Hanns Haas conducted *a cappella* sections of the work. Edward de Rivera was to have conducted the work, but due to a sudden illness his place was taken by Professor Robert Heger.

The following extracts appeared in various German newspapers. One report which appeared in the *Aschaffenburger Volksblatt* ended with the following paragraph:

> The composer, a small elderly man with a distinguished white beard, who had some difficulty climbing onto the stage, received a standing ovation and was very emotional when he shook hands with the conductor and the soloists.[9]

Another description of Dixon was given in the *Süddeutsche Zeitung*:

> The elderly, touchingly endearing Englishman J H Reginald Dixon looked like a catholic relative of the old Sibelius, who had made the journey from a country behind the mountains, where the music stopped at 'Parsifal', Elgar or the sensitive interval leaps in the recitatives of Italian opera and the diminished seventh chord.

The report continues:

> Dixon clothes the mystery of the most Holy Sacrament of the Altar with voluptuous hymn technique from the 19th century, including surging passages for strings, expressive violin solos, noble polyphony and estatically blissful melodies. The shadows of Verdi, Wagner and Rossini appear behind thick

---

9   *Aschaffenburger Volksblatt*, 9 August 1960.

clouds of incense; the hymns rise through symphonic waves and the choral writing contains well-formed harmonies.[10]

As the Oratorio was specifically composed for the Congress, the music critic writing in the *Freisinger Tagblatt*[11] was expecting a modern composition with discords and other elements associated with a contemporary work. While being relieved that there were none of the expected traits, he was disappointed with the lack of originality and felt it was a pity that Dixon felt obliged to imitate the style of the old masters associated with the development of the Oratorio. The writer mentioned that 'it was a delight to listen to the richness of the Oratorio's solemn, enchanting and celebratory melodies, which were mostly given to the strings.' He singled out for praise the solo violinist and Robert Heger was also praised for taking over as conductor at short notice.

Earlier fears of problems arising from having two entirely different choirs were soon dispelled when they came together under the direction of Hanns Hass. Sensitive and precision production as well as the musicianship of each choir member contributed to form a perfect unity of German and English voices, even in the most difficult parts. The writer went on to say:

> The extensive and explosive applause showed that the music-loving public, today as well as in past times does not merely want absolute perfection but real and pure music. They love and respect melodies that reach out to their hearts, combining minds and souls beyond any linguistic boundaries.[12]

Karl-Robert Danler writing in the *Aschaffenburger Volksblatt* felt that there was an almost symbolic unity between the choirs and the orchestra and also commented that:

> The piece itself did not produce any new musical aspects, but it presented an unspoilt, honest, religious request, which enriches the Oratorio literature.[13]

In his opinion the choir under the direction of Hanns Haas, the soloists and the conductor Robert Heger gave a worthy performance.

The reporter for the *Münchner Merkur* mistook Professor Heger for Edward de Rivera and apologised for the error the following day, but the report contained another error. It was stated that the work was composed by Dean Dixon! He was mentioned in a letter from Hinrichsen to Dr Ott as a possible conductor and one can see how easy it is to confuse the two Dixon's, a point discussed at the time.

---

10 *Süddeutsche Zeitung*, 9 August 1960.
11 *Freisinger Tagblatt*, 10 August 1960.
12 Ibid.
13 *Aschaffenburger Volksblatt*, 10 August 1960.

Dixon received an appreciation of the work from Dr H Halm which reads as follows:

> I want to write you a few words of appreciation and gratefulness for the great impression which I owe your work. Every note of it comes from the heart, and is written not because it must be written for the purpose, and so to speak for the effect, though of course you have made great effect.
>
> But what one feels most is that the inspiration and the composition are the work of a man, who feels what he says as well with a single violin or as with a whole brass band, and that all these orchestral and choir means are used exactly where you felt them to be necessary for your inner reasons.
>
> That gives to the whole work the character of truthfulness, honesty and sincerity, which I could not help feeling from the first note to the last one. Would God, we had more composers like you![14]

Dixon in one of his witty moments wrote a little ditty for Dr Halm:

There once was a doctor named Halm who found music a wonderful balm, but the modern acetic, atonal and fretic would put all his nerves in a qualm!

Example 19, Music for Dr Halm

After the success of Munich arranging a London performance was not easy. Much discussion took place regarding finance, venue and resources. Efforts were made to enlist financial support, but none was forthcoming not even from the Arts Council. Mgr Fairhall of St John the Evangelist agreed to a loan of £400 which had to be paid back in full after the performance. This left Dixon to finance the performance himself with the help of his sister and donations from local friends. Various venues were suggested including the Festival Hall, but in the end it was decided to hire the Central Hall, Westminster. While the performance of such a work might have been

---

14 Dixon archive.

more suited to Westminster Cathedral or Brompton Oratory, Dixon did not think that the performance should necessarily be in a church. It was he who suggested the Central Hall, perhaps hoping to attract a wider audience, recollecting the links he had with this building having performed there in his younger days with J Arthur Meale and taking into account the financial outlay. Some people involved with the performance arrangements had reservations about this venue, observing that only a few concerts were held there and they were not usually well supported, even when the musicians were well-known. Regarding musicians, the Choir of St John the Evangelist with their conductor Edward de Rivera were available and it was hoped to engage the same soloists who sang in Munich. It would appear that at this time the London Catholic Choir and Orchestra had been disbanded due to lack of support and there was little cooperation between Catholic Church Musicians in London, therefore no support could be guaranteed. Initially the London Philharmonic Orchestra (LPO) was contacted and Mr Bravington Manager of the Orchestra at a meeting with Edward de Rivera and Mr Swarsenski outlined certain requirements regarding resources and cost.

> He felt that the minimum strings for a creditable performance of the score should be the provincial strength i.e. 12, 10, 8, 8, 6 which would bring the total musicians to 64.
> In view of the length of the work and the fact that the orchestra did not know the conductor, Bravington would only consider it safe if the performance would be prepared with one orchestral rehearsal alone, one subsequent rehearsal with choir and one general rehearsal on the morning of the concert. Thus the fee for the orchestra consisting of 64 musicians would be £340 plus £160 each for the two extra rehearsals, i.e. a total of £660.[15]

As Dixon was financing the performance himself this cost was unacceptable. Contact was then made with the London Symphony Orchestra and Ernest Fleischmann the Secretary in reply gave the following quote:

> Strings 10, 8, 6, 6, 4 which would make a total of 54 musicians in all. The fee would be £310 15s. 09d., with extra rehearsals £153 16s. 03d. each. It was also mentioned that the Diary was already extremely full.[16]

Eventually the Kennedy Symphony Orchestra (Strings 10, 8, 6, 4, 3, woodwind 2 flutes, 2 oboes, 2 clarinets and 2 bassoons, 4 horns, 2 trumpets, 3 trombones and 1 tuba in the brass section, percussion and harp making a total of

---

15 Letter from Swarsenski to Dixon, Dixon archive.
16 Letter, Dixon archive.

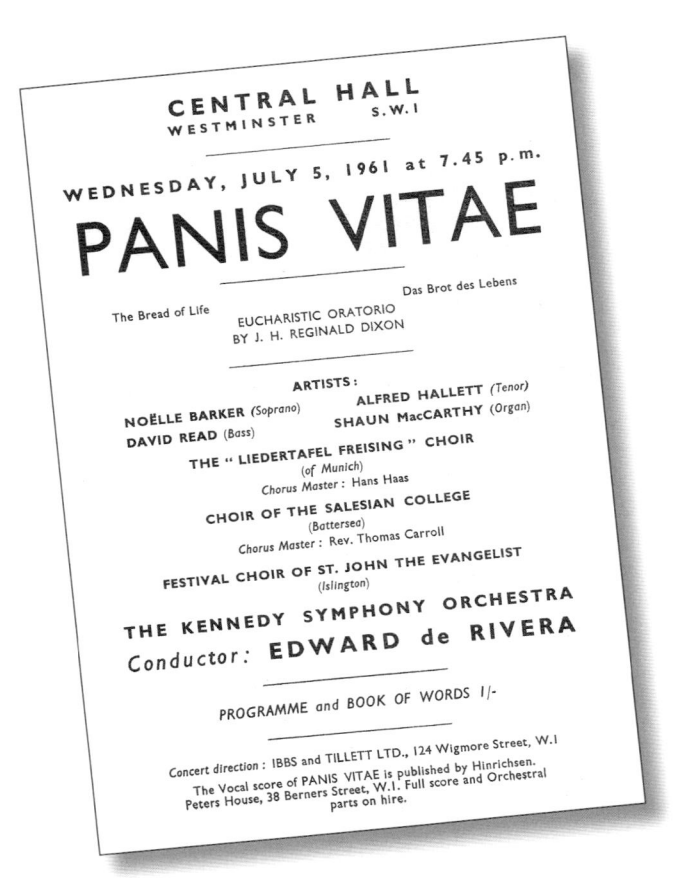

> **CENTRAL HALL**
> WESTMINSTER S.W.1
>
> WEDNESDAY, JULY 5, 1961 at 7.45 p.m.
>
> # PANIS VITAE
>
> The Bread of Life   Das Brot des Lebens
> EUCHARISTIC ORATORIO
> BY J. H. REGINALD DIXON
>
> ARTISTS:
> NOËLLE BARKER (Soprano)   ALFRED HALLETT (Tenor)
> DAVID READ (Bass)   SHAUN MacCARTHY (Organ)
>
> THE "LIEDERTAFEL FREISING" CHOIR
> (of Munich)
> Chorus Master: Hans Haas
>
> CHOIR OF THE SALESIAN COLLEGE
> (Battersea)
> Chorus Master: Rev. Thomas Carroll
>
> FESTIVAL CHOIR OF ST. JOHN THE EVANGELIST
> (Islington)
>
> THE KENNEDY SYMPHONY ORCHESTRA
> Conductor: EDWARD de RIVERA
>
> PROGRAMME and BOOK OF WORDS 1/-
>
> Concert direction: IBBS and TILLETT LTD., 124 Wigmore Street, W.1
> The Vocal score of PANIS VITAE is published by Hinrichsen.
> Peters House, 38 Berners Street, W.1. Full score and Orchestral parts on hire.

51 musicians) were engaged to play. This orchestra was specially formed for the occasion by Arthur Kennedy, Principal Viola and David McCallum, Leader who invited friends from leading London Orchestras to participate in the performance.

Ibbs and Tillet were asked to undertake the management of the Concert which they agreed to do. The total cost was approximately £1,000 which included hire fees for the Central Hall plus working expenses, fees for the soloists, the orchestra, choir expenses, management fees, publicity, tickets and programmes. Financially the performance just broke even.

The English première of the work was performed in London at the Central Hall Westminster on Wednesday, 5 July 1961 by the choirs of 'Liedertafel Freising', Munich, St John the Evangelist, Islington and Salesian College, Battersea, with soloists Noelle Barker (Soprano), Alfred Hallett (Tenor) and David Read (Bass), Shaun MacCarthy (Organist) and the Kennedy Symphony Orchestra conducted by Edward de Rivera.

Press reports of the work and this performance varied considerably. Comments on the conductor ranged from being 'carefully prepared' to being 'absorbed in the score, displaying a lack of coordination with the baton and poor communication with the singers.' While one critic thought the soloists were at their best, another

London performance of Panis Vitae
(Krishan Sharma, London)

commented on the poor production of one singer and the lack of clear diction from another. With regard to the professional orchestra, comments ranged from 'providing splendid support' to only 'adequate support.' The choir appeared to come out on top with the critics using such phrases as 'notable choral singing, impeccable tuning, clear precision in the plainsong passages and superb *a cappella* singing.'

DAWM writing in the Daily Telegraph said in his report:

> The composer has borrowed freely from the styles of the 19th century Italian and British choral writers. Even so there was no mistaking his skill in the setting of the words, his mastery of the medium and effective blend of recitatives, motets and hymns.[17]

While it was acknowledged that the performers and listeners were enthusiastic about the work JB the critic of *The Universe* wrote:

> From its Prœmium reminiscent of a more hopeful Wagner, through notions in the Lauda Sion which were worthy of Elgar at his best, to the romantic delicacy in the Pange Lingua which Ivor Novello would have been proud to have devised, delightful sound poured forth.[18]

---

17 *Daily Telegraph*, 6 July 1961.
18 *The Universe*, 14 July 1961.

Mavis Bacca writing in *The Tablet*[19] thought that the work displayed constant melodic invention and sustained interest in several parts.

According to Llifon Hughes-Jones writing in *Music and Musicians*[20] the work could have been written by any minor 19th century composer skilled in writing fluent vocal polyphony, but that apart the music is eminently singable.

The following comments were made by GM in *Musical Opinion,*

> The composer is undoubtedly a sincere musician who has carefully studied and absorbed his Verdi, Rossini, Elgar, Frank and Faure, but is almost completely lacking in invention, nearly every passage suggesting one or more of these composers. There is, too, considerable naiveté in the orchestration which is frequently so sugary as to become almost unbearable.[21]

It is true to say that all composers including well-known ones learn from one or more of their predecessors whether it is in compositional techniques, harmony, form or orchestration, and some are known to borrow melodic material intentionally or otherwise.

At any one time a new work would be expected to be written in the prevailing fashion, therefore to find that *Panis Vitae* composed in 1959 was in a late nineteenth-century style and furthermore a deeply religious work, it is perhaps understandable that it did not appeal to the critics.

Some London critics of the day maybe overlooked the fact that the work was commissioned for the Catholic World Eucharistic Congress and perhaps were not familiar with the historical religious background and spiritual significance of the text.

Criticism of any kind can only be judged fair when the critic has a true understanding of the background from where the 'seeds are sown' and views the composition as a whole.

On so many occasions the impression of a work on the listener can be affected by the building in which the performance takes place, as well as other criteria.

Mrs Beatrice Harrison, the composer's sister, wrote of the London performance:

> It was a truly magnificent performance, glorious and uplifting, with exquisite melodies and quiet passages, contrasted with the magnificent and majestic chorus particularly the finale—a fugal Amen.
>
> This is indeed an inspired masterpiece, as anyone who was privileged to hear it will agree, and although I may never live to see it, the day will surely dawn when 'Panis Vitae' will be acclaimed one of the world's great masterpieces long after its composer has passed hence.[22]

---

19 *The Tablet*, 15 July 1961.
20 *Music and Musicians*, August 1961.
21 *Musical Opinion*, August 1961.
22 *Lancaster Guardian*, 14 July 1961.

Sometime in 1961 Mr W Holden, Secretary of the Lancaster & District Musical Society wrote to the Town Clerk Mr J D Waddell suggesting that a performance of *Panis Vitae* should be given as a tribute to Dr Dixon and as a token of esteem from the City in recognition of his services for over fifty years as Organist to the Corporation. The City Council contributed to the event by giving a grant of £105 towards expenses and allowing free use of the Ashton Hall.

After months of preparation the performance of *Panis Vitae* took place in the Ashton Hall on Saturday, 6 April 1963. On this occasion the Lancaster Choral Society were augmented by the Ulverston Choral Society. The soloists for this first performance in the North of England were the same as for the London performance, Noelle Barker (Soprano), Alfred Hallett (Tenor), David Read (Bass) with Shaun MacCarthy as Organist. Herbert Horrocks conducted the Musical Society Orchestra with David Greenless as Leader and Constance Harper of the BBC (Harpist). The orchestra on this occasion was larger than usual being reinforced with professional musicians to create the right balance between singers and instrumentalists.

As the performance had received civic patronage it was attended by the Mayor and Mayoress (Ald. and Mrs E Gardener) with other members of the City Council, Earl and Countess Peel, Rev. Canon B Foley (RC Bishop of Lancaster), Canon H A Bland (Vicar of Lancaster Priory), Mr H Berkeley (MP for Lancaster) and Alderman W J Garnett (President of the Lancaster and District Musical Society).

An encore of the final chorus was conducted by the composer in response to the great ovation received.

A writer for the *Evening Post* referred to the performance as a memorable event in the cultural life of the city. He went on to describe the performance as,

> Highly commendable in a musical sense because in effect it was breaking new ground and the language barrier did not reduce the sincere character and deep religious significance which the oratorio represents in contemporary art.[23]

In contrast to the London critics Arnold Dowbiggin, music critic for the *Lancaster Guardian,* made the following comments:

> It is a great work and an impressive one, within the rather severe limitations of the medium. The dignity of the Latin text is expressed with admirable lucidity and without a trace of padding. Avoiding the obstinate adulation of the outmoded clichés of the 19th century and with understatement which is hardly characteristic in the maelstrom of contemporary music, Dr Dixon has here provided an oasis of gentle sanity in a world bent upon the strident expression of trivialities best buried. Any branch of music which becomes

---

23 *Lancashire Evening Post*, Monday 8 April 1963.

Lancaster performance of Panis Vitae (Reproduced by kind permission of Lancaster Guardian and the Lancaster Choral Society)

too separate from the main growth will rot, and it is up to Dr Dixon and composers of his calibre to face this responsibility. It was obvious throughout that the music drew its strength from conviction derived with sincere perception of the textual implications.[24]

Although some of the choral parts were a little insecure Dowbiggin felt that the choir gave a sincere and refined performance. He thought the orchestral playing was particularly impressive in the Preludes and Constance Harper made a skilful contribution throughout the score. All three soloists performed to a high standard individually and blended well together when required. Shaun MacCarthy provided an inspiring organ accompaniment. Miss Betty Wilson had made a valuable contribution to the performance by training the choir. Herbert Horrocks with one combined rehearsal had the choir and orchestra under firm control and gave a fine interpretation of the work.

Dowbiggin recalled many memorable moments:

> The 'Verbum Supernum' with the telling incursion of the soloists, the 'Ecce Panis Angelorum' with Miss Barker in splendid voice and the 'Verbum Caro' perhaps the best singing of the evening. The passages for voices in unison with the flavour of plainsong, were adroitly interspersed and made a logical punctuation of the score. A score in which nothing is wasted, nothing is allowed to interrupt the natural flow of the music or to

---

24 *Lancaster Guardian*, Thursday 11 April 1963.

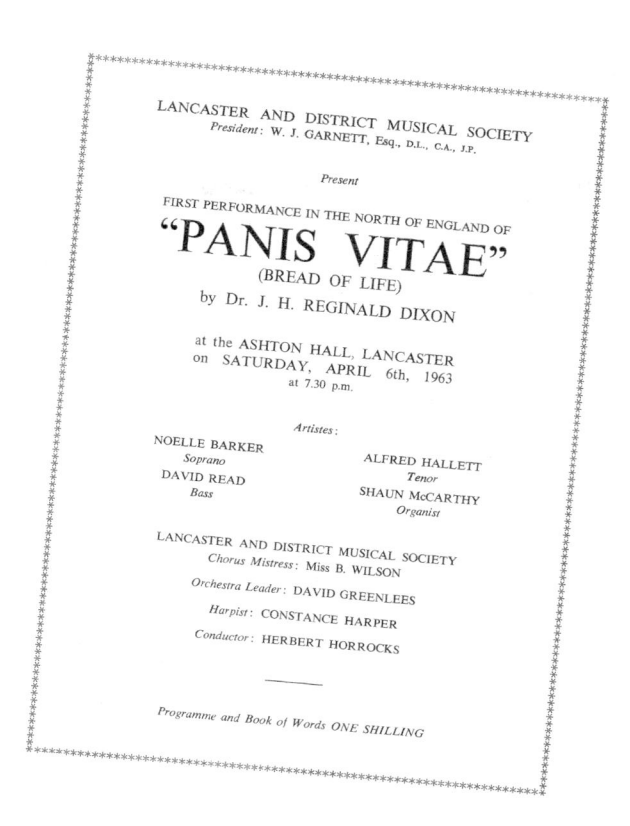

```
*************************************************************
*  LANCASTER AND DISTRICT MUSICAL SOCIETY                    *
*     President: W. J. GARNETT, Esq., D.L., C.A., J.P.       *
*                                                             *
*                       Present                               *
*                                                             *
*       FIRST PERFORMANCE IN THE NORTH OF ENGLAND OF          *
*                   "PANIS VITAE"                             *
*                    (BREAD OF LIFE)                          *
*                by Dr. J. H. REGINALD DIXON                  *
*                                                             *
*              at the ASHTON HALL, LANCASTER                  *
*               on SATURDAY, APRIL 6th, 1963                  *
*                       at 7.30 p.m.                          *
*                                                             *
*                       Artistes:                             *
*        NOELLE BARKER              ALFRED HALLETT            *
*           Soprano                     Tenor                 *
*         DAVID READ                SHAUN McCARTHY            *
*            Bass                       Organist              *
*                                                             *
*           LANCASTER AND DISTRICT MUSICAL SOCIETY            *
*              Chorus Mistress: Miss B. WILSON                *
*           Orchestra Leader: DAVID GREENLEES                 *
*              Harpist: CONSTANCE HARPER                      *
*            Conductor: HERBERT HORROCKS                      *
*                                                             *
*                        ———                                  *
*                                                             *
*      Programme and Book of Words ONE SHILLING               *
*************************************************************
```

disturb its basic mood, and both thought and atmosphere are sustained with a skill and self-discipline rare in music today.[25]

A life-long friend of Dr Dixon, Arnold Dowbiggin ended his report on the performance as follows:

> My last word must be of 'Reggie' Dixon, a term not of familiarity but of affectionate regard. In 'Panis Vitae' he has created a considerable work of art of which his fellow musicians and the City of Lancaster can be justly proud. It was fitting that this performance by a local society should have been used as an occasion to do him honour.[26]

DCF in his report on the performance of *Panis Vitae* (source unknown) writes:

> 'Panis Vitae', the third performance of which we were privileged to hear in the Ashton Hall, Lancaster, a work which though it owes something to the

---

25 Ibid.
26 Ibid.

music of the past, is nonetheless a very personal and inspired utterance, and expresses the view of the Eucharist seen through the eyes of a man, who, in the evening of his life, has set to music all that it means to him.[27]

This critic was not impressed by the orchestra, which he thought was not on its best form, but he gave the chorus much praise. He had this to say about the soloists:

Noëlle Barker, soprano sang feelingly and with purity of tone, occasionally marred by a tendency to slide, and David Read, bass, although somewhat sibilant at times, was pleasingly resonant. Alfred Hallett sang memorably.[28]

The writer referred to the work as being memorable for melody:

Dr Dixon does not wring a tune dry of all its possibilities nor does he truncate it before it has said something. In these days when two staccato C's form an entire melodic line, it is refreshing to hear a new piece of music whose composer is unashamed of melody.[29]

In works other than those with a liturgical connection where Dixon has free expression, his style varies depending on the medium for which the piece is written and the date of the composition.

Dixon was not the only composer of the twentieth century who was inspired to write lyrical melodies and use conventional harmonies.

After the London performance efforts were made to organise further performances in various towns and cities throughout the country, including York, Hereford, Gloucester and Worcester but apart from the Lancaster performance in 1963 no other full performance to date has taken place. Serious attempts were made by Edward de Rivera in 1988/89 to mount a performance in St Peter's Cathedral, Lancaster, but sadly the project was unsuccessful partly due to financial problems. Extracts from the work have been performed at St John the Evangelist Islington where Edward de Rivera was Music Director and at the Oratory in Oxford where Rivera is currently Music Director.

At the time of writing it is fifty years since *Panis Vitae* was first performed. In this rapidly changing world with the stresses and strains of modern living, many people of today are searching for that something which is missing in their lives and choral music with a religious text, instruction and lyrical melodic appeal could once more prove to be popular.

---

27 Dixon archive.
28 Ibid.
29 Ibid.

THE AUTUMNAL YEARS

IN THE EARLY 1960s Dixon was still busy composing, teaching and taking an active part in the musical life of the city.

The *Mass of St John the Evangelist* composed in March 1961 was specially written for Edward de Rivera and the Choir of St John the Evangelist, Islington, London to be performed for the Feast of the Dedication in June of that year. This work comprising six movements is scored for a five part choir (SSATB), four soloists (SATB) and organ accompaniment. Thematically each movement is based on a phrase from the Gregorian setting of the Vesper Hymn set for the Feast of St John the Apostle and Evangelist, 'Exultet orbis gaudiis'.

Example 20, Exultet orbis gaudiis

Theme A with which the melody begins is used in the 'Kyrie eleison' and the 'Agnus Dei'. The 'Gloria' and the 'Sanctus' are based on theme B, and theme C can be found in the 'Benedictus'. Theme D is one of the key motifs in the 'Credo'.

Several works dating from this period and others composed in earlier times, some having been revised, were of interest to publishers.

A work originally written for piano in 1911–12 entitled *Impromptu* was later arranged for organ by Dixon under the title *Nachtspiel*. The final version of the piece was published by Hinrichsen in 1962 entitled *Festival Postlude in G major* for organ and dedicated to Dr Francis A Jackson. This work exploits to the full all the resources of any instrument. It contains striking harmonies, contrapuntal passages with a contrasting middle section of antiphonal phrases and builds up to a thrilling climax with double pedalling, full chords, use of solo tuba if available and ends with a flourish of chords played prestissimo.

Several miniature pieces were published by Carrara of Bergamo, Italy in their monthly series of organ/harmonium and choral music. The first of these was *Solemn Procession* composed in May 1958 and published in the 1961 December issue of *Le Armonie dell' Organo* per l'azione liturgica. This was followed by a calm, expressive piece dating from June 1958 entitled *Aspiration* for manuals only included in *L'organista D'oggi*, May/June 1964. The solo melody, based on a plainsong-like motive appears in the left hand throughout and is played on a 16ft Bordone stop with a right hand accompaniment comprising sustained chords played on a 4ft Flauto stop. Also in 1964 a two-part Motet 'Ecce Sacerdos Magnus' for equal voices composed in 1938 appeared in the July/August edition of *Ecclesia Cantat*. The following year in October a *Toccata* written at the same time as *Aspiration* was published in *L'organista D'oggi*. This piece, dedicated to Joan Carter, was designed as a lesson to students in how to write a two-part invention.

An Anthem *I Rejoiced* was composed in October 1966 for a recital of organ and choral music to be given in aid of the Royal College of Organists Centenary Appeal. The recital should have taken place at St Peter's Cathedral in January 1967 with Dr Dixon at the organ and the Lancaster Priory Choir under the direction of their choirmaster Henry Walmsley. Unfortunately several of the boys were ill, so the recital was postponed until after Easter. The work is scored for SATB choir (with divisi parts for tenors, basses and sopranos), a soprano soloist and organ accompaniment.

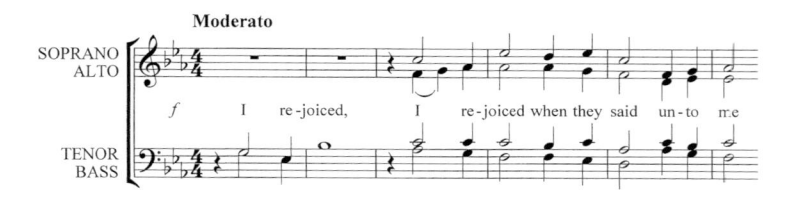

Example 21, I Rejoiced, bars 8–13

Dixon composed a new piece for organ in 1967 entitled *Vignettes* with the motto 'New wine for old bottles' (N.B. This 'wine' has been specially prepared so that it will not burst the bottles!) The piece comprises nine paraphrases on the Psalm Tune 'Coleshill' (London 1711), Prélude, Thème, Andante, Trompette, Cascade, Pastorale, Caprice, Cortège, Scherzando and Finale. Registration for the piece is indicated in both Continental and English terms and ideally requires a four manual instrument.

The Second Vatican Council (1962–65) initiated some fundamental changes, including reform of the Liturgy which now became said or sung in the mother tongue. While disappointed at the passing of the Latin, Dixon, true to his faith and wishing to conform, set about composing an English Mass in honour of *Christ the King*. The work, completed in May 1967, has six movements and is scored for a four-part choir (SATB) and congregation, but may be sung in unison throughout with organ accompaniment. There is a separate melodic line part for the congregation. It is interesting to note that the 'Kyrie' begins with the same thematic material as the 'Kyrie' in *The Dream of Gerontius*. Dixon set some responses for the Preface dated May 1968, as well as a Eucharistic Acclamation 'Christ has died' dated March 1969 which is set antiphonally for cantor (choir) and congregation in F major and G major. It is not clear if these were intended to be used with this Mass. Early sketches dating from 1967 of another English Mass which was to be Dixon's last work became known as the *Boarbank Mass*. There are two completed Eucharistic Acclamations for this Mass, 'Christ has died' and 'Dying you destroyed our death', both in A major using similar thematic material dated 24 February 1971 (the first one being a transposed version of the 1969 Acclamation mentioned above). While spending some time in convalescence in 1972 at the Convent of our Lady of Lourdes, Boarbank Hall, Grange-over-Sands, Cumbria (a place where Dixon had been on several occasions since 1965), he completed four movements of the Mass and dedicated it to the Convent.

Example 22, Kyrie from the Boarbank Mass, bars 1–2

At a later date Dixon added a Gloria and Creed composed in chant style to be sung in free rhythm, as well as four Eucharistic Acclamations (melodic line only). These Acclamations, all in various keys and with contrasting thematic material, are quite different from those composed in 1971. The Mass with organ accompaniment was intended for unison singing, but some parts could be sung in harmony. A copy of the manuscript comprising the six movements and incomplete acclamations is dated May 1973. The whereabouts of the original manuscript is unknown.

Dixon's compositions comprise a kaleidoscopic palette influenced by studying and performing many styles of music. He composed when inspired to do so, or when a particular piece was requested for a specific occasion. Some compositions were developed from an improvisation given at a recital. Dixon did not change his style of composing to follow fashion, but rather wrote the melody and harmony to suit the form and medium which came from his utmost inner feeling at different times in his life.

Speaking about the organ in one of his lectures Dixon said:

> The organ is not an instrument which is capable of much expression in detail as the violin or piano for instance, but it is undoubtedly capable of exercising great emotional effect on human beings. This power is exercised partly through the magnificent volume of continuous sound that it is capable of producing, partly through its ability to adapt its dynamic effects through gradation of tone from a mere whisper to a thrilling fortissimo at the instant demand of the organist as occasion needs, and partly through its long association with aspirations which are deeply rooted in human nature.[1]

Having been predicted a bright future by many who heard him in his younger days, could it be that he was passed by for the top positions due to the fact that he did not study at Oxford, Cambridge, or a Music College? Was his domestic situation in the early 1920s a disadvantage to securing a new post? Some may view his conversion to the Catholic Faith as a limitation on his career, but conversely it was his faith which inspired him to compose such works as *The Dream of Gerontius* and *Panis Vitae,* several Masses and Motets.

He was a brilliant organist, popular recitalist, an accomplished musician noted for his accompanying of oratorios and soloists both vocal and instrumental, as well as being a recognised local, national and international composer. Through his association with the IAO, writing articles and his earring theory he became a well-known personality worldwide.

Many people remember Dr Dixon as a grey/white haired bearded figure with his gold earrings, high-heeled shoes and a tripping gait, but he was born a redhead and in his youth was a dapper young man with curly hair.

From 1964 onwards Dixon suffered several periods of ill health and was often in hospital. On one occasion in 1965 he suffered a severe attack of pneumonia and bronchitis from which he was not expected to recover, but he rallied round and continued to play the organ and compose whenever he felt well enough.

In 1968 Dixon made his twenty-fifth visit to Lourdes, the first being in 1924. Whenever he returned home after a pilgrimage to Lourdes he would always wear a French béret for several weeks or even months.

A special Mass was held in May 1969 to celebrate his completion of 60 years as Organist and he received many letters and telegrams congratulating him on such an achievement. Although he officially retired in 1971, becoming Organist Emeritus, as mentioned earlier he was well enough to organise a concert of his music to celebrate the opening of the IAO Congress held at Lancaster in 1972.

Throughout his busy life he still found time to attend concerts and recitals given by fellow musicians.

---

1 Lecture notes, Dixon archive.

Lunehurst

Dr Dixon was a man of private means dealing in stocks and shares, but he was not a wealthy man. His faith, life, music and friends were far more important to him than money or material possessions.

From 1953 he shared Lunehurst with his sister Beatrice who attempted to take him in hand, but he had always been a very independent person from a young age and continued to do exactly as he pleased.

Many past pupils and friends will remember the Music Room. There were three instruments, a Mustel harmonium and two pianos, one a Bechstein grand and the other an upright pianola. Shelves of books and scores lined a section of two walls. Other items in the room were a bureau, a wireless, an ancient typewriter, an old settee under the window and most important a card table on which all the scores were written.

From being a young boy he was very fond of cats as seen in the family photograph taken at School House, Stockton-on-the-Forest and he always had one or more of them in the house. Bubbles, one of his favourite cats and a faithful companion during the long hours it took to write out the orchestral and vocal score of *Panis Vitae*, sadly died of old age on 28 December 1960. By 1964 Peter, a tabby, had come into the household as a stray and in the latter years there were two young cats, Fluffy the second and Sooty.

Enjoying a drink at the bar (Dixon archive)

In an evening Dr Dixon could often be found in a local hostelry having a half of bitter or a whisky, smoking a cigarette or a cigar and sometimes he was seated at the bar where a radio would be broadcasting the latest pop song from a loudspeaker near his ear. Interviewed by David Blundell he expressed strong opinions about modern 'pop' music.

> I think its rubbish. It is a low class of taste, the subjects of the songs limited, the words trite and the music itself on a similar level. I don't think it will last and it is just the same as modern dances, with a new one every few weeks. There is nothing in its nature to keep it alive.[2]

Although he could be outspoken and make controversial statements on certain topics which often attracted media attention when attending the Organists' Congress, he took his appointments on committees seriously and made a valuable contribution to those organisations of which he was a member.

During his lifetime Dr Dixon was the President of numerous local groups, including the Reform Club, the Rotary Club, the Catenian Association of which he was also a founder member and the Lancaster and District Organists' and Choirmasters' Association. He was also an Honorary Life Member of the Lancaster and District Music Society having accompanied the Choir for many years in their annual performance of Handel's *Messiah* at Christmas and other works performed at their spring concerts. During his association with the Society he worked closely

---

2 *Lancashire Evening Post*, 21 March 1963.

Doctor Dixon in his Doctorate Robes. (Dixon archive)

with honorary conductor Herbert Horrocks and chorus mistress Betty Wilson who later became conductor.

Apart from the honour bestowed upon him by the Pope, Dixon never received any official local or national acknowledgement for his services to music.

Dr Dixon was a very kind and generous person. He was a humble man and as a mark of respect always paused and doffed his hat whenever a funeral cortège passed him in the street.

In his younger days Dixon always enjoyed playing practical jokes and sharing jokes in any company. He always had a twinkle in his eye and his sense of humour could also be found in his letter writing.

After the Lancaster Congress in 1972 Dr Dixon's health declined and in 1973 he suffered a slight stroke which meant that he was confined to the house.

In 1974 Francis Kitts, who had taken over the Ainscough firm in 1973, and Jack Ainscough visited Dr Dixon regarding the proposed rebuild of the Cathedral organ. They took a selection of pipes in a basket for Dixon's approval. Kitts gives a description of Dr Dixon as they found him:

> Dixon dressed Druid-like in a long white robe, sat alongside his sick bed on
> a high backed commode, like Canute on the seashore. Here was a shadow of

Requiescat in pace.
(photo by kind permission of the Dean, Lancaster Cathedral)

the man with the same name as the organist from Blackpool Tower. He did his consultancy bit, finishing with apologies, by blowing a Walls of Jericho blast on a fruity trumpet treble. This effort caused his partial collapse, with Jack and me thinking he was about to breathe his last.[3]

James Hugh Reginald Dixon died at home in the early hours of Saturday morning 3 May 1975. On the following Tuesday evening he was received into the Cathedral and a concelebrated Requiem Mass was held on Wednesday 7 May at 10.00 a.m. In accordance with his wish Dr Dixon was laid to rest in the Cathedral cemetery in the same grave as Laurenz Schmitz.

---

3 Author's archive.

Postscript

Amongst Dixon's collection of newspaper cuttings was the following: Ronald Settle writing in the *Liverpool Evening Express*, 28 November 1949 on Music and Musicians tells of a story about an eminent musician who noticed a tombstone bearing the inscription:

> Here lies the body of a brilliant organist and a fine musician.

Turning to his companion he remarked: 'Fancy putting them both in the same grave!'

Did this give Dixon the idea of being buried in the same grave as Schmitz?

While realising that work needed to be done on the organ Dr Dixon would be greatly saddened by the changes which were made to the instrument after his death, particularly the loss of the historic console and change of position. The console, a rare example of its type in the country could and should have been saved. An inexperienced organist would find this console difficult to handle, therefore if a modern one was required then at least the old one should have been preserved either in the Cathedral or in a museum. Dixon regarded the Cathedral organ as a delightful instrument ideally suited to the building. For beauty of tone and wealth of effective combinations of stops no other organ of comparable size gave Dixon greater pleasure to play than this one.

In 1975 the contract for restoration of the Cathedral organ was awarded to Pendelbury and Co Ltd of Cleveleys. The instrument was cleaned and overhauled, worn mechanical parts renewed, a new electro-pneumatic action replaced the old one and the original console was discarded for a modern one with an array of pistons, as well as being re-sited in a new position with the organist facing south. For reasons unknown the wind pressures which were variable appeared to have been altered to become the same throughout which would certainly alter the character of the instrument, particularly the swell reeds. In a report entitled 'Swell job finished at Cathedral' (source unknown) it states 'all the original pipe work has been retained'. However it is thought that some changes did occur, the pedal violoncello becoming a principal and it is not clear why Pendelbury's altered the two great organ diapason stop names from large and small open to major and minor. The work took eleven weeks to complete at a cost of £6,500 and the instrument was in full working order for Christmas 1975. Mr Noel Smith of Cartmel Priory gave a recital on Saturday 2 February 1976 to celebrate the restoration of the organ.

Since 1999 several organs with which Dixon was associated have undergone restoration. The organ he first played at Holy Trinity Church, Stockton-on-the-Forest in 1896 was restored by Principal Pipe Organs of York in 1999. As well as replacing worn action parts tonal changes were made to the Swell. A Gedact 8, Octave 4 and Fifteenth 2 replaced the Violin Diapason 8, Salicional 8 and Salicet 4 (sadly the latter was the stop added to the organ in 1951 by Dr Dixon, his brother and sister in memory of their parents).

The organ in the Ashton Hall is in the process of being restored. A rebuild of the Great Organ took place in 2006 by Principal Pipe Organs of York and a new electrical system for the blower was installed by Lancaster City Council in March 2007. Between July and September 2008 the case was restored to its former glory by a retired French Polisher (who was employed by Gillow & Co., the original makers of the case) and an apprentice. In November 2009 new console lighting was installed. The next phase will include full restoration of the Swell Organ.

Before leaving York in 1909, Dixon gave a recital at York Presbyterian Church, now known as St Columba's United Reformed Church with Lendal. The fine Thomas C Lewis organ of 1907 has recently been restored by Andrew J Carter of Wakefield and the Inaugural Recital given by Simon Lindley took place on Sunday 31 May 2009.

An appeal was launched in 2005 to raise funds for a major restoration of the Cathedral organ. The contract to rebuild the instrument was awarded to Henry Willis & Sons of Liverpool, who completed the work in June 2009. All the leather work has been renewed, new sound boards made, pipe work restored, a new solid state action installed and a splendid new continental style terraced console has been built. The Choir Orchestral Oboe was replaced by a 2' Piccolo adding more colour and versatility to the Choir Organ. One of the improvements Dixon wished to see in 1909 was a Swell Flute. Due to lack of space it was decided to make the Swell Bourdon 16' playable at 8' pitch and also extend the pedal department to make the Bourdon playable at 16 8 4 and Quint. The Great Trumpet is now playable from the Choir and a new solo Trompette playable from both Great and Choir is an exciting addition to an instrument noted for its fine reeds. In addition to the usual divisional, combination pistons and toe pistons, the instrument is fitted with the latest technology of memory, sequencer and midi features. Through the craftsmanship, skills and dedication of the work force the instrument is now restored to its former glory. Dr Dixon would be proud and appreciative of those who had the courage to undertake such an immense project and all the donors who have made this restoration possible.

The new Willis organ console 2009 (by kind permission of the Dean, Lancaster Cathedral)

It would have been a disappointment to him that so many organists have come and gone during the last thirty years, but a new chapter began when the Very Rev. Canon Stephen Shield (Dean) who is also an organist came to the Cathedral in 2003. An adult choir and the appointment in 2008 of a new Organist and choirmaster Damian Howard, who has recruited an enthusiastic group of young choristers, all bodes well for the future.

2009 was another momentous year for the Cathedral as several special events were organised to celebrate the 150th Anniversary of the Consecration. In addition to special services events included an exhibition, a flower festival, concerts, literary and dramatic presentations and the visit of the relics of St Thérèse. On the Cathedral web site a special feature was the Billington Blog in the form of a diary which recalled many historic events and those who had links with the church in the past. A Festival of Music including a power point presentation, a concert and an organ recital devoted to the life and works of Dr Dixon was held at the Cathedral in May to mark the centenary of his appointment as organist and choirmaster. The concert presented by local musicians, included the Lancaster Choral Society and guest artists, some who knew him and some for whom singing and playing his music was a new experience. This event was attended by friends who remembered him and whose support was much appreciated.

It was also the centenary of two other well-known landmarks associated with the local philanthropist Lord Ashton: the Ashton Memorial which was opened to the public in October 1909 and the Town Hall building which includes the Ashton Hall. Dixon made his first appearance at the Ashton Hall Organ (also a gift from Lord Ashton) during the opening celebrations and became Municipal Organist, a post which he held for life.

In his will Dr Dixon left a bequest to the Royal College of Organists for a prize to be awarded to the Fellowship candidate gaining the highest mark in the improvisation test, the maximum qualifying mark being 12. This legacy and that of his compositions, teaching, lecturing and performing should ensure that the memory of this legendary figure will live on and that his music will receive due recognition.

Appendix

The Dream of Gerontius

The original 1943 score begins with a Prelude marked Largo. After two bars introduction in which the woodwind and strings (tremolo) play the note B, the trumpet announces the theme (Example 1a) set to the words 'Tuba mirum spargens sonum' in the *Dies irae* from the plainsong Requiem Mass. This theme acts as a *leitmotiv*. A short second and third phrase from the *Dies irae* (example 1b and 1c), is then taken up by the strings and woodwind, followed by a more extended theme (example 1d). These themes also occur in other movements throughout the work.

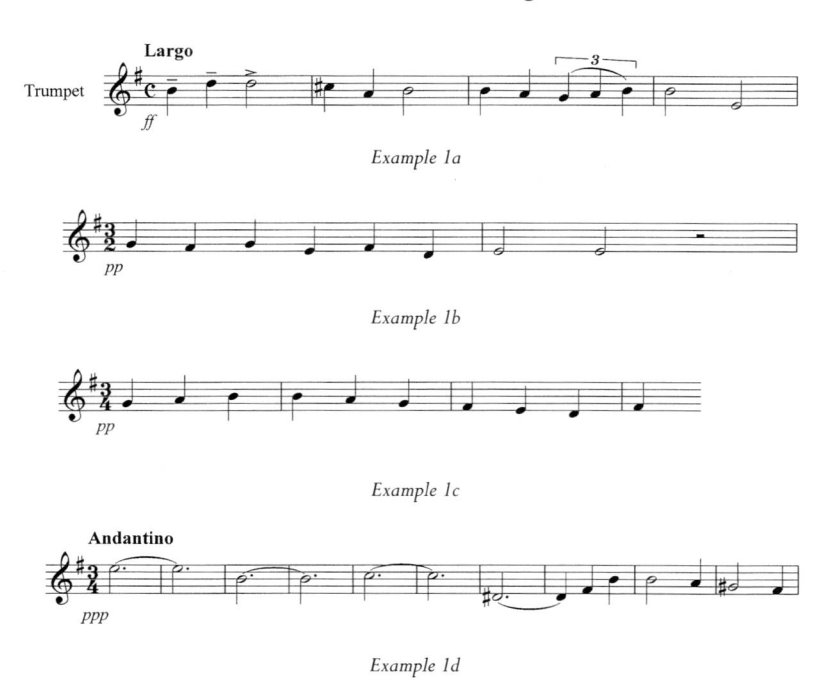

Example 1a

Example 1b

Example 1c

Example 1d

The 'Kyrie' consists of a slow rising and falling melodic phrase in minims over a crotchet moving bass part (example 2), followed by a litany in choric speaking with instrumental accompaniment, and ends with a repeat of the 'Kyrie'.

Example 2

In the next movement 'Be merciful, be gracious; spare him, Lord', the theme (example 3) is treated imitatively in the instrumental parts which are interwoven around the unison melody.

Example 3

The fourth movement 'Sanctus Fortis' (example 4) in D major is a long sustained melody over a chordal accompaniment. It is sung three times, interspersed with choric speaking of the well-known text 'Firmly I believe and truly', which is accompanied throughout and ends with an instrumental repeat of the theme.

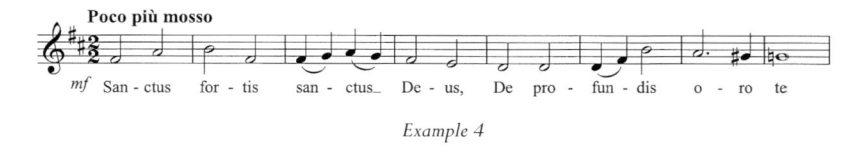

Example 4

The next movement 'Rescue him' (example 5), begins with a similar rhythmic figure to that used in 'Be merciful', and after each line of the Litany has been intoned by a soloist over a simple chordal accompaniment ending with an Amen sung by the choir, the music of the first section is repeated for the remaining text.

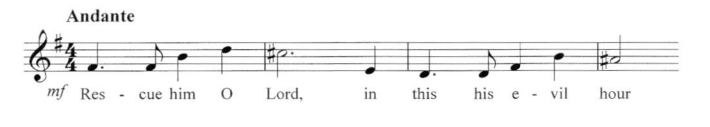

Example 5

A tremolo chord signals a change of mood and tempo to Lento and as Gerontius speaks the words 'Novissima hora est; and I fain would sleep; The pain has wearied me…. Into Thy hands, O Lord, into Thy hands….' reference is made in the accompaniment to the first three themes stated in the Prelude. A short instrumental movement of twenty bars accompanies the text beginning at the words 'Go from this world', which ends the first act. Here reference is made to a motive which appears in the Chorus of Angelicals (example 6).

Example 6

The Entr'acte and the last movement the Angel's Farewell have several features in common. Both are in the same key of B flat major and have the same long descending bass line which appears at the beginning of the Entr'acte and the end of the Angel's Farewell. There is also a similarity of thematic material in the opening bars of both movements (example 7 and 8). Does example 7 have a hint of the well-known lullaby *Golden Slumbers*?

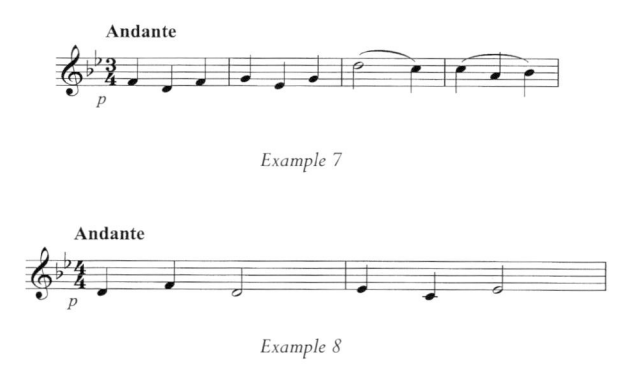

Example 7

Example 8

At the words 'And surely I heard a priestly voice Cry 'Subvenite'; and they knelt in prayer' there is a repeat of the opening bars of 'Rescue him'. One of the most spiritually moving sections of the work referred to in Chapter 8 is the 'Angel's Song'. This movement has a nine-bar introduction based on arpeggiated chords intended for the harp, accompanied by the strings playing *pizzicato* crotchets. The vocal line begins with four short phrases based on the opening four notes which are perfectly wedded to the text (example 9), each phrase punctuated by a rest before developing into a long high soaring phrase.

[Musical notation: Moderato, with lyrics "My work is done, my task is o'er. And so I come taking it home, For the crown is won, Al-le-lu-ia,"]

Example 9

A mime with music for piano solo illustrates the monologue spoken by the Angel ('O what a shifting parti-coloured scene of hope and fear, of triumph and dismay, of recklessness and penitence') performed by members of the cast representing all the emotions mentioned in the text. The music written in 9/8 consists of a series of ever changing arpeggiated dominant and diminished 7th chords. After the first ten bars there is a short cantabile melodic line which appears again at the end. All these features reflect the nature of the text. There are further spoken parts from the Soul and the Angel before movement eleven which is entitled 'Subvenite', this being a repetition of the second half of the third movement beginning with the words 'Spare him, Lord.' The lower strings play *pizzicato* this time. A theme from the first ballet is used for the entry of the demons (example 10).

[Musical notation: Con brio, pp]

Example 10

Ballet 1, entitled 'Temptation Triumphant' is in the style of a Gavotte, representing carefree mortals who are tempted by the demons to whom they yield and are overcome by remorse (example 11).

[Musical notation: Tempo di Gavotta, mf]

Example 11

The music begins in a stately manner, but soon breaks into a con brio section consisting of quaver and semi-quaver scale passages punctuated by short jagged accented *fortissimo* phrases, ending with the demon theme. After a lento section of short melodic fragments played *piano* and *pianissimo* there is a vivo passage with short scale fragments. A 16 bar section with a long sustained melody against a crotchet moving bass reminiscent of the Kyrie and a coda bring the movement to an end.

In the second ballet 'Temptation Conquered' marked Andante Grazioso, the mortals now in different costumes are tempted by the demons, but pray and resist them (example 12).

Example 12

The demons strive with ever increasing force to the climax of the movement, but the mortals prevail and the demons exit. At the words 'Before the dread tribunal' the judgment theme (example 1a) is played by the trumpet only. From indications in the score, the organ plays a four bar introduction after the words 'Hark to these sounds!' This introduces the first Chorus of the Angelicals which is sung off stage (example 13).

Example 13

The Praise Chorus, with its majestic and impressive tune is then repeated several times on stage, interspersed with spoken text from the Angel, the Soul and the Greek Chorus. Within this section there is an organ solo which accompanies the text beginning with the words 'But hark! a deeper, mysterious harmony.' At the words 'I hear the voices that I left on earth' the Kyrie is played. Music for the Judgment Scene is a repeat of the opening 50 bars from the Prelude plus the coda.

The verses of Psalm 90 ('Lord, Thou hast been our refuge') are intoned with verse 8 'Come back O Lord' being repeated three times thus acting as a sung response (example 14).

[musical example: Andante, mf, "Come back, O Lord! O Lord! how long:"]

Example 14

Following straight on from the psalm is the 'Angel's Farewell' (example 15) in which the vocal line is accompanied by the theme referred to above (example 8). Of the four stanzas the first two are sung and the last two spoken.

[musical example: Andante, pp, "Soft-ly and gent-ly dear-ly ran-somed soul,"]

Example 15

The movement ends with the descending bass line mentioned earlier (example 16) and as the curtains close the last 27 bars of the Entr'acte are played.

[musical example: bass line, p]

Example 16

In the 1955 score the opening movement, while remaining the same length, is now entitled Overture. The vocal parts and the spoken text for the soloists and chorus are written out in the full score as opposed to previously only having been written in two manuscript books. Where vocal movements have been re-scored these parts were added to the original manuscript books and the organ part now appears in a separate book. Occasionally there are some words missing, though, these can be found by referring back to the manuscript books. The Kyrie, originally in unison, is now scored in two parts for upper and lower voices. After the opening instrumental bars of the chorus 'Be merciful' which are treated imitatively, the basses enter with the theme imitated by the sopranos, then when the tenor and contralto parts are added the writing becomes homophonic. The chorus 'Sanctus Fortis' (scored for SATB), is a harmonised version of the original melody predominantly in minims. In the chorus 'Rescue him, O Lord', the first section is scored for STB, followed by the solo section, each phrase ending with a four part Amen and the movement ends with a section for SATB consisting of alternating phrases between lower and upper voices. The original sixth movement 'Go from this world', is now extended from 20 bars to 73 bars, beginning with 'Proficiscere, Anima Christiana', sung by the Priest, the solo part punctuated by the 4-part chorus singing the words 'Go from this world'. As well as comprising newly composed material, reference is made to themes 1a and 1b in the solo part. The original music for this movement using fragments from the Praise Chorus appears towards the end with additional solo and choir parts for the words, 'Through Jesus Christ our Lord, Amen', plus a coda.

Movements 7 to 15 remain the same in outline as before, but with additional instrumental parts except for 8 which is with organ accompaniment only, 10 in which the harp is used as originally intended, and 15 remains scored for solo trumpet. The stanza beginning 'There was a mortal,' was originally spoken by the Angel, but in the revised version of 1955 it becomes an aria sung by the Priest (movement 16). According to Lockwood the reason behind this was to enlarge the part of the priest and to maintain the balance between the sung and the spoken word in the work as a whole. The following three movements (17–19) are settings of the Praise Chorus. As before the first chorus in G major is sung off stage and is now scored for sopranos and contraltos with organ accompaniment. The second chorus is for SATB and the trio 'Glory to him' is scored for soprano, mezzo-soprano and tenor, followed by a repeat of the chorus. A change of key to C major and different material is used to introduce the third Praise Chorus. The next section is set for SATB, the words 'O loving wisdom' being sung unaccompanied, followed by the words 'A second Adam', in which the lower and upper voices enter in imitation and the movement ends with a repeat of the chorus. All these movements are interspersed with spoken parts of the text. The melodrama 'Deep mysterious harmony' (movement 20) remains the same as in the original score and is followed by a fourth Praise Chorus in G major, scored for full orchestra. In this chorus the section beginning 'O loving wisdom' is arranged the same as in the third chorus and the words 'A second Adam' are set as a trio with imitative entries. While the Angel speaks there is a change of key to B major and the chorus takes up the theme from the third Praise Chorus which builds to a climax before returning to the key of G major for the trio 'Glory to him'. The movement ends with a repeat of the Praise Chorus. This is followed by a repeat of the first section of the Kyrie (movement 22), sung in unison with organ accompaniment. The next movement (23) begins with long sustained chords provided by the upper strings (muted) and *pizzicato* crotchets played by the 'cellos, over which the Angel speaks the words 'It is the voice of friends around thy bed who say the Subvenite with the priest.' A change of time from 4/4 to 3/4 introduces a solo 'Jesu! by that shuddering dread which fell on Thee,' in which reference is made to the theme 1c. This is sung by the Angel of the Agony and interacts with the text spoken by the Angel. The solo continues with short phrases which are interspersed with equally short instrumental phrases. As the movement develops the solo phrases become twice as long with little or no break between them. At the words 'To that glorious Home,' there is a change of key from E minor to E major and *'senza sordini'* is indicated. The Judgement Scene (24), 'Come back, O Lord' (25) and the 'Angel's Farewell' (26), are as before with additional instrumental parts. In addition the verses of psalm 90 with the sung response (movement 25) are illustrated with a mime performed by four members of the cast representing the Holy Souls. After the final words spoken by the Angel, the chorus repeats the word 'Praise' sung in four-part harmony off stage and as in the 1943 score the last 27 bars of the Entr'acte are played for the curtain.

PRESS EXTRACTS

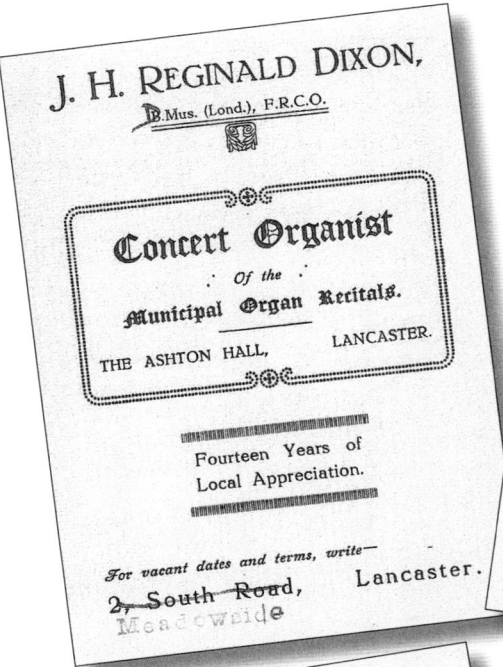

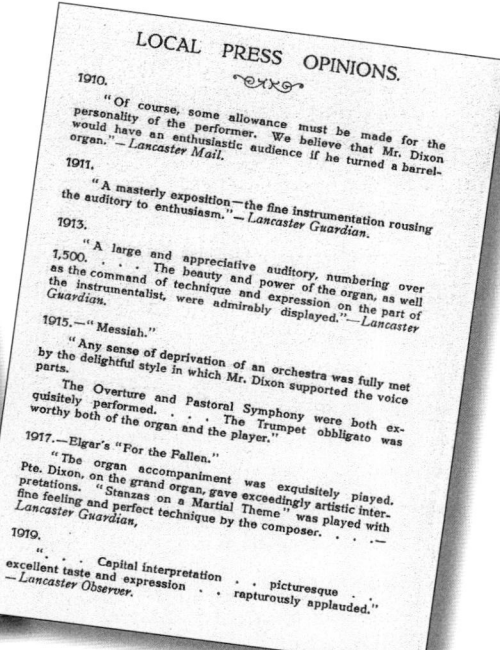

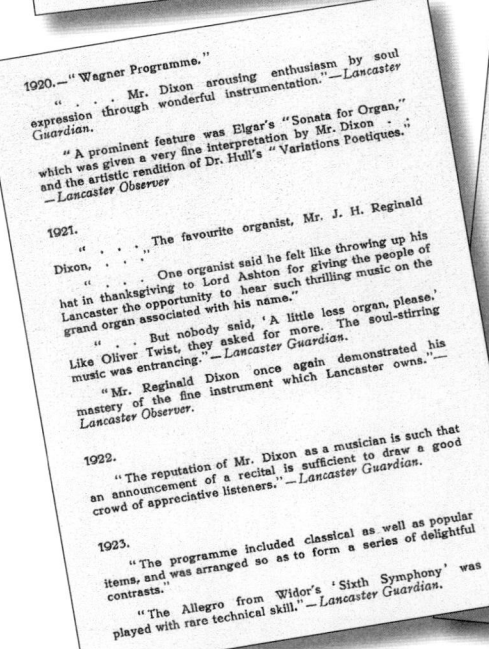

J. H. REGINALD DIXON,
B.Mus. (Lond.), F.R.C.O.

Concert Organist
· Of the ·
Municipal Organ Recitals.

THE ASHTON HALL, LANCASTER.

Fourteen Years of Local Appreciation.

For vacant dates and terms, write—

2, South Road, Lancaster.
Meadowside

LOCAL PRESS OPINIONS.

1910.
" Of course, some allowance must be made for the personality of the performer. We believe that Mr. Dixon would have an enthusiastic audience if he turned a barrel-organ." — *Lancaster Mail.*

1911.
" A masterly exposition — the fine instrumentation rousing the auditory to enthusiasm." — *Lancaster Guardian.*

1913.
" A large and appreciative auditory, numbering over 1,500. . . . The beauty and power of the organ, as well as the command of technique and expression on the part of the instrumentalist, were admirably displayed." — *Lancaster Guardian.*

1915. — "Messiah."
" Any sense of deprivation of an orchestra was fully met by the delightful style in which Mr. Dixon supported the voice parts.
The Overture and Pastoral Symphony were both exquisitely performed. . . . The Trumpet obbligato was worthy both of the organ and the player."

1917. — Elgar's "For the Fallen."
" The organ accompaniment was exquisitely played. Pte. Dixon, on the grand organ, gave exceedingly artistic interpretations. "Stanzas on a Martial Theme" was played with fine feeling and perfect technique by the composer. . . ." — *Lancaster Guardian.*

1919.
" . . . Capital interpretation . . . picturesque . . . excellent taste and expression . . . rapturously applauded." — *Lancaster Observer.*

1920. — "Wagner Programme."
" . . . Mr. Dixon arousing enthusiasm by soul expression through wonderful instrumentation." — *Lancaster Guardian.*

" A prominent feature was Elgar's "Sonata for Organ," which was given a very fine interpretation by Mr. Dixon · · ·; and the artistic rendition of Dr. Hull's "Variations Poetiques." — *Lancaster Observer*

1921.
" . . . " The favourite organist, Mr. J. H. Reginald Dixon.

" . . . " One organist said he felt like throwing up his hat in thanksgiving to Lord Ashton for giving the people of Lancaster the opportunity to hear such thrilling music on the grand organ associated with his name."

" . . . But nobody said, 'A little less organ, please.' Like Oliver Twist, they asked for more. The soul-stirring music was entrancing." — *Lancaster Guardian.*

" Mr. Reginald Dixon once again demonstrated his mastery of the fine instrument which Lancaster owns." — *Lancaster Observer.*

1922.
" The reputation of Mr. Dixon as a musician is such that an announcement of a recital is sufficient to draw a good crowd of appreciative listeners." — *Lancaster Guardian.*

1923.
" The programme included classical as well as popular items, and was arranged so as to form a series of delightful contrasts."

" The Allegro from Widor's 'Sixth Symphony' was played with rare technical skill." — *Lancaster Guardian.*

1924.
" The organist's interpretations were abounding in skill and sympathy." — *Lancaster Observer.*

" There was no doubt in any musical mind on Saturday that one had the privilege of listening to first-rate organ playing. Mr. Dixon opened in masterly fashion with some pieces of Bach, whose sonorous and majestic periods he brought out in magnificent style." — *Lancaster Guardian.*

Press Opinions:

Mr. Dixon maintains that Organ Recitals are popular when the Selections given are such as can be appreciated by the average audience, and are not of too classical an order. The large number of people who assembled in the Parish Church (Castleford) to hear him give an Organ Recital were able to bear him out in his contention, and thoroughly enjoyed the programme, which was of an ATTRACTIVE AND INTERESTING order throughout.

The opening selection was an Offertoire of the recitalist's own composition, and this was of a very BRIGHT AND HAPPY character............The Overture to Tannhauser was a VERY FINE PERFORMANCE, both in REGISTRATION and EXECUTION, and was considered his best effort ...." Sicilian Mariner's Hymn " was also an enjoyable selection, the double pedal part in one of the variations being CLEVERLY DONE. The Recital closed with Rubenstein's Russian Patrol and the Hallelujah Chorus, the representation in the former, of the gradual approach, passing by, and disappearance of a Russian Army being VERY EFFECTIVELY REALISED —*Pontefract and Castleford Gazette.*

Recital given by Mr. REGINALD DIXON, of York, which was followed with great appreciation, and delighted the large congregation gathered. This was Mr. Dixon's first visit to Goole, but he IMMEDIATELY CAPTURED HIS AUDIENCE and held their attention from beginning to end.

Another Recital followed at 7 p.m. Mr. Dixon played his part in faultless style, and undoubted testimony was given to his great abilities in the fact, that at the end of a long programme, occupying nearly two hours, THE AUDIENCE ASKED FOR MORE; and at their express wish he rendered again the ever-wonderful Hallelujah Chorus. Both Recitals were an unqualified success. It was plain that Mr. Dixon was more than a performer; he put himself into his music, and consequently HIS EXPRESSION IS MORE A SPIRITUAL THAN A MECHANICAL ACHIEVEMENT.—*Goole " Forward."*

Mr. Dixon was in fine form and gave the audience a real musical treat. His renderings of Bach and Brahms were marked by great clearness, and showed that he was besides a performer, a scholarly musician.

Wagner's Tannhauser Overture proved to be one of the treats of the evening, and Mr. Dixon's playing was said by many to be nothing short of MARVELLOUS: he was recalled four times after its conclusion. Collection realised nearly £14.—*Bridlington and Quay Gazette.*

Mr. Dixon is to be congratulated on the programme he had put forward, no less than on the EXCELLENT manner in which he rendered the various items. Mr. Dixon is no mere pyrotechnic, and the IMPRESSIVE MANNER in which he played the Overture to Tannhauser left nothing to be desired.—*Selby Times.*

A great treat was provided for those who attended the Parish Church......... Mr. Dixon showed himself to be a MASTER OF HIS INSTRUMENT, and as he is only a very young man yet we predict a great future for him.—*Pontefract Parish Magazine.*

Numerous Selections from the works of eminent composers were played by the Organist very effectively, and FULLY REALISED THE HIGH EXPECTATIONS which had been entertained.—*Selby Express.*

Mr. Dixon belongs to what may be termed the "Younger School" of Organists; being quite a BRILLIANT EXECUTANT.—*Church Porch.*

A SPLENDID performance was given on the Organ by Mr. REGINALD DIXON, who played from the excerpts.—*Hull Daily News.*

................Played with good treatment and expression.........*Huddersfield Daily Chronicle.*

The Organ Anniversary Services in connection with the Boothferry-road Wesleyan Church were held on Sunday, when an Organ Recital was given in the afternoon by Mr. REGINALD DIXON, whose MAGNIFICENT PLAYING was listened to by a large congregation.—*Goole Advertiser.*

J. H. Reginald Dixon,
B.Mus. (Lond.), F.R.C.O.

Concert Organist.

For vacant dates and terms, write—

~~2, South Road,~~ Meadowside, Lancaster.

PRESS NOTICES.

"Magnificent playing . . . ."—*Goole Advertiser.*

"A brilliant executant . . . ."—*Church Porch.*

"A splendid performance . . . ."—*Hull Daily News.*

"A thorough master of his instrument . . ."—*Pontefract Parish Church Magazine.*

"Besides a performer, a scholarly musician . . . ."—*Bridlington and Quay Gazette.*

"Mr. Dixon's descriptive work on the organ is particularly fine . . . ."—*Yorkshire Herald.*

"(Mr. Dixon's organ playing) can be characterised by one word—superb . . . ."—*Westmorland Gazette.*

"A charming selection of pieces . . . a great success from every point of view . . . ."—*Lancashire Daily Post.*

"Recital of a high order, the whole of the pieces being played from memory . . . ."—*Selby Times.*

"Wonderful ability and 'soul' . . . revealing a great depth of feeling and taste . . . ."—*Lancaster Observer.*

"Playing fully realised the high expectations which had been entertained . . . ."—*Selby Express.*

"Mr. Dixon immediately captured his audience, and held their attention from beginning to end . . ."—*Goole Forward.*

"Programme attractive and interesting . . . very fine performance both in registration and execution . . . ."—*Castleford Gazette.*

"Judas Maccabeus."—"Mr. Dixon at the organ performed a most difficult and exacting task without a fault."—*Morecambe Visitor.*

"The opening piece was a Prelude introducing the various stops, and illustrating the capabilities of the instrument in a marked degree."—*Lancaster Observer.*

"Not only was the congregation impressed by the wonderful power and beauty of the fine new organ, but with the striking capability of the organist."—*York Evening Press.*

"The Lancaster Parish Church was well filled for his recital on the new organ. . . . The programme was a varied and artistic one, and executed with all the skill and technique of which Mr. Dixon is a master. . ."—*Lancaster Guardian.*

"One of the most beautiful items on this well-conceived programme was the organ solo by Mr. Reginald Dixon, who played the finale from Vierne's Third Symphony with rare charm and delicacy of expression. . . ."—*Morecambe Visitor.*

"Mr. Dixon introduced his organ solos by explaining the construction and meaning of Guilmant's Organ Sonata . . . which certainly proved of great value, and led to a greater understanding of the piece when played on the organ."—*Lancaster Observer.*

"Mr. Dixon, of the Lancaster Corporation Organ Recitals, is well known as an executant of resource and power, and before he had played for long on Saturday afternoon it was seen how well earned is his reputation. . . . The Toccata was played with remarkable brilliance of manipulation, while the more solid virtues of the Fugue were equally finely displayed. . . The organist rose to great heights in the 'Siegfried Idyll.'"—*Eastern Morning News.*

"The organ in concert halls is so often made the medium of poor music, arrangements of hackneyed overtures and songs—anything, in short, but fine examples of the music written for it—that we have been particularly struck by the excellence of the programmes of the organ concerts given at the Ashton Hall, Lancaster. . . . . In addition to the organ works—[a list of which is given]—Mr. Dixon wisely included transcriptions of various kinds. . . . This is a combination of courage and tact that may be commended to the notice of recitalists who apparently hold that genuine organ music should be given only in homœopathic doses—if at all . . ."—*Musical Times.*

List of Works

Date of composition is only given when known.

CHORAL WORKS

Love and Music (words: Hemans, Schiller and Herrick), October 1907. Cantata: SATB Chorus, Quintette, Tenor or Soprano solo and String Orchestra.

Song for St Cecilia's Day (words: J Dryden). Mus. Bac. Exercise October 1914. Ode: SSATB Chorus, solo Quartette, Contralto solo and String Orchestra.

Mysterium Resurrectionis (words: 13th-century manuscript). Mus. Doc. Exercise September 1924. A Miracle Play set to music for Double Choir, Soprano, Mezzo-soprano, Contralto, Tenor, Baritone, Bass soli, and Orchestra.

The Dream of Gerontius (words: John Henry Newman), 1943 revised 1955. A dramatization of the poem set to music for Choir, Soli and Orchestra. First performance: 4 May 1943, Ashton Hall, Lancaster.

Anglèse de Sagazan (words: Rév. Père Vergé), 1955. Petit Oratorio: Soprano and Contralto Chorus, Tenor or Baritone solo, a Reader and Organ.

Panis Vitae (words: Bible and S Thomas Aquinas), 1960. Oratorio: Chorus, Soprano, Tenor, Bass Soli, Orchestra and Organ. First performance: 7 August 1960, Deutschen Museum, Munich. Published by Hinrichsen, 1960.

CHURCH MUSIC

Anthems

'Praise for Redemption', 1905. 4-part Choir, solo Quartette, Tenor solo and Organ. Dedicated to the Choir of St Denys, York.

'Lord who shall dwell in Thy Tabernacle?' SCTB a cappella. Gratefully inscribed to Dr A Eaglefield-Hull. Published by Robert Culley c. 1906 Choir series A27.

'O Lord, increase my faith', c. 1908. SATB unaccompanied.

'Crown Him, Christ the King' (Bridges/Dixon), 1940. 3-part men's voices.

'I Rejoiced', October 1966. SATB, Soprano solo and Organ. Dedicated to Mr H Walmsley and the Choir of the Priory Church, Lancaster.

Hymn Tunes

The World looks very Beautiful, 20 July 1907. Composed for the Selby Sunday School Anniversary Service August 1907.

We Love to Sing, 21 July 1907. Composed for the Selby Sunday School Anniversary Service August 1907. Dedicated to J A Meale. Published R Culley, Choir Series L64.

Brightly Gleams our Banner, c. 1907. Inscribed to the Rev E W Evans. Published R Culley, Choir Series L99.

Vesper Hymn, c. 1910

I need Thee, January 1911

Let us Arise

O Sacrament most Holy

Help Lord the Souls

Meadowside

Inspiration, December 1955

Carmina Missae: (words and music Dixon) 1958

  Come we all rejoicing

  Immeasurably great

  Symbols of our earthly food

  Holy, Holy, Lord most Holy

  Now on the altar of our God

  Deliver us, O Lord we pray

  Renew in me the life of grace

  Eternal thanks and praise to Thee

Published by Cary & Co., 1959

Masses

Mass in honour of St Peter, November 1909. Originally composed for men's voices a cappella and arranged for mixed voices c. 1955.

Missa Secunda in A, 'Missa in Dominicis'. SATB with organ obligato.

Mass in honour of St Wulstan originally for men's voices in B flat, adapted for mixed voices in 1956. Dedicated to the memory of Thomas Wulstan Pearson, OSB, first RC Bishop of Lancaster. Performed by the Cathedral Choir at the Cathedral, 28 August 1928.

Mass in honour of St Cecilia, 1941. Originally composed for men's voices and arranged for mixed voices in 1954.

Mass in honour of St Thomas More, October 1942.

Mass of Our Lady of Syon [sic], June 1956.

Misssa Ferialis in C, renamed Mass in honour of St Beatrice, August 1958/January 1959. Cantor/Choir and Congregation in unison. Published by Cary & Co., 1961.

Mass in honour of St Paulinus of York with separate Credo, 1958. SATB. Published by Hinrichsen, 1959.

Mass of St John the Evangelist, 1961. SSATB, SATB soli and Organ. Composed for the Choir of St John the Evangelist, Islington, London.

English Mass of Christ the King, c. 1969. SATB/Congregation in unison.

Boarbank Mass, 1973. Unison/Harmony.

Motets

Offertories 1910

> 'Afferentur regi'.
>
> 'Angelus Domini', Offertorium for 'Dom in albis'. Unison.
>
> 'Confitebuntur coeli'. Unison.
>
> 'Inveni David'.
>
> 'Justorum anima'.
>
> 'Terra Tremuit', Offertorium, for Easter Day 1910, revised 1959. Tenor I and Tenor II.
>
> 'Veritas mea'. Unison.

'Populus Meus', composed for Good Friday April 1911. 4-part.

'Domine Salvam Fac' in D major, 20 November 1913.

'Ecce Sacerdos Magnus', May 1938. Two equal voices and organ. Published by Carrara July/August, 1964.

'Ave verum corpus', September 1944. Tenor, Bass I, Bass II.

'Benedicite Sacerdotes' in A major, May 1948. Treble, Tenor, Bass. Specially composed and dedicated to Canon Brimley on his Silver Jubilee.

'Pulchra ut Luna', 22 October 1950. SATB a cappella. First performed at Pontifical High Mass in St Peter's Cathedral, Lancaster, Sunday 5 November, 1950.

'Te Sæculorum Principem', 14 September 1956. 3-part men's voices. Composed for the Feast of Christ the King.

'Ave Maria' in E flat, June 1956. Soprano solo/unison.

'Ave Maria' in F, June 1956. SATB and Soprano solo.

'Laudate Dominum', Holy week 1957. SATB and organ.

'Adoramus te Christe', Holy week 1957. SATB and organ.

'Haec Dies', Gradual for Easter Day, 1957. SATB and organ.

'Confitebuntur stetit Angelus', 1957.

'Domine Salvam Fac' in B flat major, 30 May 1958. First performed at a televised Mass from St Joseph's Church, Lancaster, 15 June 1958.

Miscellaneous

'The Lord's Prayer', c. 1906. SATB/unison. Published by Banks & Sons, York.

'Litany of the Blessed Virgin Mary' (1) in G major. 4-part choir.

'Litany of the Blessed Virgin Mary', 8 August 1910. 4-part choir and congregation.

'The Cathedral Rosary', 1910. Unison. Revised 4-part version for the feast of the Holy Rosary, 1941.

'Alma Redemptoris', 21 November 1913. 4-part choir.

'Tantum Ergo', 6 April 1918. 4-part choir. Dedicated to M. l'Abbé Blanc, Curé de St Germain au Mont d'Or.

'O Salutaris' in B flat, 26 May 1918. Duet for Soprano and Tenor. Dedicated to M. Gormetz, organiste de la Primatiale, Lyon.

'O Salutaris' in G (Melody in Easy Music for Church Choirs 1853). 4-part choir. Alternative setting for verse two with fabourdon in the bass and extended Amen. Published in the Complete Benediction Book for Choirs edited by Sir R Terry, 1933.

'Tantum Ergo' in G (Mgr Chas. Newsham 1791-1863). 4-part choir. Alternative setting for verse two with fabourdon in the tenor and extended Amen. Published in the Complete Benediction Book for Choirs edited by Sir R Terry, 1933.

'In Vigila Apostoli', 1939. Written for the Consecration of Bishop Flynn.

'O Salutaris' in B flat and A major, 12 October 1941. 4-part arrangement of the 2-part setting in B flat.

'Adoramus te Christe' (Psalm tone).

'Laudate Dominum' (Psalm tone).

'Responses' at the Preface, May 1968.

'Eucharistic Acclamations', March 1969.

INCIDENTAL MUSIC

Lancaster Pageant, 1913.

Lancaster Pageant, 'The Monks of Cockersand Abbey', 1937.

Historical Pageant, 'Beneath Hadrian's Tower', 1953.

INSTRUMENTAL MUSIC

Trio, 1905. Harmonium/Piano, Flute and Violin.

Fanfare, 1937. Two Trumpets. First performance: 2 October 1937 on the Giant Axe Field, Lancaster.

Quartet, 1938. Four Clarinets.

Légende, 1940. Violin and Pianoforte. Dedicated to Miss Hornby. First performed in 1943 at Settle High School by Miss Hornby.

Meditation (later named 'Meadowside'), 22 June 1917 revised 16 October 1957. Violin and Pianoforte.

Nocturne, 'Lunehurst', 19 October 1957. Violin and Pianoforte.

MILITARY BAND

Grand March, 'Lancastria' 1937. Composed for the visit of King George VI. First performance: 30 September 1937 in Dalton Square, Lancaster by the Band of the 5th Battalion King's Own Royal Regiment.

ORCHESTRAL MUSIC

A Christmas Fancie, c. 1916/17.

Les Fleurs de Mont d'Or. Dédie á M: Lt: Col: Trollope.

Suite Carolorégienne, June 1919. Three movements (i) L'Entrée (ii) Merci (iii) Le Départ.

Organ Concerto, August 1952. Organ and Orchestra. Dedicated to Earl Peel (Grandson of Lord Ashton). First performance: 26 November 1952, Ashton Hall, Lancaster.

ORGAN

Grand Chœur in D, 1902-3. Dedicated to J A Meale.

Grand Offertoire in B flat, c. 1906. Earliest traced performance: 9 September 1906, S. Mary's Parish Church, Tyne Dock by the composer.

Pastorale, 1907. Dedicated to E H Lemare. Earliest traced performance: 14 July 1907, Boothferry Road Wesleyan Church, Goole by the composer.

Intermezzo, 1907. Dedicated to E H Lemare. Earliest traced performance: 14 July 1907, Boothferry Road Wesleyan Church, Goole by the composer.

Bell Rondo, 1907. Earliest traced performance: 1 August 1907, Queen's Hall, Hull by the composer.

Toccata in C, Pre-1909.

A Shepherd's Idylle, 1910. First performace: 12 October 1910, Ashton Hall, Lancaster by the composer.

Melodie in D flat. First performance: 4 February 1911 Ashton Hall, Lancaster by the composer.

Impromptu, 1911-12 (Originally for piano, arranged for organ and re-named *Nachspiel*, 12 May 1959). Published as *Festival Postlude* by Hinrichsen, 1962.

Tone Poem, 'From the Alps' 1912.

Stanzas on a Martial Theme (The Minstrel Boy), March – Hope – Reflections – Lightheartedness – Sorrow – Dirge – Triumph – Consolation – Life and Glory. First performance: 1915 City Hall, Hull by the composer.

An Irish Fancie. Performed 17 March 1920, Ashton Hall, Lancaster by the composer.

Overture in G minor from 'Mysterium Resurrectionis', 1924. Performed 19 November 1924, Greaves Wesleyan Church, Lancaster by the composer.

Vox organa, vox humana, 1922. Earliest known performance: 25 March 1922, Ashton Hall, Lancaster by the composer. Also known as *Adoration* dedicated to my friend H Firth (1925).

Scherzando. Earliest traced performance: 4 April 1923, Ashton Hall, Lancaster by the composer.

Capricioso. Earliest traced performance: 2 April 1925, Lune Street Wesleyan Church, Preston by the composer.

Introduction, Variations and Fugue on the tune 'Sedbergh'. Dedicated to John Brook who composed the tune c. 1916. Earliest known performance: Saturday 16 May 1925 Ashton Hall, Lancaster by the composer. Published by Laudy & Co., 1925.

Suite Fantasie, Choral, Berceuse, Toccata. Earliest traced performance: 26 September 1926, St Mary's Church, Wigan by the composer.

An Organ Shanty, May 1927.

The Hunt, May 1927.

Meditation, 'Ascendit Deus', 1927. Composed for the Liverpool Metropolitan Cathedral Rally of 1927. Dedicated to M l'Abbé Darros, Organiste de la Basilique, Lourdes (1928).

Introibo (12 Cathedral Preludes). Dedicated to Harold Spicer Organist of Manchester College, Oxford.

Prelude and Fantasy Fugue (The Cunningham), August/September 1935. Dedicated to C H Moody. Published by Oxford University Press, 1936.

Duologue for Trumpet and Trombone, April 1939. Dedicated to S Ellingworth. First performance: 3 May 1939, St Paul's Methodist Church, Didsbury by the composer.

Toccata in E flat, May, 1940. Composed for the opening of the new organ at St Peter's Church, Lytham. Dedicated to Dr G T Thalben-Ball.

Passacaglia and Fugue on a Purcellian Theme. Originally composed in 1942 and later appeared in a new version c. 1957.

Berceuse, 8 December1953. Published by Hinrichsen, 1959.

Offertoire, 'La Reine de Massabielle' 1954. Dedicated to the Rév. Père Vergé, Chaplin de Notre Dame de Lourdes.

Suite d'Anglèse de Garaison, 1955 (i) Prelude (ii) Meditation (iii) Idylle Pastorale (iv) Chorale.

Baroque Suite, September 1957 (i)Toccata (ii) Pastorale (iii) Verset (iv) Finale. Dedications (i) Sir William H Harris (ii) Lady Jeans (iii) Ralph Downes (iv) Dr Leo Sowerby. Published by Hinrichsen, 1959.

Solemn Procession, 9 May 1958. Published by Carrara December, 1960.

Aspiration, 24 June 1958. Published by Carrara, May/June 1964.

Toccata in E minor, 25 June 1958. Published by Carrara, October 1965. Dedicated to Joan Carter.

Festival Postlude, 1959 (Originally composed for piano in 1911-12 entitled *Impromptu*, arranged for organ by Dixon and renamed *Nachspiel* 12 May 1959). Dedicated to Dr Francis A Jackson. Published by Hinrichsen, 1962.

Vignettes, 'Nine Paraphrases on the Psalm Tune Coleshill', 1967. An earlier sketch exists for a Prelude on this tune.

PIANO

Première Gavotte, April 1908. Dedicated expressively to D Fritton.

Three Flower Pieces: 'London Pride', 'Wallflowers' and 'Red Tulips', June 1908. Respectfully dedicated to H Ernest Austin.

Sonata Classique, c. 1908.

Impromptu, 1911-12.

Waltz, 'In Summer-Time', 1912. First performance: 21 December 1912, Ashton Hall, Lancaster by the composer.

Waltz, 'Wishes', 1915.

Jardins sans la Pluie, 1921.

L'apri diner d'une moustique, 1921.

Homage to Schmit, 1925.

A Glazebrook Melody, 1932. First performance: 9 July 1932, Primitive Methodist Church, Glazebrook by the composer.

Nocturne in D flat major, 'Sunset over Morecambe Bay', 1940.

Andantino in A major, 1940.

Grand March, 'Lancastria' (arranged for piano 1941).

Harvest Dance (Danse de Demétre), 1942.

Sarabande in C sharp minor, May 1942.

Quick March in G August, 1943.

Homage to J S Bach Series: Three Studies in B minor, D minor and G major, 1944.

SECULAR SONGS & PARTSONGS

Solo songs

'The Simple Sailorman' (words: Oxenford), May 1905.

'Life's Harmony', 8 April 1905. Soprano or Tenor.

'The Clang of the Hammer' (words: Oxenford), May 1906.

'Love is ever at the Spring' (words: Foster), c. 1906. Soprano. Dedicated to Miss Nellie Bolton. Published by Weekes & Co., 1906.

Two Songs: Dedicated to my friend Miss Grace Nicoll.

'Indian Serenade' (words: Shelley).

'Fair, Sweet and Young' (words: Dryden), January 1906.

'Love I know not how to say', 23 April 1906.

'Dearest Treasure of my heart', 18 January 1907.

Three Scotch Songs (words: Burns). Respectfully inscribed to Sir Frederick Bridge.

'How long and dreary is the night', 25 April 1906.

'She's fair and fause'.

'When rosy May comes in wi' flowers', 17 July 1907.

'Wintry Night', 22 November 1907.

'Come let me take thee' (words: Burns), A Monaghan/Dixon.

'Prière du Dimanche', 1908. Dedicated to ma chère Louise.

Three Contralto Songs (words: Foster), June 1908.

'The coming of Spring'.

'To a Child'.

'To a Blackbird'.

'A Ballad of Lancaster', 2 May 1913.

'Westward Bound' (words: Herbert J Brandon), 1919. Baritone. Published by Escott & Co., 1920.

'Memories' (words: Herbert J Brandon), 1919. Baritone/Tenor with optional violin obligato. Published by Escott & Co., 1920.

'Love's strong fold' (words: E Bronte), 1928. Written under the pseudonym of Pauline Meadowside.

'I'm dying for a smoke' *Cigarette Song,* May 1932.

'Auntie's Rose'.

'I wish I'd my Old Job Back', 10 March 1934. Brunley Scott and Reg Dixon.

'As I pass on' (words: J A Pickup), 1937.

'Nostalgia' (words: F C Boden), 17 January 1938. Baritone.

'Handyman' (words: Caryl Brahms), 1939.

'The Early Riser' (words: Caryl Brahms), 1939.

'Old Faithful' (words: Caryl Brahms), c. 1939.

'The Difference' (words: Caryl Brahms), c. 1939.

'Shopping' (words: Caryl Brahms), March 1940.

'Rebellion' (words: Caryl Brahms), 5 February 1941. Arranged for Voice and Guitar, 30 May 1969.

'The Poor Thing' (words: Caryl Brahms), 5 February 1941.

'Sociale' (Friendship), June 1943. Countertenor.

'Pastorale' (The shepherd and the maid), 27 June 1943. Countertenor.

'The Indian Weed' (The smokers' song), 4 July 1943. Countertenor.

'The Irishman's Home sweet home'.

'The Old Home'.

Unison Songs

'Late in Life', 3 May 1944.

'Here's to a school of a hundred years' (words: Rev. B Lockwood), 1951. Composed for the Centenary of St Peter's School, 15 June 1951. First performance: Celebration Concert 12 June 1951.

Partsongs

'Singers' (words: Will Foster), 1908. SATB. Dedicated to the members of the Selby Choral Society.

'A Request' (words: F C Boden), 1938. Alto/Tenor 1, Tenor II, Bass 1, Bass II. Also known as 'Only a Rose', arranged for SATB.

'Kitty' (words: Dixon). Dedicated to Kitty my cat and all who love them. Soprano 1, Soprano II, and Contralto.

'Achievement' (words: Dixon), date unknown revised 1965. A 3-part round. Dedicated to Joan Carter. Performed at the Schools Music Festival in the Ashton Hall, Lancaster, spring 1965.

'Transfiguration' (words: Will Foster), 1943/4. Originally set for baritone solo, later arranged for SATB 4-7 part. Published by Hinrichsen, 1959.

ARRANGEMENTS

Church Music

'O Praise the Lord of Heaven' (John Goss). Orchestrated and an introduction added by Dixon. Arranged for the Melbourne Terrace Choir Festival May 1907, York.

'As pants the hart' (L Spohr). Orchestrated and an introduction added by Dixon. Arranged for the Melbourne Terrace Choir Festival, 17 May 1908, York.

'Adoramus in æternum', 1910.

'Litany of the Blessed Virgin Mary' (Dr Armes), 1910.

'O Salutaris' (R W Oberhoffer), 1910.

'Tantum Ergo' (R W Oberhoffer), 1910.

'Tantum Ergo' (St Nathaniel: Rogers). Harmonised by Dixon c. 1910.

'Maria Mater' (Dr Newsham), February 1912.

'Adeste Fideles', December 1921. 4-part.

'Adoramus in æternum' (Allegri), 1922.

'Veni Creator', and responses arranged for the consecration of the first Bishop of Lancaster, 24 February 1925.

'Veni Sancte Spiritus', May 1938.

'O Salutaris' in C (G Joseph 1657), in D (M Wise 1646-1687), in E (Rev. S Gates O.P.), 1935.

Organ

Second Movement from Symphony No. 2 in D major (Brahms), dating from the York years.

Spanish Dance Op. 21 (Moszkowski).

Le Jardin de Pétrarque (Hahn), 8 November 1917, St Germain.

Lac Vert (V d'Indy), 14 November 1917, St Germain.

Grand Papal March 'The Silver Trumpets' (Viviana).

Passepied (Borowski), February 1928.

Invocation (Borowski), c. 1930.

Madrigal (Borowski), c. 1932.

Three Schubert Songs, December 1936.

   'Geheimes' (The Secret).

   'Ungeduld' (Impatience).

   'Haiden-Röslein' (The Wild Rose).

The Lourdes Hymn, June 1954 (Varied harmonies arranged for harmonium, organ or keyboard).

'Ave Maria' (Bach-Gounod), 1961.

Solo song

'Frühlingslied' (Merkel), 21 February 1908. Dedicated to Miss Daisie Sample.

Theatre Music

Miss Hook of Holland. Orchestral arrangement of the Overture and the Cigar song, January 1914.

Kathie (R L Smith, July/August 1945). Orchestral arrangement and additional music by Dixon including an Overture, Incidental music and extra numbers, January 1946.

Girls will be Grown-ups (R L Smith, November 1944). Orchestral arrangement, March 1949.

The Jolly Roger (R L Smith, October/November 1949). Orchestral arrangement, January 1950.

Kingdom for Cash (R L Smith, December 1950/January 1951). Orchestral arrangement, May 1951.

Bibliography

Ainscough, H, 'Organ Specifications and Testimonials' (Booklet)

Aschaffenburger Volksblatt, Aschaffenburg
    'Münchens kulturelle Mission', 3 August 1960
    '"Panis Vitae" uraufgeführt', 9 August 1960
    'Eucharistisches Oratorium "Panis Vitae"', 10 August 1960

Baines, E, *Directory & Gazeteer of the County of York*, 1823

Bamberger Volksblatt, Bamberg
    'Kirchenmusik zum Weltkongreß', 27 July 1960

Billington, R N, *A History of St Peter's* (1909)

Bulmer's, *History and Directory of North Yorkshire* (1890)

Carlisle Journal
    'Catholic Youth's Clever Performance', 11 January 1946
    'Priest's Musical Comedy on BBC', May 1946
    'Catholic Youth in Musical Comedy', 1 April 1949
    'On board the "Jolly Roger"', January 1950

Census records from 1841 to 1901

Craven Herald and Pioneer
    'School Recital', 4 April 1941

Daily Dispatch
    'Found rare Elgar work among torn music in shop', 14 December 1937

Daily Express
    'He wears 20 pairs of ear-rings', 22 August 1950
    'Ear-ring man plays at Inn', 23 August 1950
    'Dr Dixon of the Cathedral plays Handel', 23 August 1950

Daily Mail
    'The Dixon (Mr and Dr) Confusions', 3 October 1933
    'Religion on the Radio', 27 August 1934
    'Up to the ears in glamour', 29 May 1950
    Mailbag letters and replies concerning earrings, 1950
    'Jingle jangle', 22 August 1950
    'A Mus Doc mans pub organ', 23 August 1950

Daily Mirror
    '"Pendant earrings help me see" says doctor', 22 August 1950

Daily Telegraph
    'Changes his ear-rings like others ties', 22 August 1950

'Handel in the parlour', 23 August 1950

'Choral singing of note', 'Panis Vitae' DAWM, 6 July 1961

Der Allgäuer Kempten

'Oratorium "Panis Vitae" in München uraufgeführt', 10 August 1960

Deutsches Volksblatt, Stuttgart

'Geistliche Musik in München', 10 August 1960

Die Zeit, Hamburg

'Für das Leben der Welt', 5 August 1960

Dixon, George,

'Why not grow our own chicory?' *Modern Farming*, October 1919

'Chicory' A pamphlet printed by the *Yorkshire Herald*

Dixon, J H R,

Archive of programmes, newspaper cuttings, letters and miscellaneous items

'Notes on Roman Catholic Church Music', *Musical Standard*, from May 1915 to April 1916

'Continental Organs and their Music', *Quarterly Record*, July 1929, Vol. XIV, No 56

'Continental Organs and their Music', *Quarterly Record*, January 1930, Vol. XV, No 58

Incorporated Organists' Association Congress Reports

Lecture Notes

'Notes from an Organ Enthusiast's Diary', *Musical Opinion*, March, April, May 1929

The Organ, St Joseph's Seminary College, Upholland, College Magazine, 1930 pp 76–9

'The most satisfying instrument I have ever played' *The Universe*, 16 May 1930

'The Organ and Sacred Liturgy', *Music and Liturgy,* from January 1933 to April 1934

'This is truly a grand organ', *Municipal Review,* Lancaster, April 1949, p 59

Dowbiggin, E A,

'The Dream of Gerontius', *Lancaster Guardian,* 7 May 1943

'The Dream of Gerontius', *Lancaster Guardian,* 14 May 1943

Elvin, Lawrence,

'Organ Notes: The Town Hall, Lancaster', *The Choir,* 1946, Vol. 37, p 64

Flaxton Parish Church Register of Baptisms

Flaxton School Log Book, North Yorkshire Record Office

Fränkisches Volksblatt, Würzburg

'Panis Vitae' uraufgeführt, München, 9 August 1960

Freisinger Tagblatt, Freising

'Disharmonien und Synkopen blieben aus', 10 August 1960

Hughes, Bryan,

'The Organ in St Joseph's College', Upholland, *The Organ*, October 1971, Vol. L1, No 202 pp 78–82

Huntington Parish Church Register of Baptisms, Weddings and Funerals, Borthwick Institute of Historical Research, York

Jewels, E N, *A History of Archbishop Holgate's Grammar School York 1546–1946*

Kelly's Directory of the North and East Ridings Yorkshire with the City of York 1893

Lancashire Daily Post

'Working Girls in Preston Religious Play', WP, 26 October 1943

Lancashire Evening Post

'Papal Honour for Organist', 3 April 1956

'A musical tribute to Lancaster composer', 21 March 1963

'City composer honoured in musical tribute', 8 April 1963

'Man who lives for music', 13 May 1969

'Tribute to organist, Concert of own music', Anne Clement, 9 August 1972

'Death of Dr Dixon at 88', 6 May 1975

Lancaster Guardian Reports 1899–1971

'Consecration of the New Roman Catholic Church', 8 October 1859

'Opening of the new Organ at St Peter's, Lancaster', 12 January 1889

'St Peter's Church Jubilee', 9 October 1909

'Organ Recital', 3 November 1909

'Organ Recital', 10 December 1909

'Organ Recital', 1910

'Concerts for the people', 1910

'Municipal Music', 4 February 1911

'Organ Recitals', 4 March 1916

'Organist Soldier', 6 May 1916

Reports of the Dixon-Jamart Concerts from 17 March 1920 to 25 March 1922

'Organ Recital, Brilliant Programme by Mr R Dixon, of Lancaster', 12 April 1923

'Popular Concerts, Municipal musical scheme launched', 1 March 1924

'Lecture Recital, The Influence at work in modern music', 19 April 1924

'Municipal Organ Recitals, Growing public appreciation for good-class music', 10 May 1924

'Grand Festival Concert, Thousand people turned from the doors', May 1925

'Sunday's Concert, Shopping week', May 1925

'The Mayor of Lancaster Robes Dr Dixon', May 1925

'Ashton Hall Recital "What the Organ said"' 4 August 1925

'The New Lancaster Diocese', 21 February 1925

'The Consecration of Bishop Pearson at Lancaster', 28 February 1925

'Town and Country Topics', 23 December 1932

'City Celebrations in Story and Pictures', 1 October 1937

'Moving picture of stirring times in Lancaster', 8 October 1937

'Lancaster Girl Entertains', 30 July 1943

'Music Certificates Presented', January 1951

'R.C. Cathedral Concert', 15 June 1951

'Dedicated to Earl Peel', 28 November 1952

'Madrigal Society in recital', February 1954

'Cathedral organ gets a testing', 5 October 1956

'Dr Dixon's 50 years as organist at Cathedral', May 1959

'Archbishop at Cathedral centenary celebrations', 9 October 1959

'Lancaster Musical Society's tribute to Dr J H Reginald Dixon', 11 April 1963

'Celebrating 60 years as Cathedral organist', 9 May 1969

'German choir sings in London performance of Dr Dixon's oratorio', B L Harrison, July 1961

'Organists honour Dr Dixon', 11 August 1972

Lancaster Mail

'Lancaster Choristers', 25 February 1910

'Magical Music', 14 October 1910

Lancaster Musical Festival Programmes 1930–38

Lancaster Observer and *Morecambe Chronicle*

'St Peter's Church, Lancaster. Opening of the New Organ', 11 January 1889

Letters

To Dixon from family and friends

From Dixon to the Taylor sisters

Liverpool Evening Express

'Music and Musicians', 28 November 1949

Lockwood, Rev. B, 'Profile' *Church Music,* August 1977 Vol. 3 No. 10, p 15

Mills, Rev. R, *The Church of the Sacred Heart Blackpool*

Morecambe Visitor, *Heysham Chronicle* and *Lancaster Advertiser*

'A Musical Triumph', West End Wesleyan Festival, July 1925

Münchner Merker, München

'Klingendes Gotteslob zum Kongreß', 28 July 1960

'Eucharistisches Oratorium aus England', 9 August 1960

Music and Liturgy (1933–35), Articles on 'The Organ and Sacred Liturgy'

Music and Musicians, 'Panis Vitae' A review of the London performance, Llifon Hughes-Jones, August 1961

Musical Opinion, 'Panis Vitae' A review of the London performance, GM, August 1961

News Chronicle

'Ear-ringed Organist meets The Princess Royal', 22 August 1950

'Largo in a new setting', 23 August 1950

Organists' Review, J H Reginald Dixon in conversation with Basil Ramsey, July 1972, pp 17–18

Organists' Quarterly Record

Ost – West – Kurier, Frankfurt

'Gottes Wort und des Menschen Kunst', August 1960

Preston Herald

'Hippodrome "Dream of Gerontius"', 11 November 1955

Riley, M, *Percy Whitlock: Organist and Composer*, William Sessions Limited Ebor Press 2003

Roberts, W A, 'Henry Ainscough: Organ Builder of Preston', *The Organ,* April 1929, Vol. VIII, No 32, pp 211–14

Scrap Book recording information concerning the Church of Our Lady and St Joseph, Carlisle

Smith, T, Flaxton, *Over a thousand years of social history* (York 1993)

Süddeutsche Zeitung

'Ein eucharistisches Oratorium'

The Tablet

Dixon letters 1927–

Bread of Life, Mavis Bacca, 15 July 1961

The Universe

Article by Dixon 'The most satisfying instrument I have ever played', 16 May 1930

'A thrilling new work heard again', JB, 14 July 1961

Warrington Examiner

'Organists' Association, Dr Dixon's recital at Parr Hall', 24 February 1934

Westfälische Nachrichten, Münster

'Oratorium vom Brot des Lebens', 10 August 1960

White, *Directory of 1840*

Whitworth, Reginald, 'Popular recitalists and their Organs' *The Organ,* July 1931, Vol. XI No 41, pp 46–9

Widnes Weekly News

'Magnificent Organ, The opening ceremony', 13 April 1934

'Great Organ and Gifted Organist', 20 April 1934

Yorkshire Evening News

'Organist wears ear-rings at Leeds Congress', 21 August 1950

Yorkshire Evening Post

'Organist believes his ear-rings cured defective sight', 21 August 1950

'Pipe dreams', 23 August 1950

Yorkshire Evening Press

'Organists find York links', 30 August 1961

'Wedding March suits this York bride', 30 August 1961

'Practical Memorial', 31 August 1961

Yorkshire Herald

'Stockton-on-Forest'. Report of school concert, 11 March 1898

'Stockton-on-Forest'. Report of Harvest services and concert, 8 October 1898

'The Lord Mayor's Sunday Evening Concerts', 2 March 1904

'The Lord Mayor's Sunday Evening Concerts', 5 March 1904

'Lenten Sacred Concerts', 7 March 1904

'Lenten Sacred Concerts', 20 March 1905

'The Lord Mayor's Third Lenten Concert', 5 March 1904

'Lenten Sacred Concerts in York', 1905

'Remarkable Music Successes', July/August 1906

'Organ Recital by Mr J H Reginald Dixon', 28 January 1908

'York Presbyterian Church Sunday School Anniversary', 10 May 1909

'York Musicians Success', Dr J H Reginald Dixon's London Degree, 24 February 1925

'"Indignity" of Wedding March, "Unsuitable" for use in church', 1 September 1961

Yorkshire Post

'Organists' Royal Patron', 22 August 1950

'"The Dream of Gerontius" as a mystery play', Ernest Bradbury, 17 November 1955

'A Wedding March – but which one?', 31 August 1961

'This world of ours (Wedding March controversy)', 25 October 1961

Yorkshire Press

'They'll pull out all the stops at this York Congress', 28 August 1961

'Wedding March "an indignity", says Jackson', 30 August 1961

Index

Abel, Jane 2, 3
Ainscough 71, 72–73, 74, 75, 136, 171
Ainscough, Henry 23, 24, 25, 26, 28–30, 31, 32
Ainscough, Jack 171
Aldous Choir, The 34, 44
Aldous, J W 34, 79, 81, 82, 132
Allison, Arthur 38
All Saints Church, Huntington 1
Allt, Dr W Greenhouse 133
Archbishop Holgate's Grammar School, York 10, 12
Arkwright, T 79, 82
Aschaffenburger Volksblatt 154, 155
Ashton Hall, Lancaster 35, 36, 37, 38, 40, 44, 53, 56, 58, 59, 78, 79, 80, 96, 109, 121, 135, 138, 161, 163, 174, 176
Ashton Hall Organ 35, 36, 118–120, 121, 135, 174, 176
Ashton, Lord 35, 40, 138, 176
Aquinas, St Thomas 148

Barker, Noelle 153, 154, 158, 161, 164
Beeley's Dance Band 35
Bearman Bros 38
Bearman, G J H 97
Bickerstaff, Henry 84
Billington Blog 176
Billington, Canon Richard Newman 21, 27, 28, 33, 58, 95
Bishop, J C 23, 75
Blackburn Cathedral 24, 131
Blundell, Canon 59, 60, 67
Bolton, Nellie 19
Bridge, Sir Frederick 14, 19
Brimley, Monsignor R O 141
Brompton Oratory, London 45, 157
Brook, John 61, 123
Brunskill, Muriel 54
Buckfast Abbey 124 125
Burge, Prior (later Abbot) 21, 33, 58

Carrara, Bergamo Italy 166
Carlisle Journal 115, 116, 117
Carter, Andrew J, Wakefield 174
Catenian Association 57, 170
Cathedral Girls' Association, the 106, 109
Catholic Chapel, Lancaster 23, 24, 75
Catholic Youth Movement, The 115
Cavaillé-Coll, A 24, 75, 84, 88
Centenary Congregational Church, Lancaster 34, 133
Centenary Quartette 34, 37, 38, 54
Centenary Wesleyan Chapel, York 16
Central Hall, Westminster, London 45, 156, 157, 158
Chadderton, Charles 59, 60,
Charleroi, Belgium 50, 51
Child, Tom 54, 55
Christ Church, Lancaster 34
Choir of St John the Evangelist, Islington 141, 145, 147, 152, 153, 154, 157, 158, 165
Church of the Sacred Heart, Blackpool 91
City Hall, Hull 43
Clegg, David 90
Clegg, Harry 90
Compton, John 71
Crystal Palace 18
Cunningham, G D 87

Daily Express 128
Daily Mail 125
Daily Mirror 127, 128
Daily Telegraph 159
Dixon-Jamart, Alice M V, 53, 54, 56
Dixon, Beatrice Lily 4, 135, 160, 169
Dixon, Dean 152, 155
Dixon, George 2, 3, 8, 9, 13
Dixon, James Hugh Reginald
   LIFE
   Ancestors 1–2
   Birth 3

Early life 4–7
Lessons with Kinsley 4, 5
Chorister 5
Assistant Organist 6
Studies with Euston-Inman 8,
Archbishop Holgate's Grammar School 10, 12,
Music Examinations 10
Appointed Organist at St Denys 11
Academic Examinations 12, 13
Studies with Eaglefield-Hull 13
Royal College of Organists
   Associate and Fellowship Diplomas 13, 14, 15
Inter Mus Bac (London University) 14
Organist Appointment at Selby Wesleyan Chapel 15
Organist at St Edward the Confessor, Dringhouses 15
Concerts and Recitals 15–18
Early compositions 17–20
Conversion to the Catholic Faith 20
Appointed Organist at St Peter's Church, Lancaster 21
   Appointment (May 1909) 23
   Jubilee Celebrations 33
Conductor of the Yealand Choral Society 34
Conductor of the Lancaster Amateur Dramatic and Operatic Society 35
Pianist in Beeley's Dance Band 35
The Merry Ones Concert Party 35
Appointment as Corporation Organist 37
Ashton Hall Concerts and Recitals (1910–14) 37–42
Royal visit (1912) 41–42
First World War
   Joins the Royal Army Medical Corps 43
   Articles for *Musical Standard* 43–44
   Musical activities 43–45, 47–48, 49
   Bachelor of Music Degree (London University) 45
   Poems, 49–50
   Marriage, 51
After the War
   Dixon-Jamart Concerts 53–56
   Lecturer in extra mural studies (Liverpool University) 57

Honorary Conductor of the Liverpool Metropolitan Cathedral Choir 57
First visit to Lourdes 57
Local politics 57
St Peter's Church becomes a Cathedral 58–59
Doctor of Music Degree (London University) 59–60
Special Constable 62
Letters to *The Tablet* 63–64
Articles for *Musical Opinion* 64–66
St Gregory Society 66–69
Organ Adviser and Consultant 71–77
Lancaster Music Festivals 79–84
Recitals from Manchester Town Hall 84–88
Writing short stories 89
Mistaken identity 90–93
City celebrations 94–96
Inventions:
   Musical instruments 97–99
   Aural Method 99–100
   A game 100–102
   Elro Products 102–105
Collaboration with the Rev. B Lockwood 107–115
Collaboration with Monsignor Lawrence Smith 115–118
Renovation of the Ashton Hall Organ (1948) 118–121
Representative for the Trinity College of Music 133
Royal visits (1951 and 1955) 133,135
Cathedral Primary School Centenary 134
Papal Honour (1956) 136
Restoration of the Cathedral Organ (1956) 136, 137
Return visit to Lyon 137
Televised Mass 137
Compositions (1950s) 138–143,
Jubilee of Appointment 143
Composition and performances of *Panis Vitae* 145–164
Compositions (1960s) 165–167
Recollections 168–172
Death 172

WORKS
Anthems:
  I Rejoiced 166
  Praise for Redemption 17
Cantatas:
  Love and Music 19
  Song for St Cecilia's Day 43
Hymn tunes:
  Brightly gleams our Banner 17
  The World looks very Beautiful 17
  Carmina Missae 141
  Inspiration 140
  We Love to Sing 17
Masses:
  Boarbank Mass 167
  Mass in E flat 141, 167
  Mass in honour of Christ the King 167
  Mass in honour of St Beatrice 143
  Mass of Our Lady of Syon 141
  Mass of St John the Evangelist 165
Motets:
  Ave Maria 141
  Domine Salvum Fac 137
  Ecce Sacerdos Magnus 166
Oratorios:
  Anglése de Sagazan 140
  Panis Vitae 145–164
Orchestra:
  Les Fleurs de Mont d'Or 49
  Suite Carolorégienne 50, 131
  Concerto for Organ and Orchestra 131, 138–139, 143
Organ:
  A Shepherd's Idylle 39
  Aspiration 166
  Baroque Suite 90, 93, 141, 150
  Bell Rondo 18
  Berceuse 140, 141
  Festival Postlude in G major 165
  Grand Chœur in D 18
  Intermezzo 18
  Melodie in D flat 40
  Passacaglia 143
  Pastorale 18
  Prelude and Fantasy Fugue (The Cunningham) 86, 87, 88, 129
  Sedbergh (Introduction, Variations and Fugue) 60, 61, 62, 131
  Solemn Procession 166
  Stanzas on a Martial Theme 43
  Storm at Sea arr. Dixon 17, 37, 39, 53
  Toccata in C 18
  Toccata in E minor 166
  Vignettes 166
Piano:
  Gavotte 18
  Sonata Classique 18
  London Pride 18
  Red Tulips 18
  Wallflowers 18
Songs:
  Cigarette Song 115
  Here's to the school of a hundred years 135
  Love is ever at the Spring 19
  Memories 54
  Transfiguration (Part-song) 141, 142
  The Clang of the Hammer 19
  The Simple Sailorman 19
  Westward Bound 54
Musical Drama:
  Dream of Gerontius, The 59, 106–114, 131, 140, 143, 150, 152, 167, 168, 177–184
Mystery Play:
  Mysterium Resurrectionis 59
Dixon, Ronald George 4, 90, 91, 135
Dixon, Reginald Herbert 90, 91, 93
Dowbiggin, E Arnold 110, 161, 162, 163
Downes, Ralph 141

Eaglefield-Hull, A 13, 55, 57
Elgar, Sir Edward 34, 84, 88, 107, 108
Elizabeth II, Queen 135
Elvin, Lawrence 118, 119–120
Empress Ballroom, Blackpool 90
Eucharistic Congress, Munich (1960) 145, 151, 154, 160
Euston-Inman, Henry 8, 11, 12, 13

Flaxton 2, 3, 4
Flynn, Bishop T E 115, 136, 143
Foley, Bishop B 161
Foster, Will 142
Freisinger Tagblatt 155
Frost, John 153, 154

Gates, Lillian 115
Gebrüder Späth 75
George V, King 41, 42
George VI, King 94, 133
Gillow & Co., Lancaster 35, 174
Gloucester Cathedral 131
Grand Theatre, Lancaster 111, 113
Grosse, R T 34, 37, 38, 54
Gustav, Arnold 23

Hallé, Charles 23
Hallett, Alfred 153, 154, 158, 161, 164
Halm, Dr H 156
Hamilton Harty, Sir John 124
Hanns, Haas 155
Harper, Constance 161, 162
Harris, Sir William 129, 136, 137, 141
Harrison, Thomas 24
Heenan, Rev. J C, Archbishop of Liverpool 143
Heger, Robert 154, 155
Hieber Adolf 145, 152, 153
Hinrichsen, Max 141, 143, 145, 147, 150, 151, 152, 153
Hill Norman and Beard Ltd. 120, 129
Holloway, John Hughes 30
Holy Trinity Church, Stockton-on-the-Forest 4, 5, 6, 7, 45 47, 134, 135, 174
Horrocks, Herbert 135, 161, 162, 171
Huntington 1, 2

Incorporated Association of Organists 56, 94, 123–124, 131–132
  Brighton Congress 1960, 130
  Bristol Congress 1962, 131
  Edinburgh Congress 1963, 131
  Edinburgh Congress 1949, 132
  Exeter Congress 1925, 124
  Exeter Congress 1958, 129
  Glasgow Congress 1956, 128–129
  Huddersfield Congress 1931, 124
  Lancaster Congress 1928, 124
  Lancaster Congress 1972, 131, 168, 171
  Leeds Congress 1950, 126–128
  Leicester Congress 1948, 126
  Plymouth Congress 1937, 125
  Portsmouth Congress 1934, 125
  Torquay Congress 1930, 124
  York Congress 1961, 130

Jackson, Dr Francis A 130, 165
Jamart, Alice Marie Victorine 50
Jardine & Co., Manchester 91
Jean's, Lady Susi 141

Kelly, Rev. P Archbishop of Liverpool 77
Kennedy, A 158
Kennedy Symphony Orchestra, London 157, 158
Kitson, C H 59
Kitts, Francis 24, 171

Lancashire Daily Post 111
Lancashire Evening Post 161
Lancaster Amateur and Dramatic Society 35, 109, 111, 135
Lancaster and District Musical Society 135, 139, 161, 170
Lancaster and District Organists' and Choirmasters' Association 123, 131–32, 170
Lancaster Guardian 161
Lancaster Catenian Association 57, 170
Lancaster Cathedral Organ 23, 24, 25, 26, 27, 28–32, 136, 137, 173, 174, 175
Lancaster Mail 38
Lancaster Choral Society 35, 161, 176
Lancaster Male Voice Choir, The 34, 37
Lancaster Miracle Players, The 110
Lancaster Music Festival 79–84
Lancaster Orchestral Society 138
Lancaster Priory 34, 166
Lancaster Reform Club 170
Lancaster Rotary Club 57, 170

Lancaster Town Hall 35, 38, 58, 95, 124, 176
Leeming, Richard 24, 27, 28
Lewis, Thomas C 174
Liedertafel Freising Choir 153, 154, 158
Liverpool Evening Express 173
Liverpool Metropolitan Cathedral Choir 57
Liverpool University 57
Lockwood, Rev. B 20, 97, 107, 108, 109, 111, 113, 114, 133, 134, 135, 137, 143, 183
London Philharmonic Orchestra 157
London Symphony Orchestra 157
London University 13, 14, 45, 59
Lord Mayor's Lenten Sacred Concerts 15
Lourdes 57, 75, 137, 168,

MacCarthy, Shaun 153, 154, 158, 161, 162
McCallum, David 158
McElligott, Rev. J B 66
Manchester Town Hall 84, 86, 88, 90, 121, 125
Martin, Wesley 34, 35
Mayor, Ralph 75
Meale, J Arthur 15, 16, 18, 34, 40, 45, 53, 157
Melba, Dame Nellie 19
Melbourne Terrace Wesleyan Church 16
Metropolitan Cathedral of Christ the King, Liverpool 71
Monaghan, Albert 8, 16, 17
Moody, Dr Charles 82
Morecambe West End Wesleyan Choir Festival (1925) 61–62
Münchner Merkur 155
Munich 145, 152, 153, 154, 156
Music and Liturgy 67, 68
Music and Musicians 160
Musical Opinion 160
Musical Standard 43, 44, 66

Newman, Cardinal John Henry 107, 108
News Chronicle 127
Noble, T Tertius 8, 12, 14
Norman and Beard Ltd. 14, 35, 36
North Riding Technical Instruction Committee 10

Oberhoffer, R W 8, 21
Oldham, Rev. James 91, 92

Oldroyd, George 17
Ott, Dr Alfons 145, 147, 151, 152, 153, 155
Oxford Oratory 164

Paley, Edward G 23
Paley & Austin 24
Parratt, Sir Walter 14
Pearce, Dr C W 59
Pearson, Bishop Thomas Wulstan 58, 84
Pendelbury & Co. 71, 173
Philips, Gordon 150, 151
Pope John XXIII 153
Pope Pius X 44, 59, 66
Pope Pius XI 58, 66
Porter, Winifride 109, 110, 111, 113, 114
Presbyterian Church, Priory Street, York (Now St Columba's URC with New Lendal) 21, 174
Preston Herald 113
Princess Royal 127
Principal Pipe Organs, York 174

Quarterly Record 123, 132, 166
Queen's Hall, Preston 110

Radcliffe, Arthur A 13, 16
Read, David 158, 161, 163, 164
Rivera, de Edward 141, 145, 147, 150, 152, 153, 155, 154, 157, 158, 164, 165
Roberts, W A 31, 32
Royal Albert Hall, London 45, 59, 60, 61, 120
Royal College of Organists 13, 14, 15, 166, 176
Royal Hippodrome, Preston 111, 114
Rowntree, Dr John 76, 77

Sample, Daisie 17
Salesian College Choir, Battersea 158
Schmitz, Laurenz 23, 30, 172, 173
Selby 15, 20, 142
Selby Abbey 17
Selby Wesleyan Chapel 15, 17, 142
Smith, Joseph 24
Smith, Monsignor Richard Lawrence 107, 115, 117, 118
Society of St Gregory 66, 67, 68
Southlands Methodist Church 16

Southland Young Peoples' Association 16
Sowerby, Dr Leo 141
St Andrew's Parish Church, Plymouth 129
St Denys (Dennis or Dionysius), York 11, 14, 17
St Edward the Confessor, Dringhouses 15, 20
St Etheldreda's, Ely Place, London 44
St George's Chapel Royal, Windsor 136
St Germain au Mont d'Or, France 47, 48, 137
St John the Evangelist, Islington, London 141, 145, 147, 150, 152, 153, 154, 156, 157, 158, 164, 165
St Joseph's Church, Lancaster 107, 137, 143
St Joseph's College Chapel, Upholland 71
St Lawrence, Flaxton 4
St Mary's RC Church, Barnstaple 56
St Mary's RC Church, Wigan 71
St Mary and St Michael's RC Church, Garstang 71
St Mary and St Nicholas, Wigginton 2
St Peter's Church, Lancaster 21, 23, 25, 58, 75
St Peter's Cathedral, Lancaster 58, 124, 143, 164, 166, 176
St Saviour's, York 8, 11
St Thomas', Lowther Street, York 8, 11
St Wilfrid's RC Church, York 8, 20, 21
Stockton House 8, 9
Stockton-on-the-Forest 4, 47, 169
Süddeutsche Zeitung 154–155
Summers & Barnes, York 135
Swarsenski, H 150, 151, 157

Tablet The 63–64, 160
Taylor, Ethel 98, 124, 126, 136, 139
Taylor, Nora 109, 124, 133, 136, 139
Terry, Dr Richard 44, 57, 82
Tomlinson, James 27, 28, 29
Tower Ballroom, Blackpool 86, 90, 91

Universe The 159
Ulverston Choral Society 161

Walmsley, Henry 166
Waterton Hall, Carlisle 115
Waterton, Canon George 115
Westminster Cathedral, London 44, 45, 57, 68, 157
Whitlock, Percy 125
Whitworth, Reginald 118–119
Willis Henry & Sons Ltd. 71, 174
Wilson, Betty 162, 171
Wood, Henry J 34

Yealand Choral Society 34
Yorkshire Evening Post 99
Yorkshire Evening Press 130
Yorkshire Herald 9, 15, 16
Yorkshire Post 114